IN THE BEGINNING WAS A WORD

HOW LANGUAGE KNITS REALITY TOGETHER

IN THE BEGINNING WAS A WORD

HOW LANGUAGE KNITS REALITY TOGETHER

JOHN S. HATCHER, PHD

Bahá'í
PUBLISHING

Wilmette, Illinois

Bahá'í Publishing, Wilmette, Illinois

401 Greenleaf Ave, Wilmette, Illinois 60091
Copyright © 2017 by the National Spiritual Assembly
of the Bahá'ís of the United States
All rights reserved. Published 2017
Printed in the United States of America ∞
20   19   18   17   1   2   3   4

Library of Congress Cataloging-in-Publication Data
Names: Hatcher, John S., 1940– author.
Title: In the beginning was a word : how language knits reality together /
    John S. Hatcher, PhD.
Description: Wilmette : Bahá'í Publishing, 2017. | Includes bibliographical
    references and index.
Identifiers: LCCN 2016050045 | ISBN 9781618511188 (pbk. : alk. paper)
Subjects: LCSH: Language and languages—Religious aspects—Bahai Faith.
Classification: LCC BP360.9.L36 H38 2017 | DDC 297.9/32—dc23
LC record available at https://lccn.loc.gov/2016050045

Cover design by Jamie Hanrahan
Book design by Patrick Falso

for
Helen Hardman Hatcher

Thou didst wish to make Thyself known unto men;
therefore, Thou didst, through a word of Thy mouth,
bring creation into being and fashion the universe.

Bahá'u'lláh, *Prayers and Meditations*, no. 4.1

CONTENTS

ACKNOWLEDGMENTS

I would like to acknowledge the help of the editors at the Bahá'í Publishing Trust, Bahhaj Taherzadeh and Chris Martin, and manager Tim Moore, a dear friend whose encouragement keeps me going. I wish to thank my wife Lucia, who is the first reader of all my work, whose judgment is trustworthy, and who has finally given up asking if this is my last book. I would also like to express my appreciation to Martha Schweitz whose review of this work for accuracy has been extremely helpful—the breadth and depth of her knowledge are truly remarkable. Finally, I especially want to thank the principal editor for this work, Nilufar Gordon. Her attention to style, grammar, and mechanics, together with her acute sensitivity to exactitude of meaning, has been invaluable. Indeed, she has been a cherished co-worker on this project.

THE POWER OF THE WORD

No man of wisdom can demonstrate his knowledge save by means of words. This showeth the significance of the Word as is affirmed in all the Scriptures, whether of former times or more recently. For it is through its potency and animating spirit that the people of the world have attained so eminent a position. Moreover words and utterances should be both impressive and penetrating. However, no word will be infused with these two qualities unless it be uttered wholly for the sake of God and with due regard unto the exigencies of the occasion and the people.

The Great Being saith: Human utterance is an essence which aspireth to exert its influence and needeth moderation. As to its influence, this is conditional upon refinement which in turn is dependent upon hearts which are detached and pure. As to its moderation, this hath to be combined with tact and wisdom as prescribed in the Holy Scriptures and Tablets.

Every word is endowed with a spirit, therefore the speaker or expounder should carefully deliver his words at the appropriate time and place, for the impression which each word maketh is clearly evident and perceptible. The Great Being saith: One word may be likened unto fire, another unto light, and the influence which both exert is manifest in the world. Therefore an enlightened man of wisdom should primarily speak with words as mild as milk, that the children of men may be nurtured and edified thereby and may attain the ultimate goal of human existence which is the station of true understanding and nobility. And likewise He saith: One word is like unto springtime causing the tender saplings of the rosegarden of knowledge to become verdant and flourishing, while another word is even as a deadly poison. It behooveth a prudent man of wisdom to speak with utmost leniency and forbearance so that the sweetness of his words may induce everyone to attain that which befitteth man's station.

O friend of mine! The Word of God is the king of words and its pervasive influence is incalculable. It hath ever dominated and will continue to dominate the realm of being. The Great Being saith: The Word is the master key for the whole world, inasmuch as through its potency the doors of the hearts of men, which in reality are the doors of heaven, are unlocked. No sooner had but a glimmer of its effulgent splendor shone forth upon the mirror of love than the blessed word "I am the Best-Beloved" was reflected therein. It is an ocean inexhaustible in riches, comprehending all things. Every thing which can be perceived is but an emanation therefrom. High, immeasurably high is this sublime station, in whose shadow moveth the essence of loftiness and splendor, wrapt in praise and adoration.

Bahá'u'lláh, Lawh-i-Maqsúd,
in *Tablets of Bahá'u'lláh*, pp. 172–73

FIGURES AND TABLES

A GLOSSARY OF BAHÁ'Í TERMINOLOGY RELEVANT TO THE PROGRESS OF HUMAN HISTORY

God (the Creator)

A Self-Sufficient, essentially spiritual Being with neither beginning nor end, Who has created the universe so that it might bring forth beings capable of understanding His nature, becoming attracted to the Beauty of His nature, and subsequently acquiring the attributes of that nature: "Having created the world and all that liveth and moveth therein, He, through the direct operation of His unconstrained and sovereign Will, chose to confer upon man the unique distinction and capacity to know Him and to love Him—a capacity that must needs be regarded as the generating impulse and the primary purpose underlying the whole of creation. . . ." (Bahá'u'lláh, *Gleanings*, no. 27.2).

Manifestations (Prophets, Messengers, Intermediaries, Vicegerents, etc.)

An order of Beings Who manifest the divine attributes perfectly in all They say and do. Unlike ordinary human beings, the Manifestations are preexistent in the spiritual realm but appear in human form from age to age for the purpose of gradually teaching humankind the spiritual principles and attributes underlying the whole of creation, and of revealing personal and social guidance according to the capacity of humankind for the age in which They appear.

Human Being

A being endowed with self-consciousness, capable of abstract thought and of willfully manifesting all of the divine attributes: "Upon the inmost reality of each and every created thing He hath shed the light of one of His names, and made it a recipient of the glory of one of His attributes. Upon the reality of man, however, He hath focused the radiance of all of His names and attributes, and made it a mirror of His own Self. Alone of all created things man hath been singled out for so great a favor, so enduring a bounty" (Bahá'u'lláh, *Gleanings*, no. 27.2).

The Word (the Creative Word, the Revealed Word, the Word of God, the Book)

"The laws, teachings or message of God transmitted through His Manifestation to mankind" (*Basic Bahá'í Dictionary*, p. 195). Bahá'u'lláh designates the revealed Word as "a Revelation direct from God" (Bahá'u'lláh, Kitáb-i-Aqdas ¶37).

Authoritative Texts

In the Bahá'í Dispensation, this definition applies only to the authentic works of the Báb, Bahá'u'lláh, 'Abdu'l-Bahá, Shoghi Effendi, and the Universal House of Justice. The Báb and Bahá'u'lláh are inherently infallible, and They partake of "the Most Great Infallibility" ('Abdu'l-Bahá, *Some Answered Questions*, no. 45.1). 'Abdu'l-Bahá, Shoghi Effendi (as Guardian), and the Universal House of Justice possess "conferred infallibility," explained as "the unerring guidance of God" (Ibid., no. 45.4, 45.3).

The Major Plan of God

The plan of God for bringing about the Kingdom of God on Earth; the "process of world unification . . . whose operation will continue, gathering force and momentum, until the human race has been united in a global society that has banished war and taken charge of its collective destiny" (Shoghi Effendi, quoted in *Century of Light*, p. 138). It "proceeds mysteriously in ways directed by Him alone . . ." (December 8, 1967, written by the Universal House of Justice to an individual). "His Own Major Plan, using both the mighty and lowly as pawns in His world-shaping game, for the fulfillment of His immediate purpose and the eventual establishment of His Kingdom on earth" (Shoghi Effendi, *Citadel of Faith*, p. 140).

The Everlasting or Eternal Covenant

The Covenant in which God promises to send successive Prophets or Manifestations so that He will never leave humankind without sufficient spiritual guidance to bring forth an "ever-advancing civilization" (Bahá'u'lláh, *Gleanings*, no. 109.2).

Greater Covenant

The Covenant that "every Manifestation of God makes with His followers, promising that in the fullness of time a new Manifestation will be sent, and taking from them the undertaking to accept Him when this occurs" (letter from the Universal House of Justice, dated March 3, 1975, to an individual believer).

"As regards the meaning of the Bahá'í Covenant: The Guardian considers the existence of two forms of Covenant both of which are explicitly mentioned in the literature of the Cause. First is the Covenant that every Prophet makes with humanity or, more definitely, with His people that they will accept and follow the coming

Manifestation Who will be the reappearance of His reality. The second form of Covenant is such as the one Bahá'u'lláh made with His people that they should accept the Master ['Abdu'l-Bahá, His eldest son]. This is merely to establish and strengthen the succession of the series of Lights that appear after every Manifestation. Under the same category falls the Covenant the Master made with the Bahá'ís that they should accept His administration after Him.

The Most Great Covenant is different from the Everlasting Covenant" (Shoghi Effendi, quoted in Helen Hornby, *Lights of Guidance*, no. 593).

Lesser Covenant

The binding pact "that a Manifestation of God makes with His followers that they will accept His appointed successor after Him. If they do so, the Faith can remain united and pure. If not, the Faith becomes divided and its force spent. . . . It is a Covenant of this kind that Bahá'u'lláh made with His followers regarding 'Abdu'l-Bahá, and that 'Abdu'l-Bahá perpetuated through the Administrative Order that Bahá'u'lláh had already created" (letter from the Universal House of Justice, dated March 3, 1975, to an individual believer).

The Divine Plan

The name assigned to the overarching teaching plan initiated by 'Abdu'l-Bahá in 1916 with the *Tablets of the Divine Plan* and succeeded by a series of three plans by the Guardian and eleven plans (thus far) by the Universal House of Justice. The *Tablets of the Divine Plan* are considered to be the "mandate" (Shoghi Effendi, qtd. in *Messages to America*, p. 29) and "divine charter of teaching," (Universal House of Justice, Ridván Message 1993 ¶5) thus all subsequent plans follow from 'Abdu'l-Bahá's guidance and are considered subsidiary to it.

The Adamic Cycle (The Prophetic Cycle)

The cycle of Manifestations that began with the Prophet Adam. "The Adamic Cycle inaugurated 6000 years ago by the Manifestation of God called Adam is only one of the many bygone cycles. Bahá'u'lláh, as you say, is the culmination of the Adamic Cycle. He is also the Inaugurator of the Bahá'í Cycle" (from a letter written on behalf of the Universal House of Justice to an individual believer, quoted in Helen Hornby, *Lights of Guidance*, no. 1683).

The Bahá'í Cycle

Bahá'u'lláh is the "Inaugurator of the Bahá'í Cycle" (ibid.). The "Bahá'í cycle will extend over a period of at least 500,000 years" (from a letter written on behalf of the Guardian to an individual believer, November 14, 1935, in *Bahá'í News* no. 102 (August 1936): pp. 2–3).

Dispensation (also Day or Era)

The period of time during which a revealed religion is intended to guide humankind, either in a particular part of the world or the world as a whole.

The Bahá'í Dispensation (The Dispensation of Bahá'u'lláh)

A Dispensation that began with Bahá'u'lláh's intimation of His mission in the Siyáh-Chál and that is destined to endure for at least a thousand years until the next Manifestation appears (Bahá'u'lláh, Kitáb-i-Aqdas, note 62). Shoghi Effendi writes that the Bahá'í Dispensation will be acknowledged by posterity to have been "the most glorious and momentous in the greatest cycle in the world's religious history" (Shoghi Effendi, *Citadel of Faith*, p. 4).

The Three Ages of the Bahá'í Era or Dispensation

1. The Heroic Age (Apostolic Age, Primitive Age) 1844–1921
2. The Formative Age (Transitional Age, Iron Age) 1921–
3. The Golden Age (The World Order of Bahá'u'lláh)

Epochs

Distinctive periods of time within these three ages.

THE HEROIC AGE (APOSTOLIC AGE, PRIMITIVE AGE) 1844–1921

1. 1844–1853 (nine years)
2. 1853–1892 (thirty-nine years)
3. 1892–1921 (twenty-nine years)

THE FORMATIVE AGE THUS FAR (TRANSITIONAL AGE, IRON AGE) 1921–

1. 1921–1944/46 (twenty-three years)
2. 1946–1963 (seventeen years)
3. 1963–1986 (twenty-three years)
4. 1986–2001 (fifteen years)
5. 2001–

- 1 -

ROOTS, DIASPORA,
AND A FAMILY REUNION

And the Lord came down to see the city and the tower, which the sons of men had built. And the Lord said, "Behold, they are one people, and they have all one language; and this is only the beginning of what they will do; and nothing that they propose to do will now be impossible for them. Come, let us go down, and there confuse their language, that they may not understand one another's speech." So the Lord scattered them abroad from there over the face of all the earth, and they left off building the city. Therefore its name was called Babel, because there the Lord confused the language of all the earth; and from there the Lord scattered them abroad over the face of all the earth.

Genesis 11:5–9*

---

* This and all further citations refer to the Revised Standard Version of the Bible.

1

Like millions of others, I was overwhelmed by the creativity and complimentary synthesis of cultural affect manifest in Paul Simon's 1986 album *Graceland,* and no less mesmerized by some of the lyrics. Recently I saw a PBS film titled "Paul Simon's Graceland Journey" (Jan. 3, 2013)* in which he discusses breaking the UN cultural boycott of South Africa designed to help end the apartheid regime. In the documentary, the founder of Artists Against Apartheid, Dali Tambo, maintains that Simon showed a certain callous disregard for what the ANC (African National Congress) was trying to achieve. Simon replied that art, and music in particular, has the capacity to unite peoples, to overleap boundaries and barriers of every sort, whether physical, ideological, social, or linguistic.

But more impressive to me than the discussion were the interweaving voices of those at the reunion who had been among the original members of the South African Graceland tour some twenty-five years earlier. For them, this synthesis of the American lyrics of a Jewish artist from New York City with some of the most evocative African rhythms, melodies, voices, and instruments was a "miracle of rare device," a driving force by means of which they broke the sound barrier of apartheid, or, rather, ignored barriers altogether and embraced one another in unabashed fellowship that transcended time, place, beliefs, and race.

Our Family Roots

I begin this discussion about language and how it is central in making us human with an allusion to the *Graceland* album not merely because of the milestone in contemporary musical culture it proved to be. As a trained historical linguist, I had long before

---

* The critically acclaimed new film by Academy Award–nominated and two-time Emmy and Peabody Award–winning filmmaker, Joe Berlinger.

noted how the intersection and confluence of cultures seems to bring about something more powerful than either influence might have produced on its own, perhaps in the same way that mixed race children tend to be more advanced both socially and intellectually. I remember in my graduate classes discussing how English theater emerged from dividing the choral parts of the Easter Sepulcher service. Often I would have the class listen to *Missa Luba*, a version of that same Latin mass, but based on traditional Congolese songs and sung exquisitely and movingly by the Muungano National Choir of Kenya.

But it is the recent DNA projects that coalesced my thinking about how a study of language is also central to understanding our beginnings in Africa. As I listened to Simon recount how he created the songs in his album (especially the "Graceland" song itself) I realized that possibly he was not entirely aware of how much his art had accomplished by way of tracing our collective history.

In the song, he speaks of a trip he actually took with his son to visit Elvis Presley's Graceland estate. Two images in the lyrics stood out for me when I first heard the piece, and now they resonate even more profoundly after watching the interview. The first describes the speaker and his son driving along the Mississippi River: "I am following the river / Down the highway / Through the cradle of the Civil War." It struck me profoundly not only because my great grandfather fought in that most uncivil of wars but also because the tension that sparked the war centered on the debate over whether one person should be able to own another. This idea now seems utterly absurd, and yet only one and a half centuries ago, it was somehow acceptable to a good number of people in this land of the free.

Of course, it was not just any people owning any other people, but specifically White Americans being allowed to own Africans brought against their will to a foreign land for the purpose of providing free labor for plantation owners. And this song about receiving grace in a land I presumed was founded on a belief in grace—and an "Amazing Grace"* at that—thus echoed in my heart and mind the need for this country to be redeemed by grace for its still bewildering past act of enslaving foreign peoples and treating them as chattel, as well as the continuing racism that, like a virus in the blood, reemerges vehemently as soon as one thinks the disease has been conquered.

So this songwriter is traveling to be received and redeemed, not as an American but as a musician paying homage at one of the shrines of perhaps the only original American music—gospel, jazz, and blues, all originating from African cultures, emerging first in New Orleans and Memphis, and then floating up and down that same American life-vein that is the Mississippi River.

If we are to be totally honest, then, this American music, though percolating out from the mud of the delta, is not really American, but African-American—so much so that in high school (we are talking about the 1950s), I had to tune in to station WLAC out of Nashville to hear the music I loved because it was banned on most stations in Atlanta, where I lived. And I would send my money to Randy's Record Mart in Gallatin, Tennessee, to receive singles by such favorites as Muddy Waters, Etta James and the Peaches, Lightnin' Hopkins, Big Joe Turner, and so many, many others.

This was my soul's music before the term "soul music" was invented, and yet it was banned quite simply because it was "Negro music"—until, of course, white singers sneaked into Sam Phillips' studio at Sun Records in Memphis and cashed in on the sounds, the rhythms, and the "soul" that was being borne along this river. The rest is an easily traced history, and there are some fine inter-

---

* Lyrics by John Newton (1725–1807), an English slave trader who converted to Christianity and later became a member of the clergy.

4

views among Black artists such as Bo Diddley, Chuck Berry, and Little Richard talking very frankly about how they felt hearing their songs and sounds whitened and mellowed out by Pat Boone and the singers on the Hit Parade. Even the Beatles and the Rolling Stones observed the irony of "invading" America to sing songs that they had learned from Black American music. The point is that we had not only enslaved and segregated a people, we had also tried to segregate their art, the only original music that America could claim. But long before the legal barriers oppressing these talented visitors we had ferried here from another continent were adjudged to be illegal, the language of music had breached the walls and set them free to insinuate their vitality and joy into our lives. And nothing, nothing whatsoever could stop the infusion of that spirit and the power of that inner vision.

"The Mississippi delta was shining / Like a national guitar," sings Simon. This is America's heart and heartbeat, the backbeat that emerged from the forging together of souls through music created by a disenfranchised people whose solace were songs echoing a vaguely recalled homeland and a newfound hope of "crossing over Jordan" to be saved spiritually and physically from a life that offered no prospect for any sort of tangible relief.

For me, this theme of hope sounds very much like the hope Simon expresses for all humankind when, in that same song, he ends with the lines, "Maybe I've a reason to believe / We all will be received / In Graceland." This is an optimism we all can share as we aspire to fashion a place of grace for all the citizens who inhabit our orbiting blue-marble home.

The Diaspora of Humankind

Around the same time the *Graceland* album came out, two other sources of our collective connection with Africa emerged. Back in the 1960s, I had studied and researched the history of the English language and historical and comparative linguistics, and I had noted common threads among emerging peoples from the migration of the Indo-Europeans around 3000 BCE. What had been a single language became subdivided into at least ten language groups and eventually evolved into different tongues as migrations began throughout Europe, into Scandinavia, the Middle East, and the Indian subcontinent. This was not a new theory, nor was it based on mere speculation. The relationship among the Indo-European languages was substantiated during the mid-1800s and presaged what scientists studying human DNA began to discover in the 1980s.

First of all, contemporary theories of anthropology suggest that the modern human (represented by the contemporary anatomical human model) emerged in Africa no later than a quarter of a million years ago. Secondly, DNA studies beginning in the 1980s seem to confirm a theory posited by Darwin in 1871 that we all have a single point of origin, a point the Adam and Eve story in Genesis may have been describing in symbolic terms.

Often referred to as the "Out of Africa" theory, this idea has become the most widely accepted theory about the anatomical and geographical origin of humans. This hypothesis traces a theoretical migratory route from what is now Ethiopia into the southern part of the Arabian Peninsula—around present-day Yemen—approximately seventy thousand years ago. This educated guess then maps the trails that various groups took as they divided and subdivided until, over the course of time, humans had migrated to every land mass in the world. The "hard science" of DNA appears to vindicate the overall hypothesis that Africa is indeed our homeland, even as Paul Simon's music seems to suggest.

In the 1970s, Alex Haley discovered another influential popular culture perspective on the "Out of Africa" theory. Prompted by stories passed down through the generations in his family, Haley began to study how his ancestors had taken a somewhat more direct route from Africa to these shores, albeit unwillingly. The result was the widely renowned book, *Roots: The Saga of an American Family*, published in 1976.

Tracing Haley's genealogy, the story begins in Gambia in 1767 with the kidnapping of a young man, Kunta Kinte, who is then transported by ship to present-day Maryland, where he is sold as a slave. The novel goes on to trace the seven generations of Haley's forebears in a remarkably powerful drama that was made into an award-winning serialized epic television show that garnered the spellbound interest of audiences from all countries, races, and backgrounds. Naturally, it was particularly appealing to the Black pride movement in the United States, demonstrating as it does that the same people who had been regarded as mere chattel were descendants of noble families and tribes, of brave warriors and royalty.

This was not a new idea. This same theme had been recounted a century earlier by African-American intellectual pioneers, such as Frederick Douglass in his autobiography *Narrative of the Life of Frederick Douglass* (1845), or Booker T. Washington in his autobiography *Up from Slavery* (1901), or W. E. B. Du Bois in his *The Soul of Black Folks* (1903).

Among Haley's most inspiring personal experiences in the course of his research, was a visit to the African village of Juffure, where Kunta Kinte had lived. There Haley was privileged to hear a tribal "bard"* recite the oral history of the capture of Kinte,

---

* I use this term because it alludes to the fact that all tribal societies have oral history that is transferred from generation to generation, and, as the charter of Haley discovers, is often extremely accurate. Familiar examples of fables emerging from this tradition are the Anglo-Saxon epic of *Beowulf* and the Homeric epics of the *Iliad* and the *Odyssey*.

much as Haley had heard fragments of the same story passed down within his own African-American family. And while there have since been some disputes about the total accuracy of his account—even though he invested ten years of research into the project—the impact of the work was not due to its exacting authenticity as a historical documentary but rather to the life Haley breathed into the concept of the essential nobility of all human beings. Whether we migrated from Africa thousands of years ago, or were brought in chains, or emigrated to escape oppression or to fulfill the dream of a better life, we all ended up here together: a myriad stories but a single aspiration—to create a prosperous and just society.

Likewise, the importance of Africa to our hearts may cause us to return to discover our personal roots, contribute our DNA to trace our trek across the planet, or take our artistic contributions back to Africa to sing out in choral strains our common desire for freedom, justice, and fellowship among all the peoples of our increasingly contracting planetary community.

Babel, Bewilderment, and Bloodshed

It was the idea of African-American Marcus Garvey that a possible solution to the race problem in America was not integration, but a "back to Africa" movement. This too was not a new idea but similar in theme to that of the early nineteenth-century movement of the American Colonization Society, which advocated that the best avenue for complete freedom for African Americans was the creation of a colony in Africa where a freed people could establish their own country. This movement—similar in nature to the return of Jews to present-day Israel after World War II—contributed to the establishment of Liberia in 1822 and its subsequent independence in 1847.

But by the time Garvey advocated a similar resolution (early 1900s), the bulk of a very rigorous century had resulted in the horrific bloodshed of the Civil War, the emancipation of slaves, the abolition of slavery itself, and the so-called "Reconstruction" of the South. Alas, while the American Civil War resulted in the abolition of the institution of slavery, it did very little to change the racist attitudes of the American people or to establish a new place for the descendants of African slaves in American society. By the time of Garvey's movement, African Americans were several generations removed from remembering Africa. There was some further migration to Liberia, but by then, most Black people in America considered themselves Americans, even if disenfranchised by virtue of their skin color.

The difficult road to complete cultural freedom lay ahead—and still does. We are even now struggling mightily to create a society in which incidental matters of color, culture, origin, religious belief, and even language, are set aside so that we might fashion a diverse yet just and neighborly society. This experiment has been taking place for quite some time now, mostly out of necessity rather than from noble ideological imperatives or the collective transformation of human hearts.

True, the United States has now had an African-American president, and most communities in the country reflect an evolving heterogeneous conglomeration of colors, cultures, and languages. Yet social tensions resulting from matters of race, religion, and culture have been escalating in spite of an increasingly diverse blending of peoples, whether in America, in the western hemisphere, or worldwide. In fact, there are now few countries untouched by the struggle to create unity out of diversity because planet Earth itself is now a churning melting pot.

The upside of this reality is that many of the most beautiful and celebrated luminaries in the arts, sciences, sports, and government are marvelous blends of diverse racial and cultural backgrounds. Indeed, it would be accurate to say that even the standard paradigm of beauty—for both males and females—has undergone a dramatic change worldwide. The downside is that this melting pot could, with a few unwise decisions on the part of world leaders, become a roiling cauldron of chaos.

Perhaps this is precisely what the Creator had in mind to begin with. Humanity appeared at some central location where there was a temperate climate rich with natural resources, suitable for the survival of a relatively untutored species. Then, after learning the basic skills for gathering food, building shelter, and organizing ourselves—possibly through the guidance of early Manifestations of God—we followed our inherent thirst for learning about reality: "Science is the first emanation from God toward man. All created beings embody the potentiality of material perfection, but the power of intellectual investigation and scientific acquisition is a higher virtue specialized to man alone."[1]

Out of curiosity, we began to explore the reality of our environment and spread outward to examine the rest of our global home. Over distance and time, we found it harder to remember our origins. Eventually we had no time, or need, or desire to return to our original home. As we traversed lands, we became increasingly more divided. Some of us took one path, others decided to stay at various inviting places along the way, while still others continued to venture out to explore what lay beyond the horizon.

And as we populated more and more diverse territories and became separated into a variety of settlements, our communication became more diverse, so that different dialects, in time, became distinct languages. We no longer thought of ourselves as members of a single tribe or clan or people; within a few generations, each community created its own discrete identity and began to regard other peoples as "alien," as the "other."

Perhaps this is the process to which Moses alluded in the Genesis story of the mythical Tower of Babel,* even though apparently He is referring to a different time in history:

Now the whole earth had one language and few words. And as men migrated from the east, they found a plain in the land of Shinar and settled there. And they said to one another, "Come, let us make bricks, and burn them thoroughly." And they had brick for stone, and bitumen for mortar. Then they said, "Come, let us build ourselves a city, and a tower with its top in the heavens, and let us make a name for ourselves, lest we be scattered abroad upon the face of the whole earth."

And the Lord came down to see the city and the tower, which the sons of men had built. And the Lord said, "Behold, they are one people, and they have all one language; and this is only the beginning of what they will do; and nothing that they propose to do will now be impossible for them. Come, let us go down, and there confuse their language, that they may not understand one another's speech." So the Lord scattered them abroad from there over the face of all the earth, and they left off building the city. Therefore its name was called Babel,** because there the Lord confused the language of all the earth; and from there the Lord scattered them abroad over the face of all the earth.[2]

---

* We presume that while the Pentateuch may not have been written down by Moses, it was possibly passed down by oral tradition from what Moses recounted to the tribal bards.

** The word *Babel* derives from the Hebrew word *balal,* which means "to confuse" or "to bewilder."

Here the tower is mentioned, but in conjunction with the entire city, the construction of which seems to bother God because either He is not pleased with the people's hubris or, more likely, He finds that they are becoming complacent by focusing all their energy on developing only one location and not following the plan of spreading humankind and its influence throughout the earth. While this story is more emblematic of a larger theme than of some specific allusion to the "Out of Africa" migration (which would have occurred much earlier) it seems to reflect what has been happening in our collective history.

There is no mention of a Tower of Babel in the Qur'án, but there is an interesting parallel story concerned with Egypt in the time of Moses. The Pharaoh mandates building a tower of stone or clay for the explicit purpose of enabling him to mount to the heavens so that he, as a deity, might challenge the God of Moses:

Moses said: "My Lord knows best who it is that comes with guidance from Him and whose End will be best in the Hereafter: certain it is that the wrongdoers will not prosper."

Pharaoh said: "O Chiefs! no god do I know for you but myself: therefore, o Haman! light me a (kiln to bake bricks) out of clay, and build me a lofty palace, that I may mount up to the god of Moses: but as far as I am concerned, I think (Moses) is a liar!" And he was arrogant and insolent in the land, beyond reason—he and his hosts. They thought that they would not have to return to Us! So We seized him and his hosts, and We flung them into the sea! Now behold what was the End of those who did wrong! [3]*

---

* This and all further citations to the Qur'án are mostly from the translation by Abdullah Yusuf Ali as clarified at times by this author.

In the context of discussing how much change has occurred in such a relatively short period of time, Bahá'u'lláh alludes not to a tower but to a land known as Babel where, indeed, the diversity of languages began to emerge, as did the diversity of cultures and customs:

> Consider the differences that have arisen since the days of Adam. The divers and widely-known languages now spoken by the peoples of the earth were originally unknown, as were the varied rules and customs now prevailing amongst them. The people of those times spoke a language different from those now known. Diversities of language arose in a later age, in a land known as Babel. It was given the name Babel, because the term signifieth "the place where the confusion of tongues arose.
>
> Subsequently Syriac became prominent among the existing languages. The Sacred Scriptures of former times were revealed in that tongue. Later, Abraham, the Friend of God, appeared and shed upon the world the light of Divine Revelation. The language He spoke while He crossed the Jordan became known as Hebrew ('Ibrání), which meaneth "the language of the crossing." The Books of God and the Sacred Scriptures were then revealed in that tongue, and not until after a considerable lapse of time did Arabic become the language of Revelation. . . .[4]

The relationship of this story to the theme of our discussion is important, and not merely because of Bahá'u'lláh's mandate for the creation of a universal auxiliary language and script as tools to help fashion a global polity. From our contemporary perspective, within this story we can observe three distinct stages of one organic process. And it is only from appreciating at the outset the "end" or "end result" of this process that we can fully understand and thereby delight in this process and the part language plays in all three stages.

First, as we have noted, there seems to have been some point in the evolution of our social awareness when we became eager to venture out beyond the boundaries of the family, the village, or the tribe. Second, so long as land was plentiful and there remained unexplored territories with resources sufficient to sustain humankind's wandering peoples, major conflict could be averted. Likewise, when conflict did arise from the quest for power or domination, the more disenfranchised among the populace had the option of fleeing to another territory. We witness this solution, for example, with Abraham leading His people across the Jordan, or Moses leading His people out of bondage in Egypt.

Of course, the downside of this complexification of the human body politic was that we were no longer a single, unified family. Our small planet became a pastiche of thousands of peoples, cultures, languages, and beliefs. We had little more in common than we might presently share with populations on distant planets. In short, the "Babel effect" of confusion and the inability to communicate instigated much of what is turning our planet red with blood.

A Family Reunion

This mentality of alienation, of regarding certain peoples or cultures as "the other," has of late assumed major global importance as peoples in Syria attempt to emigrate to Europe, as children attempt to escape violence in Honduras and other Central and South American countries, and as the threat of global terrorism increases from fanatical Islamic terrorist organizations (such as Al-Qaeda, Boko Haram, and ISIS) seemingly bent on a nihilist approach to destabilizing nation states, with the professed objective of establishing a global caliphate that will create a sort of world unity by imposing Sharia law worldwide.

I well remember as a child during the Second World War perusing enthusiastically coloring books in which the American GI was pitted against what was portrayed as the soulless and heartless Japanese enemy. The same attitude was promulgated more vividly in comic books and movies. The Japanese were alien, the enemy— even as we Americans surely must have been depicted to them. This corollary has been dramatically demonstrated in documentary films from the battle of Saipan, where Japanese women and children were jumping off cliffs to their deaths rather than submitting to what they had been led to believe would be barbaric treatment by American soldiers.

Our global vision has experienced a degree of cleansing through postwar contact and collaboration with these same peoples whom we had so vehemently demonized and slaughtered. As we helped peoples in Japan and Europe rebuild the very infrastructure we had struggled so mightily to destroy through atomic weaponry and ceaseless firebombing, we became allied in our common desire to ensure that no such war would ever occur again. Even so, nationalism and alienation have endured worldwide, although humanity can begin to spy the first glimmering of the dawn of another stage in its settlement of its global home.

And yet, how hubristic and improbable it is to assume that humanity might describe its history while still in the midst of it. It is like trying to describe the cosmos from the point of view of our planet, situated as it is in one solar system of a million such systems, in one galaxy among countless other galaxies. For as soon as I describe what has past or is passing, a new paradigm in our constantly changing global polity emerges.

Wars still occur. Even though effectively mankind has become a single global community, we still have internecine squabbles, any one of which might quickly become capable of destroying the totality of all we are. If we have hope for a family reunion forged out of the diverse peoples and perspectives we have become, if we believe that there can be some willful cooperation to construct familial unity from our diverse appearances and tongues and oppressions, it surely is not readily apparent in light of the perilous threats to our habitat, our freedom, and our very lives. As much as we may long to return to that simple beginning in Africa when we were a single people in a single locale, speaking a single language, we know now that such a unified and placid reality must be wrought by degrees. Furthermore, while fashioning our family reunion at the community level, we simultaneously must also defeat those oppressive forces that would deter any such felicitous unity by imposing an homogeneous and dictatorial polity derived from the vain imaginations of monomaniacal fanatics.

Stated in simpler terms, before we reassemble our familial unity on a global scale, we must bear witness to and participate in the outcome of two antithetical forces at work. The one espousing the construction of a draconian, homogenous social order in the name of godliness is, in fact, creating a maelstrom of nihilism that obliterates whatever stands in its way, whether the remnants of our past achievements or the aspirations we have for global peace and coherence. The other, a carefully planned and wholesome attempt to create justice, education, and fellowship, is gradually—neighborhood by neighborhood, community by community, village by village—devising a renaissance of the human spirit from the ground up.

The former is doomed to fail, to splinter and self-destruct under the ponderous weight of its own vanity and misbegotten, twisted, and spurious doctrines. The latter, born from loins of sequential stages of manifest justice and divine altruistic love, must succeed by virtue of its obvious logic and beneficial remedies that will attract the hearts and minds of those free to assess its foundation through personal study and assay its efficacy through individual and collective experience.

So it is that the vision of a global community articulated by Bahá'u'lláh over a hundred years ago does indeed presage a family reunion. And among the essential components of that reunion is a universal auxiliary language and script whereby we can communicate with the other members of our newly emerged planetary family:

> The unity of the human race, as envisaged by Bahá'u'lláh, implies the establishment of a world commonwealth in which all nations, races, creeds and classes are closely and permanently united, and in which the autonomy of its state members and the personal freedom and initiative of the individuals that compose them are definitely and completely safeguarded. This commonwealth must, as far as we can visualize it, consist of a world legislature, whose members will, as the trustees of the whole of mankind, ultimately control the entire resources of all the component nations, and will enact such laws as shall be required to regulate the life, satisfy the needs and adjust the relationships of all races and peoples. A world executive, backed by an international Force, will carry out the decisions arrived at, and apply the laws enacted by, this world legislature, and will safeguard the organic unity of the whole commonwealth. A world tribunal will adjudicate and deliver its compulsory and final verdict in all and any disputes that may arise between the various elements constituting this universal system. A mechanism of world inter-communication will be devised, embracing the whole planet, freed from national hindrances and restrictions, and functioning with marvelous swiftness and perfect regularity. A world metrop-

olis will act as the nerve center of a world civilization, the focus towards which the unifying forces of life will converge and from which its energizing influences will radiate. A world language will either be invented or chosen from among the existing languages and will be taught in the schools of all the federated nations as an auxiliary to their mother tongue. A world script, a world literature, a uniform and universal system of currency, of weights and measures, will simplify and facilitate intercourse and understanding among the nations and races of mankind. In such a world society, science and religion, the two most potent forces in human life, will be reconciled, will cooperate, and will harmoniously develop. The press will, under such a system, while giving full scope to the expression of the diversified views and convictions of mankind, cease to be mischievously manipulated by vested interests, whether private or public, and will be liberated from the influence of contending governments and peoples. The economic resources of the world will be organized, its sources of raw materials will be tapped and fully utilized, its markets will be coordinated and developed, and the distribution of its products will be equitably regulated.[5]

Reflection, Planning, Action

Since 1938, when Shoghi Effendi so artfully examined and portrayed the blueprint for a world polity derived from the writings of Bahá'u'lláh, much about our world has changed. Many of the components cited in the above passage have come about, or else are in process. Every day, as we confront those obstacles that remain impediments to achieving this vision, we are incrementally closer to manifesting the attributes that such a family reunion will bring about, what Shoghi Effendi refers to metaphorically as "a new race of men."[6]

In one of its exhortations to the Bahá'í community to grasp the full extent to which Bahá'u'lláh intends that His followers help instigate and model this new global consciousness, the Universal House of Justice, the Supreme Institution of the Bahá'í Faith, sent the following message to the Bahá'í community in April of 1967:

> What is Bahá'u'lláh's purpose for the human race? For what ends did He submit to the appalling cruelties and indignities heaped upon Him? What does He mean by "a new race of men"? What are the profound changes which He will bring about? The answers are to be found in the Sacred Writings of our Faith and in their interpretation by 'Abdu'l-Bahá and our beloved Guardian. Let the friends immerse themselves in this ocean, let them organize regular study classes for its constant consideration, and as reinforcement to their effort, let them remember conscientiously the requirements of daily prayer and reading of the Word of God enjoined upon all Bahá'ís by Bahá'u'lláh.[7]

Sometimes, as I hear people speaking a language totally unrelated to English—or to any of the Romance languages, most of which I grasp a little—I marvel not only that these sounds have logical meaning but that ordinary human beings can fashion everyday conversations out of such diverse and beauteous music. I feel much the same when I see languages that do not use the Latin alphabet and instead use oriental or Arabic characters that seem more like art forms than graphical symbols of human speech.

And perhaps it is these profound differences that cause me to wonder about how we began as one people in Africa and emerged so different in appearance, in culture, and in the sounds and symbols with which we communicate. Perhaps our foremost craft is found and expressed in the language of daily living, this thoroughly humanizing force whereby we share these celestial melodies in our communion with friends and neighbors. This craft of becoming ever more refined in the art of being human, whether as individuals or as a body politic, requires the same sort of imagination, diligence, and perseverance as any other art.

In the chapters that follow, we will examine how language and the tools it employs are the central and foremost means by which the Creator has guided us through this three-part process and presently is exhorting us to fashion something spectacular. It is not a tower to the heavens but a "New Jerusalem" of heavenly neighborhoods and communities that set forth an increasingly delightful environment to prepare human souls for all the work that lies ahead, both in the future history of planet Earth and in the continuation of our individual lives beyond the limitations of this earthly experience.

IN THE BEGINNING WAS THE WORD

As it is said in the Gospel of John, "In the beginning was the Word, and the Word was with God." It follows then that the Holy Spirit and the Word are the appearance of God and consist in the divine perfections that shone forth in the reality of Christ. And these perfections were with God, even as the sun which manifests the fullness of its glory in the mirror. For by "the Word" is not meant the body of Christ but the divine perfections that were manifested in Him.

'Abdu'l-Bahá, *Some Answered Questions*, no. 54.5

According to the Bahá'í teachings, "it is one of the most abstruse questions of divinity that the world of existence—that is, this endless universe—has no beginning."[1] As an emanation from a Creator Who is without beginning or end, creation itself must likewise be without limit with regard to time or space, even though it has at least two distinct dimensions or realms of which we are aware—the physical and the metaphysical (or spiritual).

As 'Abdu'l-Bahá explains, these two realms are not separate but are, instead, different expressions of a single coherent reality: "The spiritual world is like unto the phenomenal world. They are the exact counterpart of each other. Whatever objects appear in this world of existence are the outer pictures of the world of heaven."[2]

This counterpart relationship does not mean that these twin expressions or dimensions of reality are coequal or interdependent. The Spiritual Realm is, effectively, the "real" world, the primary reality, while the physical dimension is the outer expression or sensibly perceptible expression of that unseen or concealed realm. This relationship is, effectively, similar to the human reality in which our spiritual essence, or soul, is the source of the self and of all our distinctly human powers. But during our earthly experience, this essential reality associates with phenomenal reality by means of its intimate relationship with the human body or temple. During this brief formative period of our existence (brief in relation to the eternality of our spiritual existence), this physical expression of our essential reality might be likened to an avatar of ourselves by means of which we gradually come to understand our true nature and the nature of reality itself. We also come to appreciate how we can best advance and sustain our personal and collective development by expressing this new knowledge in creative personal and social action.

But the importance of communication during the physical stage of our existence and the importance of language as the means for that communication is the heart of our objective in this discussion, especially as language is understood in its more refined function as the principal medium for human enlightenment and advancement.

Before we examine how language works to elevate our existence and knit together these twin dimensions of reality, let us begin with a brief but important overview of some of the major premises on which our observations and conclusions will be based, especially from the point of view of the Bahá'í Faith, where we find some of the most lucid and profound discussions about "the Word" and its powers.

Premise #1—All Points of Beginning Are Relative

The first important premise we need to understand is that from the Bahá'í perspective, all points of beginning, or "creation," are merely the inauguration of systems—or their upgrading—within the context of a universal system that is limitless and timeless, that has neither beginning nor end.

From this perspective, all creation myths from world religions relate solely to the beginning of human awareness on planet Earth, or the beginning of one of the successive stages in collective human development, but not the beginning of the universe nor of physical reality as a whole. We know this because the Bahá'í teachings assert that the Creator is eternal, has always been a Creator, and, therefore, has necessarily always been creating.

And since the Creator's purpose of this eternal process is to bring forth beings capable of benefiting from knowledge of their Creator and subsequently willfully participating in a relationship with Him, and since human beings are uniquely endowed with these twin capacities, then we must logically deduce that human beings have always existed. Naturally, this proposition does not mean that "human beings" must inevitably appear in the same material form in every solar system or even on every planet within a solar system. It does mean that by "human being" we are alluding to a being capable of these twin capacities. In brief, the human being has always existed—somewhere, in some form—in the created universe as the loftiest being in any given planetary system.

Put even more simply, we humans are the reason for creation in the first place, because God wished to fashion a being capable of understanding and receiving the gift of His love—a motive we may better come to comprehend and appreciate through our inherent wish to bring forth progeny. Obviously, in humans this motive is not always altruistic; it can become distorted or perverted into a selfish act. But in its purest form, this desire stems from an inherent wish to have a love relationship in which we participate in bringing forth something truly remarkable: another human being capable of knowing that our love is unconditional and that we desire nothing more than assisting this being to become enlightened, virtuous, and thoroughly happy.

To conclude this first premise, we can observe that if this process has always been in motion and its fruit has always been bringing forth and refining human souls, then logically, there have always been planets on which this process has occurred. Allied to this observation is the equally unavoidable logical conclusion that bringing forth human life on planet Earth was neither a random nor a unique process in the universe.

Premise #2—In His Image

A second important premise related to creation and the Creator's methods for educating us derives from His purpose in fashioning beings "in his own image."[3] Going back to the parental analogy, we might take great joy in rapport with a lesser being than a child—for example, in having a pet upon which we can bestow love and with which we can have an important relationship. But the joy derived from participating in bringing forth human life is that we are contributing to the development of beings who, like us, can understand and discuss ideas, become enlightened, contribute to the common good, and attain relative degrees of independent thought and self-motivation, especially regarding their spiritual development.

Hopefully, this process brings us joy, not because we take credit for the accomplishments of our offspring but because we participate in the inherently enjoyable process of assisting a being to rise from essential nonexistence and evolve through the limitless stages of understanding, communication, and refinement. Certainly, we will always be tempted to have less altruistic motives in parenting. We may feel that our progeny's accomplishments increase our own influence. We may even assume that producing those who will attribute their success to our training will bestow upon us some earthly immortality by proxy. All this notwithstanding, in our inmost being is the motive to emulate the Creator's altruistic impulse, even as this premise is set forth in Bahá'u'lláh's statement regarding the primary purpose of marriage: "Enter into wedlock, O people, that ye may bring forth one who will make mention of Me amid My servants. This is My bidding unto you; hold fast to it as an assistance to yourselves."[4]

But what we are to bring forth in this emulation of the Creator's own powers is not an end in itself. Even as we are exhorted to become good or "Godly" and show forth the image of God latent within us, so we are mandated to assist our progeny in understanding, appreciating, acquiring, and manifesting in their character and actions those attributes that are the qualities of God.

Another corollary of this premise is that the Creator has fashioned us with sufficient free will and discernment that each of us is capable of recognizing God, either directly through the teachings of His Intermediaries—the Prophets or Messengers that successively and progressively enlighten humankind and advance civilization—or indirectly through Their perfect manifestation of all the divine attributes: "I have perfected in every one of you My creation, so that the excellence of My handiwork may be fully revealed unto men. It follows, therefore, that every man hath been, and will continue to be, able of himself to appreciate the Beauty of God, the Glorified. Had he not been endowed with such a capacity, how could he be called to account for his failure?"[5]

Premise #3—The Perfect Altruism of the Creator's Motive

We cannot really grasp the logic of these axioms without first appreciating the logic underlying the Creator's motive in all that He does, especially in creating us. For while it is clear in every Revelation that our individual purpose is to become "good" and that the collective purpose of this process is to emulate, in social organization and relationships, the spiritual principles of the heavenly kingdom, the Creator's motive behind His universal process may not be clear.

As I have noted in much of my writing, at the heart of understanding the enigma of why a self-sufficient Being would wish to create anything is a simple but endlessly abstruse tradition in which the Creator states: "I was a Hidden Treasure. I wished to be made known, and thus I called creation into being in order that I might be known."[6] Discussed at length by both 'Abdu'l-Bahá and Bahá'u'lláh, as well as by several Bahá'í scholars, the core of this statement is the reason or motive behind the Creator's desire to be known.

According to the implicit and explicit portrait of God in every revealed religion, the Deity is omnipotent, omniscient, all-forgiving, loving, yet totally independent and self-sufficient. In short, it is solely from God's love that His desire to be known proceeds, not from any selfish motive. By definition, He is neither lonely nor in need of being worshipped—at least, not in any common sense of these terms as we might understand them in human relationships. Rather, like a perfect parent, He knows His own capacity to make others benefit from a relationship with Him, experience His perfect love, and thereby advance physically, mentally, and spiritually.

Thus, we should not infer from this tradition that God suddenly decided that creating a being in His image (that is, with powers such as abstract thought, free will, and creativity) might be a good idea, nor that there was a specific point in time when this process was instigated by Him. If this decision is a good idea, then it was always a good idea. If the Creator has always existed, then this idea has always existed. If this objective is the central purpose underlying all the Creator has brought forth, then human beings have always existed and everything in creation plays a part in accomplishing this purpose. And, finally, if bringing forth a being capable of knowing and worshipping God is the central purpose of creation, and if the Creator is a perfect creator, then we must conclude that not only is the infinite universe useful in accomplishing this task, but that this outcome could not have been accomplished in any other way.

This image of the Creator is so strategically important because it helps us abandon the notion of God as simply an exponentially superior sort of human being. The fact that He created us in His image does not mean we should return the favor by creating Him according to our limited, anthropomorphic notion of Him. Unlike us, the Creator has no limitations, no hidden agenda, no self-serving purpose. And while the Bahá'í writings affirm that the human being is superior to the rest of creation because we are capable of manifesting *all* the attributes of God, the most complete expression of the Creator is the Manifestation of God, Who not only manifests all the divine attributes but does so perfectly. The perfection of the Manifestation is an inherent and inseparable part of His nature, whereas human beings strive for perfection, but never attain it—not even in a single attribute, let alone the entirety of the divine attributes. This distinction is one demonstration of why the Manifestation is portrayed in the Bahá'í writings as another order of being belonging to another "kingdom."

Again, possibly the best understanding we can have of experiencing some degree of this sort of altruistic love is as parents. It is for this reason that God says in Genesis 9:7 that we should be "fruitful, and multiply," and Bahá'u'lláh adds the deeper insight into this process, that the same urge that causes our greatest delight (bringing forth children) is also the greatest source of human progress, both individually and collectively.

It is through the refinement of that creative urge into an altruistic desire to advance the enlightenment and progress of our children—and society as a whole—that this process becomes "an assistance" to ourselves. And, as I mentioned earlier, it also allows us to experience some inkling of the perfect love the Creator has for us and to understand why that love is unconditional. For, indeed, all we need to do to receive God's love is to recognize and choose that love freely—to become active participants in this relationship: "O Son of Being! Love Me, that I may love thee. If thou lovest Me not, My love can in no wise reach thee. Know this, O servant."[7]

Premise #4—How Creation Takes Place

Even though we have acknowledged that creation is a process, not a single point in time or space, there are points of beginning relative to the various parts of this eternal universal system—the physical dimension of reality. Therefore, when scripture describes creation, it is alluding to the formation of our particular planet or the beginning of some important stage in our spiritual and social evolution, not to the formation of reality itself.

As we read the portrayal in Genesis of specific parts of this progression within a specific time frame (six days), we can reasonably conclude that this narrative may be describing a creative process accurately but in symbolic terms.* In other words, since we

---

* "In the beginning God created the heaven and the earth. And the earth was without form, and void; and darkness was upon the face of the deep. And the Spirit of God moved upon the face of the waters. And God said, 'Let there be light: and there was light.' And God saw the light, that it was good, and God divided the light from the darkness. And God called the light Day, and the darkness He called Night" (Genesis 1:1–5).

know that the Earth's formation took millions of years, the "days" to which Genesis refers possibly symbolize cycles of time. Likewise, the image of God's humanlike direct structuring of material reality is a useful analogy for the indirect process by which the Creator employed physical laws to set in motion the evolution of human life on our planet. Subsequently, once human beings were sufficiently evolved to benefit from direct assistance, the Creator provided an educational system for our refinement—namely, the sequence of Manifestations (Messengers) Whose Revelations instigate and sustain the successive stages of our development. Indeed, the Bahá'í teachings affirm that this progressive Revelation is the motive force in human history, not merely an afterthought or an ancillary program that might be useful for some.

In the New Testament, Christ Himself does not say anything explicit about how creation occurred, but the author of the Gospel of John does. He begins his chronicle of the life and ministry of Christ with the following enigmatic statement: "In the beginning was the Word, and the Word was with God, and the Word was God." As if this were not sufficiently abstruse, this same author goes on to assert that "the Word became flesh and dwelt among us. . . ."[8]

The books of the New Testament were written in the Greek of the first and second centuries CE. Therefore, we first encounter this notion of the "Word" as discussed in terms of "Logos," a symbol in this passage of the Word of God revealed to the people via the Prophets or Manifestations of God. The idea of the Logos taking on human form alludes to the process whereby these same Emissaries from God become the means by which the will of God is transmitted into language and by which the teachings set forth in His words are exemplified through Their own exemplary character and actions.

Effectively, They "manifest" the meaning and intent of the Word that God inspires Them to convey. It is precisely for this reason that the Bahá'í teachings refer to these Beings as Manifestations rather than by more ambiguous terms, like "prophet" or "messenger."

In the Qur'án, Muhammad accords with this notion, alluding to all the followers of the successively revealed religions as "People of the Book," the "Book" in this case being the "Logos" or "Word"—the successive Revelations of God. As regards creation and the genesis of human life, Muhammad says that God "created all things, and He hath full knowledge of all things." In surah seven, Muhammad asserts, "our Guardian-Lord is Allah, Who created the heavens and the earth in six days, and is firmly established on the throne (of authority)." Muhammad goes on to allude to the creation of the rest of the universe, or at least our particular solar system: "He created the sun, the moon, and the stars, (all) governed by laws under His command. Is it not His to create and to govern? Blessed be Allah, the cherisher and sustainer of the worlds!"[9]

The authoritative Bahá'í writings—which include the revealed works of the Báb, as well as the writings of Bahá'u'lláh, 'Abdu'l-Bahá, Shoghi Effendi, and the Universal House of Justice—explicitly state that there is a Creator, that He brought creation into being, that He has been going about this same task forever and ceaselessly, and that He will continue doing so eternally. The Bahá'í notion of the nature, powers, and methods of the Creator is quite distinct from most other theological doctrines, especially when compared to the literalist understandings that have sometimes come to dominate previous Revelations after the Manifestation—or any other authoritative interpreter—was no longer available to set things right.

Premise #5 — Why the Creator Refines His Work Indirectly

Before we begin to understand how the "Word," as symbolic allusion to divine guidance, knits together the twin aspects of reality, let us first review a few of the major components comprising the foundation of the Bahá'í perception of how reality is logically structured for the specific objective of human enlightenment and spiritual advancement.

According to the Bahá'í discussion of creation, in the beginning was one word, the command "Be!" indicating the wish of the Creator that this process of bringing forth human life be commenced. And while the Creator is exalted beyond physical properties, this implicit command is sufficient to bring about whatsoever the Creator thinks might be required in order to realize His desire of creating a being capable of spiritual enlightenment and willful transformation.

Since the Creator is omnipotent, He could simply order that we exist instantly and already in some refined condition. But because He wishes to have us discover His bounty on our own and thence willingly aspire to know the nature of His reality so that we might strive to emulate His attributes, He has devised an indirect method for this process. We are thus given every opportunity to acquire this insight and instigate our own transformation, but we are never forced or compelled to do so.

This indirection, understood more generally, is precisely what any good teacher knows to be the most efficacious instructional method. Unless the student wants to learn and is willing to acquire the tools for learning, authentic or meaningful education is impossible. For example, were a student coerced to memorize the answer to a certain question—say, the sum of 345 plus 678— this information might conceivably be valuable were he or she ever to encounter this precise problem. But true enlightenment occurs when the student is taught how to acquire the conceptual tools of math and thus becomes capable of solving all manner of problems.

So it is with our individual and collective spiritual enlightenment. The Creator could have devised a plan whereby we are compelled to follow exacting laws without having the opportunity to question or understand the basis for this guidance. But true religion is neither oppressive nor dictatorial. It maximizes our opportunity to learn and develop while minimizing any sort of mindless exercises, which all too often, in the past, have been contrived by clerics to sustain their self-gratification and satisfy their hunger for power by maintaining control over the laity.

Thus, the need for indirection conveyed through a wise and subtle Teacher, an Emissary from God, becomes apparent. We can become autonomous in our desire for enlightenment only under the ceaseless tutelage of Teachers trained by the Creator to function on His behalf to uplift us, guide us, and provide us with the essential tools and methods that will foster and sustain this endless process:

> . . . since there can be no tie of direct intercourse to bind the one true God with His creation, and no resemblance whatever can exist between the transient and the Eternal, the contingent and the Absolute, He hath ordained that in every age and dispensation a pure and stainless Soul be made manifest in the kingdoms of earth and heaven. Unto this subtle, this mysterious and ethereal Being He hath assigned a twofold nature; the physical, pertaining to the world of matter, and the spiritual, which is born of the substance of God Himself.[10]

This indirect methodology by which the Creator educates human beings (on whatever planet we may dwell in the created universe) is the same one we apply in our school systems where we employ capable intermediaries to teach our progeny to comprehend all aspects of reality. Similarly, we teach them ourselves how to navigate the social and spiritual aspects of reality because it is our fond hope they might begin where we leave off in advancing civilization by degrees.

The Manifestations thus possess two stations that explain the dual nature of Their personal experience and the dual function of Their mission. They are inherently superior Beings. They preexist in the realm of the spirit and thus comprehend the nature of reality from a perspective we will never attain, even in the life to come. Indeed, the Bahá'í writings state that They will remain intermediaries between us and God in the continuation of our lives beyond this brief physical period: "We will have experience of God's spirit through His Prophets in the next world" because "God is too great for us to know without this Intermediary."[11]

I often think of the Manifestations as being like a teaching team because in this loftiest realm of Their existence, They are not only aware of God but are also aware of the mission They willingly undertake in becoming incarnate in the guise of ordinary human beings. Likewise, being in a station of essential unity, They are also aware of Each Other and of the overall plan whereby Each will impart and exemplify teachings geared to the capacity of human civilization during the age or "Day" when each particular Manifestation appears.

Put another way, any Manifestation appearing at the time of Moses would have had to do the same job Moses was exhorted to do by God, and in a manner similar to the teaching plan Moses was inspired to devise. Likewise, while some Christian scholars have found it hard to understand how Muhammad could participate in battles, the Bahá'í writings assert that any Manifestation (including Christ) appearing in the historical context and conditions Muhammad faced would have responded in the same manner:

If Christ Himself had been placed in similar circumstances and among such lawless and barbarous tribes; if for thirteen years He and His disciples had patiently endured every manner of cruelty at their hands; if they were forced through this oppression to forsake their homeland and take to the wilderness; and if these lawless tribes still persisted in pursuing them with the aim of slaughtering the men, pillaging their property, and seizing their women and children—how would Christ have dealt with them? If this oppression had been directed towards Him alone, He would have forgiven them, and such an act of forgiveness would have been most acceptable and praiseworthy; but had He seen that cruel and bloodthirsty murderers were intent upon killing, pillaging, and tormenting a number of defenceless souls and taking captive the women and children, it is certain that He would have defended the oppressed and stayed the hand of the oppressors.

What objection, then, can be directed against Muhammad?[12]

Naturally, this same principle applies to the station and mission of Bahá'u'lláh. His appearance signals the culmination of all previous stages in the process of bringing about the maturation of our global community into a world commonwealth. In this sense and in this context, Bahá'u'lláh's Revelation and guidance is superior to all those Revelations that appeared before Him. However, as He carefully notes in the Kitáb-i-Íqán, there is no ontological distinction among the Manifestations.[13] Therefore, we can infer that any Manifestation appearing at this time would have been guided by the Creator to do the same job and would have been endowed with the same powers to accomplish this task.

It is precisely in this context that Bahá'u'lláh asserts that were He to be killed, God would raise up Another to complete His mission, even as Bahá'u'lláh was faced with having to finalize the Bábí Dispensation before He could reveal His own station to the Bábís: "Give heed to My warning, ye people of Persia! If I be slain at your hands, God will assuredly raise up one who will fill the seat made vacant through My death, for such is God's method carried into effect of old, and no change can ye find in God's method of dealing."[14]

It is in this sense that I tend to think of the Manifestations assigned to enlighten and advance human civilization on our planet as a teaching team; I envision these exalted Beings as consulting, as praying for One Another as Each takes on an incarnate persona to pursue the ostensibly thankless task of teaching obstinate beings like ourselves. Yet, They necessarily undertake this charge without disclosing the full nature of Their powers and without being coercive or becoming discouraged or distracted.

It is likewise in this context, I imagine, that They rehearse in perfect candor, in Their communication with the Almighty, all They are being made to endure, and yet They *thank* the Creator for the privilege of having been appointed to carry out this sacred duty on His behalf. Note how this sentiment is portrayed in the following passage from a prayer in which Bahá'u'lláh thanks God for all the adversity that has befallen Him in the path of His mission: "I give Thee thanks, O my God, for that Thou hast made me to be a target for the darts of Thine adversaries in Thy path. I offer Thee most high praise, O Thou Who art the Knower of the seen and unseen and the Lord of all being, that Thou hast suffered me to be cast into prison for love of Thee, and caused me to quaff the cup of woe, that I may reveal Thy Cause and glorify Thy word."[15]

Bahá'u'lláh thus distinguishes between the two stations that the Manifestations occupy and makes it clear that the Manifestation is not transmuted from one category of being to another and then back again. In His preexistent state, in His incarnate state, and afterward—when He continues to guide His Cause from the celestial realm—the Manifestation, as a Soul, undergoes no change. He is ever the same essential reality as He was when, prior to becoming manifest in the material world, He dwelled in the realm of the spirit and, as Bahá'u'lláh explains it, entered the "School of God":

> O people of the Bayán! We, verily, set foot within the School of God when ye lay slumbering; and We perused the Tablet while ye were fast asleep. By the one true God! We read the Tablet ere it was revealed, while ye were unaware, and We had perfect knowledge of the Book when ye were yet unborn. These words are to your measure, not to God's. To this testifieth that which is enshrined within His knowledge, if ye be of them that comprehend; and to this the tongue of the Almighty doth bear witness, if ye be of those who understand. I swear by God, were We to lift the veil, ye would be dumbfounded.[16]

Continuing this same theme, Bahá'u'lláh then explains that this "School" existed from the beginning that hath no beginning, before the Creator issued the creative command "Be!":

> Were We to address Our theme by speaking in the language of the inmates of the Kingdom, We would say: "In truth, God created that School ere He created heaven and earth, and We entered it before the letters B and E were joined and knit together." Such is the language of Our servants in Our Kingdom; consider what the tongue of the dwellers of Our exalted Dominion would utter, for We have taught them Our knowledge and have revealed to them whatever had lain hidden in God's wisdom. Imagine then what the Tongue of Might and Grandeur would utter in His All-Glorious Abode![17]

Much of this passage might seem difficult, especially the reference to conjoining the letters "B" and "E." We will explain this in the next chapter, after we establish with greater specificity the two primary methods by which the Manifestations teach us.

Premise #6—Twin Methods Require Twin Responses

While the attributes that constitute spiritual reality are in themselves changeless, the understanding of these attributes and our subsequent expression of them in patterns of physical and social action are constantly evolving and becoming ever more refined. In this sense, those essential teachings of the Manifestations explaining what it means for us to be "good" or "spiritual" never change from age to age or from Dispensation to Dispensation, although we gain a more complete and profound understanding of that guidance. This constancy is the source of similarity in the themes and guidance we find among all the world's revealed religions.

But the social teachings of the Manifestations—as They operate within the constraints of a particular stage in the development and advancement of the collective human experience—do change and accord with time, place, and historical context. Thus, the stage we are now experiencing is a unique milestone in the advancement of civilization on our planet—a period characterized by the emergence of a universal understanding of the purpose and role of religion in advancing the human condition, and by a culmination of the learning from all previous Revelations. However, in the future, there will still be a need for further guidance, inasmuch as our collective civilization is capable of infinite refinement.

Thus, while the administrative paradigm that Bahá'u'lláh has designed for planetary governance will always remain essentially the same, this global polity will, like the individuals that comprise it, become ever more refined over the course of time: "The emergence of a world community, the consciousness of world citizenship, the founding of a world civilization and culture—all of which must synchronize with the initial stages in the unfoldment of the Golden Age of the Bahá'í Era—should, by their very nature, be regarded, as far as this planetary life is concerned, as the furthermost limits in the organization of human society, though man, as an individual, will, nay must indeed as a result of such a consummation, continue indefinitely to progress and develop."[18]

This stage is a marked change from all that has preceded it, though it is, in fact, the predestined and longed-for culmination and logical outcome of the foundation established by all the previous Revelations and all the dedication and sacrifice that took place during the myriad Dispensations leading us to this point of crucial change. And our universal awareness and acceptance of this realization will help lay the foundation for institutions essential to the establishment of a global unity emerging from a just and lasting peace.

This quantum leap forward is characterized in the Bahá'í texts as the stage of maturation in the advancement of human civilization. However, this maturation in no way designates the "end" of progress, but rather a period in which the rationale for the process becomes apparent and the tools for all future progress are understood and utilized. Consequently, what had previously been experienced or perceived only in glimpses of spiritual and social transformation will become modeled by ever more advanced degrees. What previous Dispensations were only able to prophesy, we will finally begin to witness and assist: Bahá'u'lláh's vision of the earth becoming a single country and all humankind alike the full-fledged citizens of that country in which the physical or social aspect of reality will mirror forth ever more exquisitely the metaphysical kingdom.

- 3 -

THE WORD THAT WAS THE BEGINNING

I testify unto that whereunto have testified all created things, and the Concourse on high, and the inmates of the all-highest Paradise, and beyond them the Tongue of Grandeur itself from the all-glorious Horizon, that Thou art God, that there is no God but Thee, and that He Who hath been manifested is the Hidden Mystery, the Treasured Symbol, through Whom the letters B and E (Be) have been joined and knit together.

Bahá'u'lláh, *Prayers and Meditations*, no. 183.10

In the previous chapters, we have established the foundational premises and principles underlying the Bahá'í view of reality. We have also seen that, from this perspective, religion is the principal educational process devised by God to fulfill the purpose of creation. We can now begin to examine how language comprises the central tool whereby the Manifestations of God accomplish the task of knitting together the attributes of the spiritual realm with their physical or social counterparts.

Kun fa Yakúnu ("'Be!' and it is")

In the writings of Bahá'u'lláh, we find the following passage from a prayer describing the Manifestation of God: "He who hath been manifested is the Hidden Mystery, the Treasured Symbol, through Whom the letters B and E (Be) have been joined and knit together."[1]

The word "Be!" in this passage represents God's command calling creation into being. The implications of this imperative relate to the concept that the Creator has but to will something to occur, and whatsoever He desires will happen: "Thou didst wish to make Thyself known unto men; therefore, Thou didst, through a word of Thy mouth, bring creation into being and fashion the universe. There is none other God except Thee, the Fashioner, the Creator, the Almighty, the Most Powerful." These words of Bahá'u'lláh echo Muhammad's explanation of God's exalted station: "To Him is due the primal origin of the heavens and the earth; when He decreeth a matter He saith to it: 'Be!' and it is."[2]

Obviously this allusion to the power of God to bring creation into being—to guide and nurture the entire process by which creation evolves and increasingly manifests the attributes of the spiritual world—is not meant to imply a phenomenal event, even though it ultimately brings about phenomenal results. As Muhammad also explains, far be it from this exalted and essentially unknowable Being that He would take on physical properties, such as uttering a command in audible sound or directly (that is, physically) causing a phenomenal event to occur. Rather, His will or wish sets in motion powers that will function on His behalf to bring about whatsoever He desires. And as we also previously noted, because God is inherently just, benign, and loving, whatsoever He desires is unvaryingly that which is just and felicitous for humankind. Furthermore, since the celestial realm is timeless, God can foresee the end of the process at the beginning point of His command.

It is in this sense that the station of the Manifestations is also exalted, because it is They, working as the Creator's Emissaries or Vicegerents, Who become incarnate in the physical realm in order to gradually implement the details of God's plan. Yet Their task is not to undertake this work firsthand, but rather to guide Their followers by means of language and example whereby human beings themselves can become the principal agents in the process of the individual and collective advancement of humankind. We thus can discern in the revealed words of the Manifestations two categories of guidance: teachings about spirituality as manifest in human character, and specific laws regarding practices that will cause spiritual attributes to become manifest at every level of society.

Here we can distinguish between the will of the Creator, emanating from the realm of the spirit—the metaphysical aspect of reality—and that wish becoming realized in the created world, in the physical realm where the constraints of time and space apply. As the Manifestations carry out the will of God over the course of human history, They are constrained by time and space as they affect the gradualness of human progress. Accordingly, the Manifestations must adapt Their message, language, and methodology to befit the capacity of human civilization at a given time and place. It is likewise in this sense that in the long obligatory prayer revealed by Bahá'u'lláh and mentioned earlier, the suppliant recites and thereby acknowledges the following axiom about the function of Manifestations: "I testify unto that whereunto have testified all created things, and the Concourse on high, and the inmates of the all-highest Paradise, and beyond them the Tongue of Grandeur itself from the all-glorious Horizon, that Thou art God, that there is no God but Thee, and that He Who hath been manifested is the Hidden Mystery, the Treasured Symbol, through Whom the letters B and E (Be) have been joined and knit together."[3]

In this verse, the "Hidden Mystery" and the "Treasured Symbol" are epithets or titles of "He Who hath been manifested," the Manifestation of God come to dwell among us to exemplify and reveal in carefully chosen words a new Revelation. In the terms of Christ's prayer—the so-called "Lord's Prayer"—this process enables the kingdom of God to become manifest in earthly form in a progressively more encompassing, refined, and exquisite manner over the course of human history. We can thus come to appreciate this manifestation of God's will "on earth as it is in heaven" as exemplifying how the letters B and E become "joined and knit together"—the conjoining of heavenly or spiritual attributes expressed in earthly or human terms.

It is understandable, then, that when this prayer is translated into other languages, the imperative "Be!" is divided into whatever letters constitute this same command in that language:

> Shoghi Effendi, in letters written on his behalf, has explained the significance of the *"letters B and E."* They constitute the word "Be," which, he states, "means the creative Power of God Who through His command causes all things to come into being" and "the power of the Manifestation of God, His great spiritual creative force." The imperative "Be" in the original Arabic is the word "kun," consisting of the two letters "káf" and "nún." They have been translated by Shoghi Effendi in the above manner. This word has been used in the Qur'án as God's bidding calling creation into being.[4]

Language as a Teaching Tool of the Manifestations

The Manifestations employ two primary tools in the methodology by which They instruct humankind—Their exemplary pattern of a perfectly spiritual human being and Their revealed utterances They leave for Their followers. As we noted earlier, They are endowed by God with whatever powers are needed to accomplish both of these tasks, even though They find it necessary to conceal Themselves in the guise of ordinary human beings for a number of strategically important reasons.

For example, were They to demonstrate Their power through spectacular and miraculous works, then the followers might be attracted to Them solely on the basis of these sensational displays of superhuman powers, and not because they recognize in these Beings signs of spiritual transcendence. For the same reason, the Manifestations never aspire to or accept positions of temporal power. Outwardly, They most often appear among us as the least likely figure to be a Prophet of God. For example, Moses stuttered and was reputed to be a murderer. Christ appeared as a mere carpenter's son. Muhammad was an unlearned leader of caravans in the desert. The Báb was a simple merchant. Bahá'u'lláh, though the son of a member of the court of the shah, rejected political offices and honors, spent His time helping the poor, and later became an avowed follower and teacher of the Bábí Faith, which was considered by many to be an heretical sect.

Across the centuries, personalities with mass appeal have been most often those who flaunt their wealth and whose lifestyle, while specular in its opulence, is often devoid of moral substance. Indeed, the most heralded figures often turn out to be shallow, unscrupulous, and completely entranced by material possessions, power, and public acclaim. Consequently, in whatever age the Manifestation appears, He must confront the rejection of those whom we would think most capable of recognizing His station— such as learned scholars of the day and students of religion.

Even many of the most devout followers of a previous Revelation, who have at their disposal explicit teachings, prophecies, and traditions meant to lead them to recognize the next Revelation from God, usually fail to do so. Veiled by their own lofty station and public acclaim, and often resistant to any change that might threaten their status, these individuals are often the most vicious opponents of the new Manifestation, even though He inevitably fulfills the precise proofs foretold by their own scriptures. And among these proofs are the two principal tools of exemplary character and exquisite language.

As Christ forewarns His own followers, if they are searching for a Prophet, they should look for someone who is Christlike, who is fearless, who rejects earthly ascendancy in all its forms, and who confirms the validity of the previous Manifestation.* Thus, while we might wish that the Manifestations were more obvious in displaying Their station and power, Each demonstrates the precise proof that He is prophesied to bring and that is most appropriate for those whom He wishes to attract. Therefore, They purposefully conceal Their identity until it is timely for them to declare Their station and begin Their ministry. Once They publicly proclaim Who They are and what They have come to do, They acknowledge Their rank, speak with authority, and reveal and exemplify the precise standards for personal behavior that They call upon Their followers to emulate. They then reveal, for the ordering of society, a new code of conduct and laws, guidance that is designed for the individual, the family, community life, and even the more inclusive levels of social governance.

It is in this manner, then, that the Manifestations conjoin the dual aspects of the human reality—the spiritual with the phys-

---

* See Matthew 12:33–37 and Luke 6:43–45: "Beware of false prophets, which come to you in sheep's clothing, but inwardly are ravening wolves. By their fruits ye shall know them. Do men gather grapes of thorns, or figs of thistles? Even so every good tree bringeth forth good fruit; but the corrupt tree bringeth forth evil fruit. A good tree cannot bring forth evil fruit, neither can a corrupt tree bring forth good fruit. Every tree that bringeth not forth good fruit is hewn down, and cast into the fire. Therefore by their fruits ye shall know them."

ical—thereby fulfilling the will of the Creator's command "Be!" And among the most prominent symbols of this dual nature of the Revelations of the Manifestations is the symbolic calligraphy designed by 'Abdu'l-Bahá. Sometimes referred to as the ring-stone symbol, this calligraphic design of the "Greatest Name" (Bahá) consists of two letters, *B* (ﺏ) and *H* (ﻩ) in the following arrangement:

Figure 1. Greatest Name Symbolic Calligraphy

The symbolism in this design is simple but exquisitely profound. Viewed from top to bottom, the highest horizontal line of the letter "b" represents the celestial realm or the abode of the Creator from which command emanates. The bottom level represents the created realm of existence, material reality. The descending or vertical "b" represents the Holy Spirit being conveyed to the material world. And yet its descent achieves translation into language and action by means of the middle or intermediary "b" that represents the level of the Manifestation of God. Finally, the two stars (*haykal*) at this intermediary level symbolize the human temple through which the Manifestation appears on earth and represent the twin Manifestations of the Báb and Bahá'u'lláh:

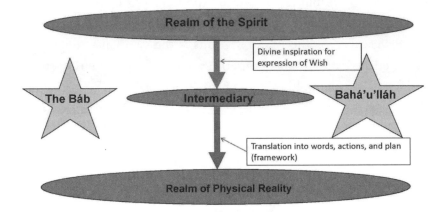

Figure 2. An Interpretation of the Ring-stone Symbol

In light of this analysis, we can observe that the wish articulated by the Heavenly Father is implemented by these Divine Emissaries. From such a perspective, the Manifestations might thus be said to be functioning *in loco parentis*. For while it would be incorrect to assert that the Manifestations are incarnations of God, They are perfect incarnations of all the *attributes* of God, even as a perfect mirror would convey all the attributes and powers, the light and heat of the sun without itself becoming the sun.

Like the perfect or flawless mirrors that They are, the Manifestations provide us with all the access to God that we need (or will ever need or be able to utilize), whether in this life or in the life to come. It is the context of this relationship that Manifestations function for us as the Word made flesh. That is, They are the means by which we understand God and godliness and the path by which we gain access to His plans for us. Thus, the mirror analogy might be another way of examining and understanding the structure of the ring-stone symbol:

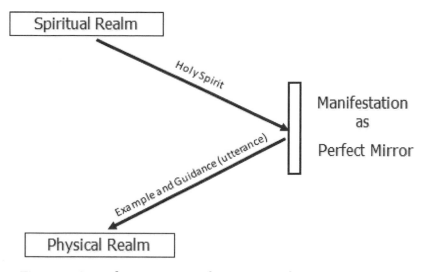

Figure 3. Manifestation as Perfect Mirror of Divine Attributes

It is precisely in this context that Bahá'u'lláh makes the following remarkable observation about how we should regard the Manifestations as we respond to these Beings and the teachings They reveal:

> The essence of belief in Divine unity consisteth in regarding Him Who is the Manifestation of God and Him Who is the invisible, the inaccessible, the unknowable Essence as one and the same. By this is meant that whatever pertaineth to the former, all His acts and doings, whatever He ordaineth or forbiddeth, should be considered, in all their aspects, and under all circumstances, and without any reservation, as identical with the Will of God Himself. This is the loftiest station to which a true believer in the unity of God can ever hope to attain. Blessed is the man that reacheth this station, and is of them that are steadfast in their belief.[5]

I suspect this is precisely what Christ meant when responding to Thomas's question about where Christ was going and how they could know the way to follow Him: "I am the way, and the truth, and the life; no one comes to the Father but by me. If you had known me, you would have known my Father also; henceforth you know him and have seen him."[6] Not understanding exactly the concept of a Manifestation and His function, Philip then asked again to be allowed to see this "Father" to Whom Christ was soon to return:

> Philip said to him, "Lord, show us the Father, and we shall be satisfied."
>
> Jesus said to him, "Have I been with you so long, and yet you do not know me, Philip? He who has seen me has seen the Father; how can you say, 'Show us the Father'? Do you not believe that I am in the Father and the Father in me? The words that I say to you I do not speak on my own authority; but the Father who dwells in me does his works. Believe me that I am in the Father and the Father in me. . . ."[7]

In His Surah of the Temple, Bahá'u'lláh reiterates this same theme regarding the physical appearance of the Manifestation as He specifically applies this axiom to Himself and to His Revelation. In this tablet, the use of the term "temple" is a symbolic reference to the temporary association of the spirit or soul of the Manifestation with a human body. The following passage from that work is particularly useful in expanding this concept of the Manifestation as the perfect incarnation of the attributes of God: "Say: Naught is seen in My temple but the Temple of God, and in My beauty but His Beauty, and in My being but His Being, and in My self but His Self, and in My movement but His Movement, and in My acquiescence but His Acquiescence, and in My pen but

His Pen, the Mighty, the All-Praised. There hath not been in My soul but the Truth, and in Myself naught could be seen but God."[8]

In the Beginning was the Creator

Of course, just because the reality of the Manifestation and the truth He reveals may be veiled or concealed within the shell of signs and symbols does not mean that the truth of the accounts of creation are any less valid or valuable. Interpreted properly, creation myths contain a great deal of insight, even for a contemporary audience. A cursory review of some of 'Abdu'l-Bahá's explicit elucidations collected in the book *Some Answered Questions* demonstrates how rich and rewarding these analogies and symbolic explanations are for a process whereby creation comes into existence under the mandate and guidance of a Supreme Being.*

But our most immediate concern, as we begin to examine how words and language function in the process of Revelation, is not to attempt a catalogue of elucidations of specific passages. Our purpose here is to examine the foundational statements about these same subjects as they are articulated directly in the Bahá'í texts for a contemporary and a future audience fully aware of the divine process, an audience willing and able to understand the nature of reality directly through comprehensive logical methods. Therefore, let us begin with the source of reality, the Creator.

According to the Bahá'í portrayal of reality, the Creator is an actual Being; "God" is not merely a term devised to represent the sum total of the spiritual powers in the universe. And the Bahá'í

---

* In *Some Answered Question* (Part 1, "On the Influence of the Prophets in the Evolution of Humanity") 'Abdu'l-Bahá gives wonderfully lucid explanations of the symbolism found in prophecies contained in both Old and New Testament, including proofs from the Book of Daniel, chapter 11 of Isaiah, and chapters 11 and 12 of the Book of Revelation.

texts affirm that this Being is beyond any direct or complete understanding, even though we can learn an endless amount about His names, powers, and attributes. In fact, it is axiomatic that everything we learn in this life can inform us about some aspect of the nature of God since everything in existence emanates from God, bears the imprint of God, and is thus expressive of the Creator: "Know thou that every created thing is a sign of the revelation of God. Each, according to its capacity, is, and will ever remain, a token of the Almighty. Inasmuch as He, the sovereign Lord of all, hath willed to reveal His sovereignty in the kingdom of names and attributes, each and every created thing hath, through the act of the Divine Will, been made a sign of His glory."[9]

I WAS ALONE

In this sense, we might want first to expand the notion of God's uniqueness to appreciate that He is singular: the single Source from Which emanates all reality, whether physical or metaphysical. Likewise, because God is entirely spiritual and thus indivisible, none can claim to be a part of God or to share God's powers. By definition, God is the dispenser of powers and capacities to whomsoever He wishes.

In a highly respected and thus far unrefuted proof of the existence of God, William S. Hatcher* demonstrates that logically there must exist a Being Who is the Source of all other sources, the Cause of all causes. He argues that since all existent beings in reality are either other-caused or self-caused, ultimately we are left with only one possible being that is Self-caused, and it is this Being Whom we call God.

Hatcher's argument is more encompassing than this brief summary. It goes on to demonstrate how we can also deduce the nature

---

* My brother and colleague in Bahá'í studies.

of that Being, that God is a cognitive Being and not simply some physical energy or phenomenal event—such as a Big Bang—that brings creation into existence.*

In consideration of this characteristic of the Creator, we can appreciate the poetic expression of this condition in the sayings "attributed to the Prophets of old, such as, 'In the beginning was God; there was no creature to know Him,' and 'The Lord was alone; with no one to adore Him.'" Bahá'u'lláh explains that "the meaning of these and similar sayings is clear and evident, and should at no time be misapprehended. To this same truth bear witness these words which He hath revealed: 'God was alone; there was none else besides Him. He will always remain what He hath ever been.'"[10]

It is important here that we immediately distinguish between the "aloneness" that is an eternal condition of God and the "loneliness" we use to designate one who is isolated and in need of companionship. For example, various clerics of some religions tend to interpret this concept as implying that God brings creation into being because He *needs* companionship and depends on our love, or that God is constrained by His own laws and limitations. This interpretation is totally at odds with the logic of God as an entirely Self-Sufficient Being:

> By this [God being alone] is meant that the habitation wherein the Divine Being dwelleth is far above the reach and ken of any one besides Him. Whatsoever in the contingent world can either be expressed or apprehended, can never transgress the limits which, by its inherent nature, have been imposed

---

* See William S. Hatcher, *Minimalism: A Bridge between Classical Philosophy and the Bahá'í Revelation.*

upon it. God, alone, transcendeth such limitations. He, verily, is from everlasting. No peer or partner has been, or can ever be, joined with Him. No name can be compared with His Name. No pen can portray His nature, neither can any tongue depict His glory. He will, forever, remain immeasurably exalted above anyone except Himself.[11]

Language as a Central Tool of Revelation

'Abdu'l-Bahá observes that the Manifestations are the intermediary between the Creator and His creation, and They are the means by which particular systems in creation are wrought, monitored, and sustained. The character of the Manifestations is one indirect means by which we learn about what it means to be a "good" or "godly" person because everything the Manifestations do is replete with some educational significance. However, language is Their direct teaching method, the conduit through which the guidance of God is translated from abstraction to sensible form, from spiritual concepts into words accessible to humankind at each stage of our continuous social and spiritual evolution.

Consequently, 'Abdu'l-Bahá indicates that one meaning of the passage about the Word being the "beginning" is an allusion to the fact that the Revelation of the Manifestation through His utterances is "the cause of all life":

The enlightenment of the realm of thought proceeds from these Centres of light and Exponents of mysteries. Were it not for the grace of the revelation and instruction of those sanctified Beings, the world of souls and the realm of thought would become darkness upon darkness. Were it not for the sound and true teachings of Exponents of mysteries, the human world would become the arena of animal characteristics and qualities, all existence would become a vanishing illusion, and true life would be lost. That is why it is said in the Gospel: "In the beginning was the Word,"; that is, it was the source of all life.[12]

Of course, unlike the single word "Be!" symbolizing the wish or will of the Creator, the Manifestation is challenged to devise specific strategies and programs appropriate for the "Day" of human enlightenment in which He appears. He will not be able to effect, during one era or Dispensation, the final expression of the Creator's will because the advancement and spiritual refinement of human civilization is a neverending process. But each Manifestation will do all that is in His power to advance God's plan, given the historical exigencies and capacity of humankind during the age in which He appears. Likewise, the longevity of His Dispensation will similarly depend on how faithfully His followers promulgate His teachings and what degree of change is possible at that stage of human history. So it is that Christ's Dispensation was destined to endure only about six centuries, whereas the Dispensation of Muhammad lasted twice that long.

In this sense, from the perspective of the Revelation of Bahá'u'lláh and His explanation of how the entire process of progressive Revelation works, we can in retrospect study the logic underlying the words of previous Manifestations and better appreciate how ingenious Their translation was of the Divine Plan of God for planet Earth into specific "Days" or Dispensations. We can further discern how each "Day" or Dispensation sets forth a "minor" or subsidiary plan to advance the successive stages of this abiding purpose. So it is that the words of the Manifestations differ according to the specific guidance and language They devise for the particular stage of human development in which They appear since, as previously stated, Their guidance is geared to the needs and capacities of the people who will receive this Revelation.

In this sense, each Manifestation speaks in terms that are alluding to the message of the previous Manifestations and what They had previously taught. Yet Each also carries forward these ideas to introduce further enlightenment and more advanced practices to humanity. By this means, the human condition has become incrementally more refined and sophisticated over time, though in order to discern this progress we need to view history from the perspective of the spiritualization of humankind, as opposed to confining our assessment to material progress.

It is in this context that Bahá'u'lláh observes how, even in this age of the maturation of humankind on planet Earth, His own Revelation needs to adapt teachings and language to befit the capacity of the people of this day, rather than unleash upon us the full extent of His own capacity: "O son of Beauty! By My spirit and by My favor! By My mercy and by My beauty! All that I have revealed unto thee with the tongue of power, and have written for thee with the pen of might, hath been in accordance with thy capacity and understanding, not with My state and the melody of My voice."[13] Thus, each Manifestation must masterfully employ the art of language to comply precisely with the task at hand, shaping His instructions and His enhanced vision of reality. Both the substance and forms of His guidance are conveyed, therefore, in language that, while accessible, exhorts and challenges us to advance spiritually.

The Twofold Nature of the Revealed Verses

As we have noted, language is not the only tool with which the Manifestation shapes society and prepares humankind to advance spiritually, both individually and collectively. The Manifestation has the power to do whatever is appropriate. But while there are some miraculous events associated with the lives of each of these Messengers, Bahá'u'lláh states that the exercise of Their material powers is not the principal means by which the Manifestations demonstrate Their station or attract human hearts: "We entreat Our loved ones not to besmirch the hem of Our raiment with the dust of falsehood, neither to allow references to what they have regarded as miracles and prodigies to debase Our rank and station, or to mar the purity and sanctity of Our name."[14]

'Abdu'l-Bahá expands this cautionary admonition by explaining that miracles were never intended as a primary proof of the station of the Prophets: "Of course, a miracle may be a proof for the eyewitness, but even then he might not be sure whether what he beheld was a true miracle or mere sorcery." Furthermore, 'Abdu'l-Bahá explains, the true importance of miracles associated with the Manifestations is their symbolic or inner significance: "our meaning is that many marvelous things appeared from Bahá'u'lláh, but we do not recount them, for not only do they not constitute a proof and testimony for all mankind, but they are not even a decisive proof for those who witnessed them and who may ascribe them to magic."[15]

The two most essential proofs of the Manifestation, then, are Their person (They are immaculate exemplars of Godliness manifested in human form) and Their utterances (the message God has inspired Them to reveal). As mentioned previously, it is in this context that the analogy of the Manifestation as perfect mirrors works well to illustrate Their function as Intermediaries between God and us.

And yet because the example of the Manifestations is, after Their ascension, perceived entirely through Their words—or through observations by others—at the heart of each Revelation is the Word, the exquisite language with which the Manifestations teach us. And at the heart of that language is what Bahá'u'lláh refers to as the "inner meaning" of the words, not the obvious literal or surface meaning of what They say.[16]

Part of Bahá'u'lláh's Kitáb-i-Íqán is indeed dedicated to explaining the nature of the language of the Manifestations—how the symbolic or metaphorical "inner meaning" can be studied and discovered. In this context, toward the end of this informative discourse, He makes the following helpful statement about the language of revelation:

> It is evident unto thee that the Birds of Heaven and Doves of Eternity [the Manifestations] speak a twofold language. One language, the outward language, is devoid of allusions, is unconcealed and unveiled; that it may be a guiding lamp and a beaconing light whereby wayfarers may attain the heights of holiness, and seekers may advance into the realm of eternal reunion. Such are the unveiled traditions and the evident verses already mentioned. The other language is veiled and concealed, so that whatever lieth hidden in the heart of the malevolent may be made manifest and their innermost being be disclosed. Thus hath Sádiq, son of Muhammad, spoken: "God verily will test them and sift them." This is the divine standard, this is the Touchstone of God, wherewith He proveth His servants.[17]

It is important to observe in this passage that one purpose of concealing the inner meaning in the outer garment of symbol, metaphor, or parable is to coax us to think for ourselves, to train us to reflect on the deeper significance of what is being said. Indeed, it would be correct to acknowledge that one of the most vehement causes of chauvinism and discord among various religions is the insistence—from their followers, clerics, or leaders—that scripture should be accepted at face value, as being literal and having no veiled or analogical meaning.

But for the individual, merely reading and reciting the sacred verses has no enduring value. The Manifestation exhorts us, instead, to reflect on the inner meaning of the revealed word. Criticizing the "feeble souls" at the time of His Revelation who read, memorized, and recited the Qur'án without understanding the inner meaning of these verses, Bahá'u'lláh (just like Muhammad Who criticized the literalism of Christian believers for the same failure) states the following:

> Twelve hundred and eighty years have passed since the dawn of the Muhammadan Dispensation, and with every break of day, these blind and ignoble people have recited their Qur'án, and yet have failed to grasp one letter of that Book! Again and again they read those verses which clearly testify to the reality of these holy themes, and bear witness to the truth of the Manifestations of eternal Glory, and still apprehend not their purpose. They have even failed to realize, all this time, that, in every age, the reading of the scriptures and holy books is for no other purpose except to enable the reader to apprehend their meaning and unravel their innermost mysteries. Otherwise reading, without understanding, is of no abiding profit unto man.[18]

In a very explicit response to the question of *why* the Manifestations choose to use symbolic language and speak in veiled or concealed terms, Bahá'u'lláh observes that while one purpose is to teach us to think for ourselves, a second purpose is to challenge or test the sincerity of our motives: "Know verily that the purpose underlying all these symbolic terms and abstruse allusions, which emanate from the Revealers of God's holy Cause, hath been to test and prove the peoples of the world; that thereby the earth of the pure and illuminated hearts may be known from the perishable and barren soil. From time immemorial such hath been the way of God amidst His creatures, and to this testify the records of the sacred books." From this observation, we must necessarily infer that those who are spiritually enlightened will be capable of learning how to discern the true meanings underlying the obvious ones. Bahá'u'lláh also warns us that such enlightenment should not be confused with that learning which derives from scholarly or academic training: "The understanding of His words and the comprehension of the utterances of the Birds of Heaven are in no wise dependent upon human learning. They depend solely upon purity of heart, chastity of soul, and freedom of spirit."[19]

Finally, another reason for the poetic nature or indirection of the language of the Manifestations is that by speaking in symbolic or metaphorical terms, this exalted Teacher is able to present various levels of meaning and thereby satisfy and edify individuals, whatever their level of intelligence or education.

The Twofold Nature of Reality

Now that we have begun to touch upon the variable levels of meaning in the language that the Manifestations employ, we can more easily approach the central theme of this entire discussion— that there is a precise parallel between the dual aspects of reality, between the outer physical dimension and the concealed inner or spiritual dimension. As we have already noted, from a Bahá'í perspective, physical reality is only a dramatized version or "outer display" of the essential reality, which is metaphysical in nature.

This view—somewhat reminiscent of the Socratic view of our physical experience as but a shadowy reflection of the true nature of reality—plays upon and bestows meaning onto everything we do, say, or think. Most obviously, this view of reality alludes to the fact that our first experience of self is as physical beings although our actual self is a metaphysical essence, the soul—the principal or most obvious power of which is the conscious mind operating through association with our physical body during the foundational or earthly stage of our existence.

In a very important sense, then, our body and the totality of our physical experience are the expressions of an instructive illusion the Creator has devised to teach us our first and most basic lessons about our eternal reality and enduring purpose—to know and to love God. Stated differently, it is the Creator's intention that while our bodies go through dramatic and difficult changes (especially as they deteriorate over time), our minds and our sense of self develop according to our own willful choices and metaphysical practices, regardless of whether we are young or old, healthy or feeble, ordinary or extraordinary.

As part of this training program, the Creator has crafted our physical experience in such a way that the process of ageing is a truly ingenious teaching device because it exhorts us to attend to our enduring or essential reality (our soul) rather than become obsessed with or emotionally attached to our physical self, which is inexorably doomed to falter, fail, and return to dust.

As Bahá'u'lláh lovingly assures us, this ageing—together with any other disabilities that might seem to encumber or deter our development—in no way impairs the advancement of our true self (our soul and all its powers). In a succinct but entirely helpful analogy, He compares such impediments we might encounter in this life to the placing of a shade or globe over a light—an act that does not impede the properties or powers of the light itself:

> Know thou that the soul of man is exalted above, and is independent of all infirmities of body or mind. That a sick person showeth signs of weakness is due to the hindrances that interpose themselves between his soul and his body, for

the soul itself remaineth unaffected by any bodily ailments. Consider the light of the lamp. Though an external object may interfere with its radiance, the light itself continueth to shine with undiminished power. In like manner, every malady afflicting the body of man is an impediment that preventeth the soul from manifesting its inherent might and power.[20]

Bahá'u'lláh concludes this logical distinction with a heartening reassurance. He states that when the soul dissociates from the body, "it will evince such ascendancy, and reveal such influence as no force on earth can equal. Every pure, every refined and sanctified soul will be endowed with tremendous power, and shall rejoice with exceeding gladness."[21]

Here again, we are dealing somewhat simplistically with an infinitely complex relationship between these two realms and how we experience them. Clearly, reality is one coherent and integrated and astonishing construct. There are not several realities loosely bound together, nor is our experience of the various dimensions or aspects of reality compartmentalized. According to the Bahá'í teachings, we begin our spiritual experience in the "afterlife" more or less where we leave off here. Bahá'u'lláh describes this transition as analogous to the passage from life in the womb to our more advanced physical experience after birth. In like manner, upon dissociation from our physical experience, we will most certainly be amazed by the differences, by our expanded vision, by our clear understanding of reality, and by how the totality of existence works in concert to fulfill the will of the Creator. We will also suddenly comprehend how what we imagined to be two separate dimensions are but distinct expressions of a single reality.

It is precisely in teaching us this logical and relatively simple concept that the Manifestations find it valuable to begin this lesson by first helping us comprehend that the central tools they employ in our enlightenment—the example of Their own character and the utterances they bequeath as guidance—have both a surface or literal meaning and a concealed or inner meaning.

It is thus through language that these Emissaries convey "the Word" and simultaneously are "the Word." It is likewise by this means that They teach us how we also can knit these two aspects of reality together in ourselves, whether in our individual efforts at growth or in our collective and collaborative attempts to replicate the attributes of the celestial realm in the dramatic and progressive creation of social forms and relationships.

Language in the Realm of the Spirit

One interesting consideration—before we examine human speech in relation to our spiritual nature and purpose—is the idea of language *without* sound. There have long existed theories propounding that without speech we cannot think or conceptualize, that even our most internal reflections are carried out silently in words and that until we have developed language skills, such reflection or intellectual activity is not possible.

In one sense, there is clearly a reciprocal relationship between thought and word—the thought precedes the word, and the more words we learn, the more sophisticated we can become in articulating our complex ideas, perhaps even to ourselves. But from a Bahá'í perspective of human reality, clearly both powers emanate from the same source, the essential metaphysical reality that is the human soul. If a child ascends to the spiritual realm before attaining language skills, is the child then unable to communicate?

Obviously, the logical and instinctive response is that the soul, once dissociated from the relationship with the human temple, is no longer dependent on physical sounds or ordinary language to communicate thought. Communication takes place, but it occurs directly from soul to soul, not through the complex intermediary process of an idea being translated into electrical impulses and then into vibrations of the air, and so on.

Our only thoroughly reliable knowledge of the afterlife is derived from the allusions of the Manifestations, Who purposefully limit what they tell about what awaits us: "The nature of the soul after death can never be described, nor is it meet and permissible to reveal its whole character to the eyes of men."[22] However, the scientific community is beginning to pay greater attention to the accounts of those who have undergone a near death experience (NDE) and their description of communicating wordlessly complex thoughts and ideas to souls. While some materialist scientists attribute these recalled experiences to hallucinations or to attempts of a dying brain to comfort itself, there is increasing evidence supporting the possibility that these experiences may be accurate portrayals of the initial stage of the afterlife experience, subjective though they may be. In other words, just as each of our lives in the material world is unique, so we must assume that the exact nature of the continuation of our lives would reflect all the variables that have brought us to this point of transition.

NDE accounts began to be popularly acknowledged and discussed in the 1970s in works by Kübler-Ross, Moody, and others. More recently, I examined Eben Alexander's account of his own NDE, *Proof of Heaven: A Neurosurgeon's Journey into the Afterlife*. As a man of science, he purports to prove scientifically why his personal NDE offers indisputable evidence that there is an afterlife, and he gives detailed arguments why he believes his proof to be sound.

My own opinion, after having studied a good number of these narratives, is that I am fairly satisfied that many of them provide us with insight into some of the aspects of the nature of the transition to the afterlife. It is important, though, that we take into consideration that these experiences, though timeless and extensive from the perspective of those who have them, are describing only a few minutes of dissociation from their physical selves. For our purposes here, I will refer to the NDE experience and these accounts for the single purpose of one consistent observation all of these individuals note—that in this experience, all participants report unambiguous conversations that take place without sound or words and are instead communicated from mind to mind.

Those who experienced an NDE do not attempt to explain the mechanics of how these conversations take place—they don't feel the need to. They focus, instead, on the import of the information shared in these exchanges of ideas. Furthermore, all are totally confident that the dialogues occurred, and they are able to report these conversations with great clarity.

Of course, by definition, a spiritual realm possesses no material properties, but neither is it constrained by physical limitations. For example, in addition to conversations, many of those who have experienced an NDE report hearing delightsome heavenly sounds, perhaps something akin to the philosophical notion of the "Music of the Spheres."

Alexander describes his own experience regarding a nonverbal conversation in which he was pondering what had occurred to him, where he was, and why he was there:

Each time I silently posed one of these questions, the answer came instantly in an explosion of light, color, love, and beauty that blew through me like a crashing wave. What was important about these bursts was that they didn't simply silence my questions by overwhelming them. They *answered* them, but in a way that bypassed language. Thoughts entered me directly. But it wasn't thought like we experience on earth. It wasn't vague, immaterial, or abstract. These thoughts were solid and immediate . . . and as I received them I was able instantly and effortlessly to understand concepts that would have taken me years to fully grasp in my earthly life.[23]

Related to this description of language without words is a passage by Bahá'u'lláh in the Kitáb-i-Aqdas where He alludes to the "School of God" which, He states, He entered prior to His incarnation and where He read the revealed Word before it was revealed in human language: "We read the Tablet ere it was revealed, while ye were unaware, and We had perfect knowledge of the Book when ye were yet unborn. These words are to your measure, not to God's. To this testifieth that which is enshrined within His knowledge, if ye be of them that comprehend; and to this the tongue of the Almighty doth bear witness, if ye be of those who understand. I swear by God, were We to lift the veil, ye would be dumbfounded."[24]

Bahá'u'lláh's reference in this passage to "lifting the veil" has various possible meanings. It could allude to the fact that He reveals only so much of His station and powers as will benefit His hearers, but it also could allude to removing that veil that prevents us—in this physical stage of our lives—from being able to understand directly the process Alexander and others have tried so desperately to put into words. In this regard, it is interesting to note that without exception, those who have experienced an NDE state emphatically that words and language are incapable of conveying their experiences. It is thus obvious from these accounts that the ineffable nature of spiritual reality in general, and these conversations in particular, elude or transcend the capacity of ordinary language to convey them, and that accurate understanding can be attained only by undergoing the experience of the afterlife.

But perhaps equally important in our attempt to comprehend fully the nature of spiritual reality is Bahá'u'lláh's caution that even were such an experience capable of being conveyed while we are in the physical stage of our lives, the result could be detrimental, not beneficial or inspiring. He affirms that were we to experience the nature of that reality—even momentarily—we would be overwhelmed with the desire to attain that state: "If any man be told that which hath been ordained for such a soul in the worlds of God, the Lord of the throne on high and of earth below, his whole being will instantly blaze out in his great longing to attain that most exalted, that sanctified and resplendent station."[25]

Of course, it is important that we not ignore the context of this passage, particularly the fact that Bahá'u'lláh is referring not to just any soul, but to a soul "which, at the hour of its separation from the body, is sanctified from the vain imaginings of the peoples of the world."[26] Nevertheless, the sense of exaltation portrayed by Bahá'u'lláh in these passages seems invariably experienced and recounted by virtually all those who have experienced an NDE.

Some say they are given a choice—to remain or return—and choose to return only because they feel a need to care for loved ones. But almost all those who experience the bliss of the afterlife express regret at having to leave that realm and return to the material one. No doubt the ineffable nature of experience in the realm of the spirit helps explain why the Manifestations are compelled to translate allusions to the afterlife into analogical terms of a paradisiacal physical environment. That they succeed is evidenced in part by the number of religious fanatics willing to sacrifice their mortal lives to attain a paradise that has been described only in terms of sensual delight.

- 4 -

THE MIND AS INTERMEDIARY

> As for the mind, it is the power of the human spirit. The spirit
> is as the lamp, and the mind as the light that shines from it.
> The spirit is as the tree, and the mind as the fruit. The mind is
> the perfection of the spirit and a necessary attribute thereof,
> even as the rays of the sun are an essential requirement of the
> sun itself.
>
> 'Abdu'l-Bahá, *Some Answered Questions*, no. 55.6

How, then, does one come to understand that the language of
the Manifestations has this twofold nature, and, even more importantly, how does one acquire the skills necessary to discern the
concealed meaning of the revealed Word? Is this not a capacity
more likely to be found among the learned who have studied the
great works of the past in which symbol, metaphor, allegory, and
other similar literary devices have been employed? How can the
Manifestation expect the ordinary follower to possess or acquire
such acumen?

As we have already noted, Bahá'u'lláh states that understanding
His words depends on "purity of heart, chastity of soul, and free-

dom of spirit" rather than on academic learning,* the "learning current amongst men."[1] But let us examine more precisely what is intended by this distinction.

Socrates to the Rescue

In Plato's *Republic,* the character Socrates employs a simple but effective technique in trying to define justice as it applies to the individual. In order to teach his students what justice means for the individual, he suggests that it might be easier first to examine justice as it is manifest in larger proportions. Therefore, since the state is effectively the individual "writ large," he suggests that they should first design the components of a just social order and then see how these same attributes could be applied to a just individual.

While this work has lent itself to various interpretations and applications, Socrates' analogy is a simple and ingenious approach to assessing how justice works at both the individual and collective levels. The overriding conclusion about justice observed in the work is that while all parts of the state are essential and collaborative in a properly functioning society, all functions or tasks are not interchangeable. A farmer is essential in order to provide the community with nourishment, but the farmer might not be capable of assuming the function of a teacher of mathematics or of a physician. In this sense, while all people and all tasks are important, it is necessary to realize that not everyone has equal capacity, especially when it comes to matters of governance. The qualifications for the rulers in a just society are their wisdom, their manifest virtue, and their altruistic desire to serve society without concern for reaping any kind of reward.

---

* See page 58.

These conclusions about what constitutes a just society parallel the qualities and relationships that constitute a just individual. That is, even as a just social order derives from the collaboration among those who carry out the various functions required for a properly ordered polity, so the just individual must ensure that his own self-governance is properly ordered and subordinated: for example, the rational soul guides and rules over the emotions, passions, and other aspects of the appetitive nature. Similarly, all the organs in the body are essential for wellbeing, but the organs are not interchangeable—the liver cannot do the work of the lungs, nor can the stomach do the work of the brain.

At the heart of this analogy is clearly the notion that the highest capacity we possess—the rational mind as a power of the soul—should function as the "ruler" of the individual, rather than those organs that maintain the life of the physical body. Obviously, this observation relates most importantly to the fact that the just individual is one who does not let passions or other emotions usurp the duties of the "higher" aspect of the self. By virtue of this higher capacity, justice in the individual is achieved and sustained when all organs and capacities collaborate in subservience and obedience to the decisions of the rational mind, which itself must function in accord with those virtues that befit the "good" individual—selflessness, kindness, refinement, beneficence, magnanimity, and so on.

In other words, underlying Socrates' concept of an "aristocracy" governing the "republic" is that ruling should be done quite literally by those best qualified for the job rather than those who are born into a superior social class or have inherited a great fortune. This is not the brave new world of Aldus Huxley, a dystopia where we are "designed" or trained from birth to be relegated to some station or task, nor is this an abnegation of affluence or striving for excellence, even though some have interpreted the *Republic* this way.

But regardless of our interpretation of the political implications of Socrates' analogy, the analogy between the individual self and the collective self is valuable on its own, especially in our attempt to discern a parallel between the divine plan at work in civilization and the same plan at work in our individual lives. For example, we have observed that according to the Bahá'í theory of the evolution of human civilization, the primary cause of collective enlightenment and progress—whether material, spiritual, or intellectual—is the system of progressive Revelations from God as conveyed by the Manifestations, who might usefully be compared to the "Philosopher Kings" in Plato's *Republic*. We have further observed that it is in this sense that the Bahá'í writings interpret the concept of the Manifestation as the "Word made flesh." The Manifestation instigates the next stage in human progress, not simply through some vague objectives or exhortations but by restating and exemplifying the eternal and changeless spiritual teachings and by conveying flawlessly specific social laws and practices that are designed to implement the plan of God for humankind.

It may be that we can best observe this pattern of advancement from a distance, because as each plan becomes ingrained, and especially once it extends beyond the time it was intended to serve, it may well become distorted or perverted by those whose primary motive is to gain power or prestige rather than to uphold social order and advance the wellbeing of the humankind. This ostensible faltering of the successive stages in the Divine Plan occurs because no single stage is intended as the complete or final stage in human development. Each Revelation and the civilization that subsequently emerges from that infusion of enlightenment and empowerment is properly viewed as a part of one coherent and organic process, not as an end in itself, nor as the sole or final expression of divine guidance.

Thus, we might come to appreciate how the teachings of Moses instruct a specific people about how best to establish justice in the context of a tribal society—a polity of strict laws and precise order as conveyed symbolically through rigorous forms of ritual and worship. With the successive advent of Christ, the concept of law is not abandoned, nor are all the practices from the previous Dispensation left behind, but there is a quantum shift from the strict legalisms that had become associated with the Jewish religion to a more affective expression of religious belief with an emphasis on personal spiritual transformation rather than rigorous attention to ritual, custom, and form.

The new path defined by Christ thus focuses on the process by which one can establish an intimate personal relationship with God as a Father, rather than the stark fear of God as a jealous and vengeful tribal Chieftain. Not that this image of a personal God is a new idea with Christ. In the Psalms of David some five centuries earlier, we find God portrayed as a loving Shepherd, though in safeguarding His sheep, He employs both rod (to urge the sheep onward) and staff (to rescue those who have fallen in the bramble).

Even without delving into a precise analysis of how the progressive Revelation of God is geared to the advancing capacities and requirements of the human race on our planet, we can begin to understand how, from the Bahá'í view, God is a cognitive Being Who is well aware of the condition and needs of His people and consequently inspires His Messengers to tailor each Revelation accordingly. So it is that each Manifestation plays an active role in determining precisely what information and what educational practices will best propel forward the next stage in human enlightenment and development, and—perhaps even more pertinent to our primary focus—what linguistic tools will best convey His guidance, inspire His followers, and enable them to commune with God.

It is in this sense that the Word proceeds from God—His wish conveyed by means of the Holy Spirit—empowering these celestial Beings, the Manifestations of God, to become incarnate in human guise and inspiring Them to shape God's will into plans and language designed to befit a particular stage in our progressive education and advancement. Shoghi Effendi employs a wonderfully effective analogy to portray the role of the Manifestation in this process:

> Not ours, the living witnesses of the all-subduing potency of His Faith, to question, for a moment, and however dark the misery that enshrouds the world, the ability of Bahá'u'lláh to forge, with the hammer of His Will, and through the fire of tribulation, upon the anvil of this travailing age, and in the particular shape His mind has envisioned, these scattered and mutually destructive fragments into which a perverse world has fallen, into one single unit, solid and indivisible, able to execute His design for the children of men.[2]

This conceit is so valuable because it provides us with a visual referent to a complex spiritual and intellectual process whereby the Manifestation creatively translates the will of God into a specific plan for a given stage of human social and spiritual development. In the case of Bahá'u'lláh and the Bahá'í Era (Dispensation), the "particular shape" is the fabrication of a fully functioning global commonwealth from the "scattered and mutually destructive fragments" of our present world condition, a body politic that is "one single unit, solid and indivisible, able to execute His design for the children of men":

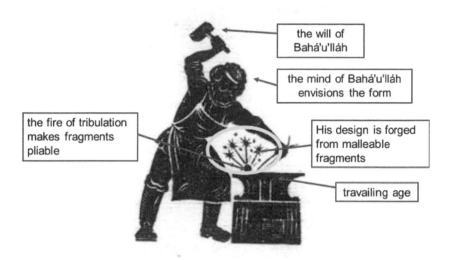

Figure 4. Bahá'u'lláh's Part in God's Plan

But let us now return to how this same process is analogous to the part our soul, mind, and body play in carrying out our own mandate as followers of God's plan in this age. In effect, let us follow the same analogy Socrates employs in the *Republic*. This time, though, we will compare the method by which the Creator fosters human progress to how our soul employs our mind to bring about personal spiritual progress in our daily lives. By so doing, we can discover how language on the individual level functions similarly to link or knit together our essential spiritual reality (our soul and its powers) to our physical reality (our body and its powers).

Therefore, let us again utilize a graph of the descending line representing the Holy Spirit as it becomes translated by the mind operating in association with the brain to create words and logical syntax.

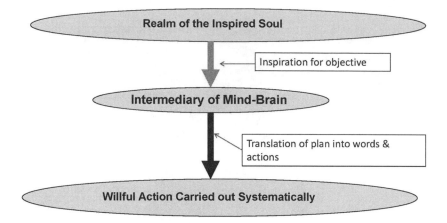

Figure 5. Symbolic Representation of Soul in Relation to Action

Of course, we could also employ the metaphor of the mirror, except instead of the perfect mirror (representing the Manifestation's flawless conveyance of the Divine Will into human language and action), we would use the image of a mirror obscured by dust* to portray the imperfect means by which we struggle to convey an approximation of what we think and feel, whether to our conscious self or to others:

---

* "What is the dust which obscures the mirror? It is attachment to the world, avarice, envy, love of luxury and comfort, haughtiness and self-desire; this is the dust which prevents reflection of the rays of the Sun of Reality in the mirror" ('Abdu'l-Bahá, *The Promulgation of Universal Peace*, pp. 341–42).

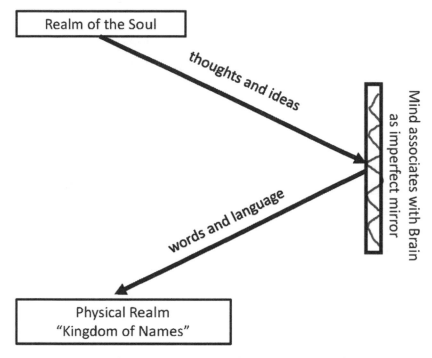

Figure 6. Mind in Association with Brain as Imperfect Mirror

The Basics of Communication

The tools associated with the early advances in human civilization were as simple as shaping a stick or stone for digging in the earth, for hunting or fishing. Doubtless, language itself evolved according to similar pragmatic exigencies. The more complex human life became, the more complex became the terms needed to communicate experiences.

We might well ponder at what point human thought became sufficiently complex that words developed to represent emotion or abstract thought, such as theoretical notions about how reality works, or instructions about how to start a fire or draw pictures on the wall of a cave.

In the Beginning was a Sentence

The foundation of all communication in every language, even the language of animals, is the sentence, whether explicit or implicit. This is understandable for two reasons. First, the word *sentence* derives from the Latin *sententia,* the most fundamental meaning of which in Latin is *thought,* though employed in contemporary discourse of literature the term alludes to "a short, pithy statement of general truth."[3] Thus, any communication expressing a thought—whether that cognition be a mere emotional outburst or a complex observation—necessarily requires the mechanism for expressing thought or feeling as sound.

A sentence is usually defined as a construct requiring a subject, a verb, and the expression of a complete thought. But, of course, while all thoughts may be said to be complete, often the subject is implicitly understood. For example, in the grammatical construction "Go!" the subject is evidently "you." Even in less obvious examples of communication where both the requisite subject and verb are understood, we can still discern the implied sentence. If someone asks us to accompany them and we reply "Yes," it is clear that we mean "I will accompany you." If we respond enthusiastically "Yes!" then implicitly we are saying "I will gladly and wholeheartedly accompany you!"

And if we turn our attention to the animal kingdom, the call of a bird or the bark of a dog is communicating to those of its own kind a variety of "sentences" (complete thoughts) with varying pitches, tones, and sequences of sound. The sound may be inquiring, "Where are you?" Whereupon a response sound may say, "I am over here" or "I'm in trouble! Come help me!" So it is with movements of head or ears by a horse, the stomping of feet by a rabbit, and on and on.

Some might note that this all-encompassing notion of the sentence as implicit in all communication is not so much a discourse about human language as it is about the field of semiotics, or signs. In effect, whether by body movement or by the articulation of sound, one being is creating a symbol or sign that conveys meaning to another being capable of understanding the same semiotic system. Thus, while I am not a donkey (at least, not literally), I have come to recognize that when Gin-Gin (my pet donkey) puts her ears back, I would do well to stay out of kicking range.

And so have emerged a plethora of studies in biology and zoology attempting to read the semiology or language of plants and animals, sometimes with the hope that we might communicate with them, whether it be our favorite houseplant or furry pet, Koko the gorilla, or a pod of humpback whales. Like the "horse whisperer" Buck Brannaman, or Barbara Woodhouse (the late dog trainer who demonstrated a remarkable ability to communicate with all canines), or Jane Goodall and her gorilla families, we are constantly trying to figure out the extent to which we humans can express ourselves to other life forms and, more importantly, understand what they might wish to say to us.

Alas, while some sentient beings other than humans seem capable of expressing emotions such as affection, anger, or grief, or basic animal appetites such as hunger, felicity, or sexual desire, none is capable of producing, expressing, or understanding what humans are uniquely capable of: conceptual thought. For while our pets may feel love and demonstrate affection, they cannot discuss the idea of love. Birds may welcome the morning with a glorious chorus of calls and songs, yet they cannot conceive or discuss what the morning represents—either literally for them or figuratively for us. They know only that they feel like singing, and that is sufficient for them.

Of course, from the perspective of the Bahá'í teachings, and of all those who have come to believe that there is some fundamental ontological distinction between human beings and the animal kingdom, this barrier is not surprising. Because of the powers with which we have been endowed, we not only can welcome the morning, but we can reflect on why the new day brings with it hope and joy.

Or perhaps sometimes it doesn't. Perhaps we feel oppressed by the monotony of having to go through the same routine as yesterday. Or we may muse about how joyful yesterday was and relive in our mind's eye the beauty of a landscape we saw, or recall a conversation we had with a close friend about some happy experience or interesting theory, perhaps about how the morning light is both particulate and a wave.

Consequently, we may understandably ponder the source of the distinguishing characteristics that give us the ability to develop speech for the explicit purpose of conveying complex feelings and abstract theories. Or conversely, we might want to know why theoretical mathematicians choose to escape the vagary of words and resort instead to signs and symbols that, they feel, are more precise because there is an exact one-to-one correlation between symbol and meaning. They develop a formal language of notation to express precise sentences without the distraction of nuances.

I remember all too well trying to coerce my brother William—a theoretical mathematician and philosopher—to translate into straightforward English his article proving the existence of God. Finally, I understood that while people can misunderstand words or rhetorically twist a sentence in order to bend it to their will, a sentence stated as a proof in formal notation cannot be refuted unless one can demonstrate that some part of the equation or formulation does not "add up." And thus he is cited in Wikipedia for having achieved a proof that mere words would have failed to express equally well.

In the Beginning was a Teacher

A child does not learn to speak until exposed to other humans who speak. Speech in human beings does not emerge autonomously or instinctively, although sounds—such as expressions of discomfort, hunger, or various emotions—do. Clearly, therefore, we possess inherent capacities to acquire speech that other mammalian life does not—a child raised side-by-side with a chimpanzee will acquire speech, but the chimp will not. This axiom is obvious, but one among many important proofs showing that while we are endowed with capacities that lesser beings do not possess, we require a teacher to learn to exercise just about every distinctly "human" power we possess, whether it be abstract thought or the language to express it.

Another importantly related axiom regarding the acquisition of speech, whether for an individual or for humankind collectively, is that learning to exercise distinctly human capacities is a process, not a point. Consequently, if we accept the notion that the evolution of our individual skills in the context of a family or community parallels the evolution of human skills collectively, then two ancillary propositions must also follow.

First, it seems obvious that throughout early human history, the emergence of speech capable of expressing complex ideas and emotions was gradual. Those of us who have taught language skills—particularly writing—might well argue that the process is ongoing and that, in time, even more exquisite and refined forms of language will emerge to fashion an increasingly refined familial and social milieu. But it is the second ancillary proposition that is most crucial to appreciate as it relates to our theme, however obvious it may be: For human beings to acquire and exercise appropriately the skills derived from our higher capacities—skills such as speech, refined comportment, and virtues—we human beings require teachers. And because this principle is operative at the individual level, it must also be valid at the collective level; all advancement of civilization must have been prompted by some sort of "teachers."

Put another way, if the understanding and exercise of our higher powers must be acquired through willful effort, and if this process does not occur autonomously, then our progress requires other beings to demonstrate the understanding and use of these powers to us, whether in the family, the community, or the society at large. When we apply this axiom to the advancement of civilization as a whole, we must further conclude that the beginning of all major progress is necessarily instigated by someone who propagates enlightenment about some form of advanced behavior or skill set and who also demonstrates, as an individual already in possession of the skill or behavior to be imparted, that same capacity in action.

This obvious but logical conclusion is the central thesis of the Bahá'í view of the evolution of human civilization—that all forward motion at every major stage of human progress has been and will continue to be the result of the advent of Manifestations. These Emissaries appointed by God teach humankind—by words and example—the appropriate social structures and laws, as well as the most advanced understanding of human spirituality a given civilization is able to utilize for a given duration of time—a Dispensation or era.

While the guidance of the more recent Manifestations—the Báb and Bahá'u'lláh—is intended to reach, teach, and unify the world as a whole, we can conclude from various discussions in the Bahá'í writings (as well as from certain passages in the Qur'án) that during the past ages—when human civilizations were developing independently of one another—Manifestations doubtlessly appeared more or less simultaneously in various parts of the world. This does not mean their message or Revelation was not intended to be spread abroad, but it does mean that the number of peoples and the geographical area the religion could reach was limited by the obvious constraints of the era.

In this connection, Shoghi Effendi restates the Báb's affirmation that "every religion of the past was fit to become universal." But clearly the Báb was referring to the acceptance of the Revelation among the generality of the populace to whom that Manifestation came, since, as 'Abdu'l-Bahá notes, physical and material constraints of the past meant that "understanding and unity amongst all the peoples and kindreds of the earth were unattainable" when the world was "widely divided."[4]

With these fundamental principles regarding the development of human civilization in mind, we can imagine how at least one of the tasks of these Messengers was to advance the capacity of language. With this new toolkit at our disposal, They could eventually convey to us an ever more expansive and sophisticated understanding of the existence and nature of metaphysical reality and of the unremitting relationship between the twin aspects of reality that encompass our eternal journey of enlightenment.

Certainly this concept of the critical function of language in human enlightenment is one interesting interpretation of the reason that Adam (Who, according to Bahá'í texts* and the Qur'án** is the first in the Abrahamic line of Manifestations) is portrayed as having been given by God the power to ascribe "names" to creation. Of course, this story might also be symbolic of how Adam taught others to discern the evidence (names or spiritual attributes) of the Creator as manifest in physical reality—what Bahá'u'lláh sometimes alludes to as the "Kingdom of Names," an appellation well worth a brief explication.

---

* See Shoghi Effendi, *God Passes By*, p. 100.
** Qur'án 38:71–72, 7:11.

In the Bahá'í writings, the so-called "Kingdom of Names" alludes to the physical world where spiritual powers and attributes are manifest in specific objects and actions, or "names." Conversely, in the celestial realm, reality is readily understood in its pure or essential unity, and all creation is perceived to be but an expression of the attributes and powers of the Creator. In the physical world, therefore, spiritual attributes are discovered indirectly through free will and effort. Likewise, most often we discover the attributes veiled in physical reality one at a time, through personal experience and study, as we perceive the particular "names" of God manifested in physical objects and in our relationships with them and with one another. In fact, Bahá'u'lláh asserts that there is nothing in the physical world that does *not* manifest some sign or attribute of the Creator: "Consider, in like manner, the revelation of the light of the Name of God, the Incomparable. Behold, how this light hath enveloped the entire creation, how each and every thing manifesteth the sign of His Unity, testifieth to the reality of Him Who is the Eternal Truth, proclaimeth His sovereignty, His oneness, and His power."[5]

Because Adam appeared approximately six thousand years ago—ages after human civilization had already evolved to a condition of being able to acquire important knowledge—we know that He was hardly the first Manifestation. However, according to the Bahá'í teachings, He was the first Manifestation in this particular cycle of human development, a cycle that concludes with Muhammad and is designated as the "Adamic" or "Prophetic" Cycle in the Bahá'í texts. As 'Abdu'l-Bahá notes, before Adam there were entire cycles that are entirely lost to our collective memory since no written records from that time survive to inform us: "When a cycle is ended, a new cycle begins, and the old one, on account of the great events which take place, is completely forgotten, and not a trace or record of it will remain. As you see, we have no records of twenty thousand years ago, although we have before proved by argument that life on this earth is very ancient. It is not one hundred thousand, or two hundred thousand, or one million or two million years old; it is very ancient, and the ancient records and traces are entirely obliterated."[6]

But even if we assume that one of Adam's functions as a Manifestation was to bestow names—or, more likely, to reveal the names (the inner or symbolic meaning) of an action or object—we can be sure that the allusions to this function are not so much concerned with the origin of language but with the more refined or complex possibilities of language usage. Thus, Adam explained to His followers the "names" or "attributes" of God, particularly as they become apparent in the physical realm, whether manifest inherently in nature or as discovered through our focused efforts to understand moral concepts—such as human righteousness—and express them in daily actions.

What these scriptural allusions might also be portraying with the story of Adam is a Revelation in which ineffable spiritual concepts—the "names" of God—are explained by demonstrating how they can become manifest in patterns of action. By such a method, Adam could have employed the Word to explain subtle spiritual concepts such as the love of God and His creation. It is in this sense, we might conclude, that one meaning of the "kingdom of names" is the physical realm in which spiritual powers and attributes are understood indirectly as they become apprehended through sensibly perceptible forms or expressions, things and actions that language can portray.

Adam's capacity to discern—and subsequently to teach humankind—the concealed or inner significance of reality (even as He was taught by God) is illustrated in the Qur'án where God is described as informing the celestial hosts that Adam is an exalted figure of great knowledge, Who understands the "nature" of things in themselves:

"He said: 'O Adam! tell them their natures.' When he had told them, Allah said: 'Did I not tell you that I know the secrets of heaven and earth, and I know what ye reveal and what ye conceal?'"[7]

Perhaps in time we will discover more precisely how language evolved to accord with the refinement and advancement of the human condition, with the complexification of human understanding of reality, and with the increasingly strategic need to express insights and share knowledge so that all progress could become collaborative. And doubtless in time we will discover something more about the role that the Manifestations played in the evolution of the terminology necessary to portray the dual aspects of the human experience—the physical and the spiritual/intellectual. So far, it is clear that there must always have been an inextricable link between the gradual increase in knowledge and human social organization and the advancement in the sophistication of language as a principal tool for this process.

In this sense, we need not ask which came first—language or learning. Obviously, this is a reciprocal relationship—they promote and advance each other in concert. Thus, when we accept the idea that the capacity for language is inherent to humans—though undeveloped or latent until prompted by an external source of education—then we realize the necessity of an educator of superior kinetic capacity, such as a parent or teacher, or, for the collectivity, a Manifestation. Only by means of such external assistance can this inherent capacity become manifest and freely utilized, a power that is evidence of powers that distinguish human reality from less advanced species of life—even the most highly developed members of the animal kingdom.

The Recapitulation Theory

The biogenetic theory, that ontogeny recapitulates phylogeny, asserts that there is a discernible and logical parallel between the evolution of the child in the womb and the evolution of the human species on our planet. Whether or not one accepts this theory as being literally true, it nevertheless provides us with a thoroughly useful analogy in theorizing how the various stages of human development take place. Certainly this analogy has value for us as we ponder how language develops along with the evolving understanding of self-consciousness and other abstract concepts and capacities.

For example, if we examine how a child develops language skills, we are hard-pressed to distinguish whether words are only a means of conveying the emerging concepts in the child's mind or whether they are also what enables the child to conceive abstract notions— such as colors, shapes, numbers, feelings, desires, and other affective states. Clearly, this specific pattern of development varies from child to child according to the personality, inherent capacities, and parental instruction and nurture. We can observe that no two children follow precisely the exact same path in learning how to apply words to understanding and communicating abstraction.

We might benefit from observing the developing skills of our own children or grandchildren as they proceed through various stages of learning and communicating. When we do, I suspect we will conclude that thought precedes expression of thought, that the urge to communicate something is what causes articulation of any sort, be it a particular sort of cry or the early formation of a word.

Another phenomenon we can also observe from studying children who are challenged by physical or emotional problems—such as loss of hearing, deprivation of early care and training, abuse, or neglect—is that they will develop their own language, some combination of signs and sounds. In short, while thought and language are integrated and reciprocal, it seems logical and empirically demonstrable that the need to communicate precedes the development of words, even as the wish or will of the Creator precedes the "Word" conveyed to humankind through the Manifestations.

But perhaps what is more interesting to observe, as we interact with and teach children, is that while concepts can be taught, they also will be encountered and subsequently learned as a matter of course through inference. The concept of the roundness of a circle, for example, will occur as the child begins to observe what diverse circular objects have in common, such as the letter *o*, a picture of the moon, or a ball. Naturally this process will be greatly accelerated with the help of parents using various games and exercises devised to teach these concepts, but this inferential or inductive process of going from particular to general is an inherent capacity of the human mind.

Starting from an understanding of material concepts of shapes, colors, and sounds, a child can, fairly early on, begin to progress to distinguishing more abstruse notions and feelings, such as fairness, beauty, piety, cleanliness, and so on. We are thus quite aware at this stage when the child is sad, happy, in pain, or confused. These feelings are conveyed through communication—if not through words, then through facial expressions and sounds, all of which are an integral part of semiotics, signs that include all symbolic forms of expression. Consequently, the developing child can start identifying emotion and can learn to recognize when another person is happy, sad, or perplexed. Furthermore, in this process of learning, the child is acquiring the equally important skill of responding to others with sympathy and empathy, even if it may be some time before the child can articulate these lofty attributes with appropriate words.

Here again, we recognize the inextricably strategic role of the parent and teacher in initiating and accelerating the process by which spiritual attributes are understood and practiced. Virtues like kindness, gentleness, friendship, and cooperation can be expressed in games played with stuffed animals, dolls, and other imaginary figures. Whether by guiding the child in the appropriate ways to respond to stories or relationships with others, creative and instructive parenting becomes simultaneously the most challenging and the most rewarding skill one can acquire.

As the child grows and develops, he or she can also be trained to express and experience these same virtues and abstract notions in more inclusive social environments, such as in relationships with other adults and children. From these interactions, concepts of friendships, justice, sharing, gentleness, or kindness can be acted out with others, especially when the parent / teacher begins to apply names to the various complex experiences: "You were very kind today in sharing your toys. I am proud of you!" "That was not nice of you to hit your friend; you should be nice to others and use your words to express how you feel."

Here again we do well to revert to the myth of Adam as identifying and teaching His followers the names of God. While we may take for granted that every child is taught attributes that constitute "goodness" and characterize "the good person," clearly not all children enjoy such a beneficial and enlightened upbringing. Regardless of what they may be exhorted to be, they will infer more from what they observe in the behavior of those in their immediate surroundings than they will from miscellaneous admonitions: "Be good or I will punish you!" "If you get in trouble again, you will not get a present for your birthday!"

One injunction that summarizes so well the paradox between the "names" of virtues and the manifestation in action of that same virtue is "I don't *ever* want to see you hit anyone again!" delivered by a clueless parent who strikes the child on the backside to emphasize this stellar lesson in ethics. To put this concept in the most common of terms, the child will learn more from what we do than from what we say, and they may develop concepts and behaviors that they deem to be expedient rather than any character traits we might wish them to acquire.

In contemporary society, for example, teaching morality is extremely difficult because there no longer exists much in the way of any standardized or shared notion of morality. As a result, most children and youth perceive that the negative outcome of a deplorable action is being caught (and consequently being subject to punishment), as opposed to damaging one's character by being "bad," "naughty," or "immoral."

Another phenomenon related to the language of moral instruction of children has to do with definitions of abstract terms as they are assigned to virtuous actions, thereby capturing the essence of an attribute in symbolic and memorable behavior. Perhaps the most important point in this relationship between language and learning is that the mind of the child is inherently logical. It is capable of both inductive and deductive thinking from the beginning of its awareness. These capacities are inherent gifts, powers of the mind that, while associating with the brain, emanate from the soul. And this observation clearly implies that our logical mind remains with us after we depart this physical stage of our infinite lives.

In fact, it is extremely important for us to note—as we consider the formation of language related to virtues, capacities, and attitudes—that logic must be trained *out* of a child in order to coerce the young one to accept such irrational attitudes as revenge, selfishness, and prejudice toward various categories of human beings. One memorable expression of this axiom can be found in lyrics from Rodgers and Hammerstein's *South Pacific*:

> You've got to be taught
> To hate and fear,
> You've got to be taught
> From year to year,

It's got to be drummed
In your dear little ear
You've got to be carefully taught.

You've got to be taught to be afraid
Of people whose eyes are oddly made,
And people whose skin is a different shade,
You've got to be carefully taught.

You've got to be taught before it's too late,
Before you are six or seven or eight,
To hate all the people your relatives hate,
You've got to be carefully taught!

Prophets as Parents

Whether we like it or not, the most powerful teacher of our children is the community. Consequently, even though as parents we may readily recognize the moral flaws in the norms and mores of the society in which we live—and try to safeguard our children from assuming these unfortunate and debasing attitudes—we cannot simultaneously safeguard our progeny and also have them become active participants in that same society. What we can do is provide them with an alternative home environment and training that will render our children capable of sorting out for themselves what parts of this social harangue they will accept and emulate and what parts they will reject and guard against.

Inasmuch as we cannot effectively invent a code of conduct or moral attitude to combat the incessant ambient noise of denigration and base behavior that afflicts society, we must find a viable alternative based on logical responses to this indoctrination. Contemporary educators no longer possess nor—assuming they acquired some shared moral perspective themselves—would they ever be allowed to purvey any uniform code of virtue to combat our morally barren landscape.

Clearly, in such a morass of negativity, only a few noble and divinely guided children can escape unscathed, even with the most ardent and devoted oversight of loving parents. Among these children, only an even smaller percentage will be capable of exemplifying an alternative path of nobility and upright conduct sufficiently attractive to their peers that it will inspire them to follow their lead. But with the support of an enlightened and transformed community, these same children will become empowered and will delight in their own distinctive behavior.

In light of these observations, we can better appreciate that, because we are by nature and necessity inherently social beings, the Manifestations come to instruct us collectively in order that we might transform the entirety of society, not merely a discrete group of "believers." The revealed utterances of Bahá'u'lláh thus articulate the objective of refining human virtue for this entire age. Likewise, they guide us in establishing a process by which this goal can be attained by the individual, the family, the local community, and the global community as a whole.

For while the major theme of this "Day" is the creation of a global commonwealth established on spiritual principles, it matters little how well-wrought its design may be or how smoothly it functions if our experience at the local level of family and community is not also changed for the better. Because though we may think globally, we live locally. It is precisely for this reason that the Bahá'í community—under the continual guidance of the Universal House of Justice—is presently focusing so much attention on the grassroots level of community-building, as opposed to attempting to legislate global change from the top down.

From the Manifestation, Bahá'u'lláh, and from the "Word" He revealed—together with the authoritative texts from His appointed successor (His son 'Abdu'l-Bahá), from the Guardian Shoghi Effendi (appointed by 'Abdu'l-Bahá), and the Universal House of Justice (the Supreme Institution designated and designed by Bahá'u'lláh's "Word")—the Bahá'í community is acquiring a new vocabulary. This new language is designed to describe and coordinate new and renovated concepts of justice, fellowship, love, and piety, even as all the previous Manifestations themselves introduced Their own terminology to communicate revised notions of personal ethics, of community life, and to further the education, enlightenment, and advancement of human society during Their "Day." So it is that in the Bahá'í texts we find terms such as "Manifestation," "Eternal Covenant," "Most Great Peace," "New World Order," "global commonwealth," "oneness of humanity," "equality of men and women," "unity of science and religion," "progressive Revelation," "unity of religions," "abolition of prejudice," "universal auxiliary language," "universal compulsory education," "universal human rights," "abolition of the extremes of poverty and wealth," and so on.

These and many other phrases and concepts introduced by Bahá'u'lláh well over a century ago are infused into the current worldwide Bahá'í discourse. The "Word" has become translated into specific terms representing concepts and processes created to advance civilization for this age, and this increasingly large but eminently useful vocabulary allows both Bahá'ís and friends of the Faith to discuss and implement a rapidly emerging new reality as citizens of a global community and as coworkers in constructing a new World Order from the ground up.

The current status of this global community reminds me of Gregory, my youngest grandchild, who is almost two years old. He always seems to know exactly what he wants or needs, but he has not yet acquired all the words or syntax necessary to express his thoughts. Consequently, he usually points at what he wants, or at something related to it, and says "Dat! Dat!" Because he is confident that we will get him "that," he is presently content to not give more specific names to his reality.

In this same vein, I feel that at this moment, a large majority of the citizens of the world are pointing to their hungry children or their makeshift houses or empty water jugs and saying "Dat! Dat!" And we know exactly what they mean and what they need—food, shelter, clothing, medicine, freedom, justice, peace, the sufficiency whereby to live some quality of life that all too many are denied.

This is also an important aspect of the parlance of this Day, the solutions to which are proffered in the "Word" carefully penned by God's Emissary in direct and unambiguous terms. Bahá'u'lláh set forth eloquently what we should be studying and implementing in pursuit of our divinely ordained purpose as present-day members of the human family and as coworkers in the vineyard of God in order to respond to this plaintive but justifiable request for "Dat! Dat!"

- 5 -

THE PROCESS OF CREATING WORDS

All the powers and attributes of man are human and hereditary in origin—outcomes of nature's processes—except the intellect, which is supernatural. Through intellectual and intelligent inquiry science is the discoverer of all things. . . . Science is the first emanation from God toward man. All created beings embody the potentiality of material perfection, but the power of intellectual investigation and scientific acquisition is a higher virtue specialized to man alone.

'Abdu'l-Bahá, *The Promulgation of Universal Peace*, p. 49

Despite incredible advances in the sciences of archaeology, anthropology, and linguistics, the centuries-old scholarly debate about the origin of language in the human species seems hardly any closer to arriving at a consensus about when the advent of exercising this critical human capacity took place.

While linguistic studies can be traced back centuries, the publication of Darwin's theory of evolution in 1859 set in motion the quest for a point in our development that would account for the acquisition by humans of language skills that other mammalian species do not possess, or at least not to the extent that we do. As we previously noted, animals can convey basic sorts of communication within their own species by means of symbolic sounds. However, even the more advanced species in the animal kingdom, though capable of learning to respond to various human signs or sounds, are not able to engage in a conversation about abstract concepts.

The fundamental obstacle to reaching any substantive conclusions about the origin of human speech is that no obvious evidence supports or refutes the various theoretical notions that have emerged. The result of this dilemma is that, as early as 1866, the Linguistic Society of Paris banned debates on the subject, a decision to which the generality of scholars in this field of study largely consented.

In effect, the origin of language was deemed to be so entirely reliant on conjecture that most theories and studies were set aside. Without empirical evidence of any kind, and without the hope of ever gaining access to such information, the subject lay dormant until the latter part of the twentieth century.

Theories about the Origin of Language

We can generally divide most of the arguments about the origin of human language that have emerged in the past few decades into two broad categories—"continuity" theories and "discontinuity" theories. Those advocating the continuity theory propose that the capacity for language was inherent and thus developed quite naturally as a result of the continuous evolution of the human species. The advocates of the discontinuity theory suggest instead that the capacity for speech is unique to human beings and must have appeared in the wake of some sudden change or external influence that resulted in a quantum advancement of the human ability to articulate thought.

Prominent linguist and philosopher Noam Chomsky advocates the discontinuity approach. He has theorized that a chance mutation occurred, possibly some hundred thousand years ago, that instantaneously set in motion a dormant faculty in what was, by then, the complete or perfected form of the fully evolved human being.[1] This theory plays off a foundational theory that a given biological change in a species can be instigated by a random change or chance mutation in a single being, whereupon this change rapidly spreads throughout the species.

Opposing this concept of some random mutation or the virtually instantaneous infusion of capacity is the more widely accepted continuity theory. According to this view, the capacity for language is innate, and the practice and subsequent advancement of this inherent potentiality emerged gradually as the collective human experience became more complex and diverse, thereby requiring more complex linguistic skills, even as we proposed in the previous chapter with the analogy of the child's development of language skills. Of course, this theory presents an obvious problem if its proponents accept the commonly held view that human beings are merely an advanced form of animal. Why do we not presently observe this same capacity beginning to manifest itself among more highly developed animals as they are exposed to interaction with human beings?

This question has prompted several well-known experiments in which apes were taught to employ signing to communicate with humans, rather than rely on the sounds and movements they instinctively already use to communicate among themselves. In other words, if they, like us, possess the latent physiological and intellectual skills we possess, then should we not be able to teach them to utilize this capacity even as the Manifestations have taught us? And once being taught, would they not then be capable of passing this knowledge along to their companions and offspring?

For example, if one ape learns to sign, would he or she not then teach other apes or offspring to do the same?

The result of maintaining the theory that human beings are simply highly evolved animals is that exhaustive experiments have attempted not only to teach animals to speak, but also to interpret what they are saying to each other with the sounds they employ to communicate among themselves. The findings in such experiments have value in that they allow us into the animal world to discover how animals issue commands, share experiences, and even express affection. But no part of their system of communication seems to have the ingredients that relate to human speech: words invented to represent ideas or concepts, complex syntax to represent conditionality, extended discourse in a sequence of exchanges to resolve a problem, or discussion of ideas about reality. In short, animals seem to have only precisely enough capacity to communicate their own immediate experience.

We delight in the charming and varied songs of the birds and are amazed by the precision with which parrots can mimic the sound of our words. Likewise, we can find joy in the mesmerizing beauty of the amazingly long symphonies of the humpback whales in the ocean deep. But ultimately we must conclude that we will never get any animal—however advanced—to engage in an extended conversation about anything more than its immediate needs or concerns, no matter how hard we try. The fact is that the capacity for articulating abstract thought seems confined to the only species capable of having such thoughts—the human species.

The reason lies not in hubris about what we have accomplished, or in the infinitesimally minute bit of DNA we do not share with chimps, nor is it solely due to the size or superior complexity of our brains. From the Bahá'í perspective, the distinctly human powers and capacities—such as speech, free will, abstract thought, reflection, concepts of morality, or the continuity of life beyond the physical realm—derive from the essential spiritual reality of man: the soul.

The loftier question thus is not whether we evolved from lesser species—clearly we did. Human life was not here in the beginning, and at some point it emerged from the same water and clay that brought forth all other mammalian life. Rather, the question becomes: At what point did human life become sufficiently distinct from animal life and capable of establishing an associational relationship with the spiritual essence that is the soul?

The Bahá'í writings assert that the soul emanates from the spiritual realm and establishes an associative relationship with the human temple during the process of conception.* Consequently, we may ponder if earlier forms of our ancestral lines (such as *Homo erectus* or *Homo neanderthalensis*) were likewise endowed with the same associational relationship with this distinctive spiritual essence, as opposed to the sort of spirit that animates lesser forms of life.

As science and the methodology and tools of scientific study advance, we seem to grow closer to discovering some insights that may help us find the answer to these enigmatic questions. But for now, we can safely conclude that there is some stage in our evolution when this process of being endowed with this subtle associational relationship did not exist—or else existed in some incipient or precursory form—before we transitioned to a more advanced stage during which it fully took form, possibly when we finally emerged as distinctly *Homo sapiens*.

---

* "It should be pointed out, however, that the Teachings state that the soul appears at conception, and that therefore it would be improper to use such a method, the effect of which would be to produce an abortion after conception has taken place" (from letter written on behalf of the Universal House of Justice to an individual believer, May 23, 1975, in *Lights of Guidance*, no. 1155).

If so, this transformation might account for the fact that *Homo sapiens* is the sole surviving species of the genus *Homo* and that our current "wisdom" or sapience derives from the power of this associative relationship with the soul. Given the analogy of how knowledge and powers evolve in a child, we can imagine that the powers of the soul were evolving in consonance with the final physical features that distinguish the fruition of the *Homo* genus. In short, we can do little more than have some logical discourse that is necessarily speculative, at least until such time as the studies of the physical and metaphysical aspects of reality become more collaborative.

Consequently, while broadly placed within the "continuity" category, the Bahá'í view is slightly different from most other theories because of the foundational Bahá'í premise that the human being, once having reached a certain stage of evolution, has effectively emerged as a different order of being from other mammalian life. This belief necessarily sets the Bahá'í view apart from most strictly materialist theories.

Restated from another perspective, if the human being (*Homo sapiens*) is not a chance mutation of another order of being but rather the fruition of a particular branch of hominid* possessing distinct powers and capacities, then any theory about our evolved capacities that does not take into consideration the interaction of strictly physical powers with the spiritual resources of the soul will in the long run prove inadequate.

So it is that from the Bahá'í point of view, the power of speech derives from the power of ideation and abstract reflection, but these powers themselves are emanations of the human soul. There-

---

* "Hominid" now designates the group consisting of all forms of Great Apes, whereas "hominin" designates a branch of hominid that includes *Homo sapiens* and our more immediate ancestors.

fore, capacity for abstract thought necessarily precedes the need or desire to communicate such thought. Furthermore, from this same point of view, it is the existence of an associative relationship with the soul that enables humans to have self-awareness and other abstract ideation, thereby distinguishing the human reality from that of the animal kingdom. For once having come into our own as the fruition of eons of physical and spiritual evolution, we became set apart, even as the Bahá'í teachings purport that God's purpose in creating us was to form a being capable of knowing its Creator and benefiting from its relationship with Him.

As 'Abdu'l-Bahá observes in the epigram for this chapter, "All the powers and attributes of man are human and hereditary in origin, outcomes of nature's processes, except the intellect, which is supernatural."[2] Consequently, in the most general sense, the Bahá'í view of the human capacity for abstract thought as expressed in the symbolic form of language is inherent, even if it was latent in the beginning. The use of language then developed over time, but only by means of direct or indirect influence or instruction—the capacity is inherent, but the development of the latent potential into language skills must have come from an external influence, just as all our other major advances in capacity.

Consequently, the higher brain function is not causative in the transference of ideas into language; rather, the mind is the intermediary between the soul and the physical tools of articulation. True, the more sophisticated powers of language emanate from the mind, but as already noted, from the Bahá'í view, the mind or consciousness is also a power or function of the soul.

Of course, we might find it useful at this point to set out on an extended discourse about the Bahá'í theory of the soul in relation to the brain, especially as opposed to most materialist views of human powers as originating in the brain. But all this discussion already exists in a number of studies purporting to prove the nonlocality of human consciousness.* Furthermore, scientists are beginning to question the notion that human will and the "self" or self-consciousness are the spontaneous and random outcome of the circuitry connecting the approximately hundred billion neurons in the brain. For however miraculously devised this most complex of physical creations might be, some researchers are beginning to conclude (largely from applying the law of parsimony) that this most logical explanation for human consciousness is a theoretical model in which the "operator" of this marvelous electronic organ is "outside" and distinct from the brain.** This theory necessarily involves a concept of a metaphysical essence, whether or not we ascribe to it a religiously connotative epithet, such as "soul."

Put another way, the more we examine the brain and brain function, the less likely it seems that this complex composite of neurons can, alone and spontaneously, create our sense of self, autonomously produce thought, retain abstract ideas, and instigate plans of action. In all likelihood, the simplest and most logical explanation for the source of these human powers is that they derive from an essence other than the physical brain, because matter—alone and unaided, however complex and ingeniously arranged—is incapable of producing a metaphysical result.

---

* Among my own published works, the work *Close Connections: The Bridge between Spiritual and Physical Reality* (2005) deals with this subject in some depth, especially Chapter 11 entitled "The Ghost in the Machine: Some Proofs of the Soul." Also see Stanislav Goff, *Holotropic Breathwork: A New Approach to Self-Exploration and Therapy* (Albany: State University of New York Press, 2010) and Pim Van Lommel, *Consciousness Beyond Life: The Science of the Near-Death Experience* (New York: HarperCollins, 2010), and, of course, the more recent study by Eben Alexander, *Proof of Heaven: A Neurosurgeon's Journey into the Afterlife* (New York: Simon & Schuster, 2012).

** Daegene Song, "Quantum Theory, Consciousness, and Being." https://arxiv.org/pdf/physics/0703034.pdf.

In his book *The Character of Consciousness*, David J. Chalmers observes, "It is undeniable that some organisms are subjects of experience, but the question of why it is that these systems are subjects of experience is perplexing. . . . It is widely agreed that experience arises from a physical basis, but we have no good explanation of why and how it so arises. Why should physical processing give rise to a rich inner life at all? It seems objectively unreasonable that it should, and yet it does."[3] He then goes on to suggest that in order to bridge the apparent chasm between our physical reality and its non-physical manifestation, a new order of concepts needs to be introduced, what he calls "fundamental entities":

> Fundamental entities are not explained in terms of anything simpler. Instead, one takes them as basic and gives a theory of how they relate to everything else in the world. . . .
>
> I suggest that a theory of consciousness should take experience as fundamental. We know that a theory of consciousness requires the addition of *something* fundamental to our ontology, as everything in physical theory is compatible with the absence of consciousness. We might add some entirely nonphysical feature from which experience can be derived, but it is hard to see what such feature would be like.[4]

Of course, if the Bahá'í assertions about this spiritual essence and its relation to the brain and body are true, we can be confident that science will in due time prove the existence of the soul and become capable of discerning and describing in broad terms how the soul exercises its powers.* And while some individual researchers may have a vested interest in supporting their own theories,

---

* See chapter 11, "The Ghost in the Machine," in *Close Connections*, pp. 169–200.

science, as one of the noblest bodies of learning, will in time ultimately discover the truth about reality, regardless of whose feelings or reputations get hurt in the process.

The Recapitulation Theory and Language Development

Perhaps Chomsky is not in error when he theorizes that the human capacity for language seems to have emerged all of a sudden, as if an influx of enlightenment effected a transformation. And yet, perhaps the continuity theory is also correct in that this sudden change is part of the ongoing process of human ascent.

The theory that I derive from my understanding of the Bahá'í writings is that the nascent capacity for language is an inherent property emanating from the human soul—and thus specialized for the human being. This approach seems capable of synthesizing aspects of other theories regarding the origin of language. Most importantly, it provides the missing ingredient to explain this process—a teacher from "outside" the universal set, the intervention of a Being who is able to set in motion this latent or potential human capacity, even as do the parents, the family, and the community with the evolving child once the child has emerged from its prenatal condition. In other words, it is possible that the emergence of *Homo sapiens* might be, anthropologically, equivalent to the "birth" of the human species from its "prenatal" stage of development. At this point, the species attains a stage where knowledge and teaching can be accomplished directly—that is, by means of a Manifestation who appears as one among them.

As discussed briefly in the second chapter and reiterated throughout our discussion, the Bahá'í view about all human progress is that the advent of successive Manifestations promotes and sustains all forms of human development, even in the activation of latent powers, such as language and invention. In an oft cited observation by 'Abdu'l-Bahá regarding this process, we find a profound overview of this dependence of human progress on these divinely-appointed Teachers: "Were it not for the sound and true teachings of those Exponents of mysteries, the human world would become the arena of animal characteristics and qualities, all existence would become a vanishing illusion, and true life would be lost. That is why it is said in the Gospel: 'In the beginning was the Word'; that is, it was the source of all life."[5] This single theory about human advancement, when combined with the equally weighty premise that the essential human reality is spiritual or metaphysical in nature, is capable of resolving many of the major questions regarding human history and the advancement of civilization.

At the heart of this overview of progress is another foundational premise about human reality, one which, while implicit in all we have thus far examined, is well worth reiterating here with greater specificity: Each one of us is endowed with free will and the sufficient ability to recognize independently and thence follow the truth and enlightened guidance revealed by the Manifestations. However, without this instruction from a Being of superior capacity, we would not be capable of individual or collective progress. In short, our study, determination, and rational faculties will get us nowhere unless and until they are first primed and nurtured by a teacher. This premise does not mean that our individual teachers must inevitably be superior to us in capacity (as are the Manifestations), but it does require that all our essentially human powers be stimulated and trained before they can become useful tools that we can employ at will.

And here is where the recapitulation theory can become valuable—at least as an analogy—whereby we can better understand how we become empowered to employ and perfect our inherent capacities, including the ability to learn and use language. As we have already observed, the recapitulation theory is a biogenetic concept which suggests that there is a parallel between the embryological development of a child in the womb and the evolution of the human species on Earth: "ontogeny recapitulates phylogeny." Or, stated in ordinary terms, the origin and development of the human being repeats the same pattern of development that can be observed in the development of the phylum as a whole. Though somewhat discounted by contemporary science, this theory still has analogical value in appreciating the Bahá'í concept of the evolution of both the human species (as noted above) and human society—in both instances we observe a parallel to the growth and development of the child while it resides in the womb and after it emerges from it fully formed from the womb:

> Just as man progresses, evolves, and is transformed from one form and appearance to another in the womb of the mother, while remaining from the beginning a human embryo, so too has man remained a distinct essence—that is, the human species—from the beginning of his formation in the matrix of the world, and has passed gradually from form to form. It follows that this change of appearance, this evolution of organs, and this growth and development do not preclude the originality the species. Now, even accepting the reality of evolution and progress, nevertheless, from the moment of his appearance man has possessed perfect composition, and has had the capacity and potential to acquire both material and spiritual perfections and to become the embodiment of the verse, "Let Us make man in Our image, after Our likeness." At most, he has become more pleasing, more refined and graceful, and by virtue of civilization he has emerged from his wild state, just as the wild fruits become finer and sweeter under the cultivation of the gardener, and acquire ever greater delicacy and vitality.

The gardeners of the world of humanity are the Prophets of God.[6]

Always in Need of an Educator

It is not merely the appearance of the fully evolved physiological form of the human being we are trying to understand here, but rather the evolution and development of specific intellectual skills after the mature or final stage of human physical evolution occurred. In other words, we are theorizing that the possibly sudden appearance of speech in humankind was the result of the same process by which a child acquires these same abilities after it is born into this world. While we may not as yet possess the means for understanding exactly how language first emerged or precisely how this capacity became disseminated among various populations, we do have a fairly reliable sense of how the families of languages evolved throughout the world.

One obvious and indisputable axiom we seem to have derived from all we have thus far discussed is that unlike most animals, which are born with most of the instincts and capacities they need to survive, a human being is entirely dependent on physical and intellectual nurturing from the beginning of its life until roughly the age of maturity. Clearly it is not coincidental that the higher a form of animal life is (that is, the closer it is to humans in mental capacity), the longer the progeny must remain with the mother to learn the skills necessary to survive on their own.

Thus, if we assume that this recapitulation of the individual experience in learning is applicable to the early stages of human development as a species, then the first conclusion we might deduce is that individually and collectively, we are in need of guidance to develop certain behaviors, even though the mental and physical capacity is inherent. Otherwise, we would be like a child who, though given sufficient sustenance to survive, is raised without exposure to speech and other forms of human education. Such a child would be less capable of surviving on its own than would the beasts of the field. As 'Abdu'l-Bahá notes, "Now, we need an educator who can be at the same time a material, a human, and a spiritual educator, that his authority may have effect at every degree of existence. And should anyone say, 'I am endowed with perfect reason and comprehension, and have no need for an educator,' he would be denying the obvious. It is as though a child were to say, 'I have no need of education, but will act and seek the perfections of existence according to my own thinking and intelligence,' or as though a blind man were to claim, 'I have no need of sight, for there are many blind people who get by.'" In his further discussion of this subject, 'Abdu'l-Bahá notes that such an educator must be concerned with imparting all forms of enlightenment, from social organization to education: "He must likewise lay the foundations of human education—that is, he must so educate human minds and thoughts that they may become capable of substantive progress; that science and knowledge may expand; that the realities of things, the mysteries of the universe, and the properties of all that exists may be revealed; that learning, discoveries, and major undertakings may day by day increase; and that matters of the intellect may be deduced from and conveyed through the sensible."[7]

'Abdu'l-Bahá concludes this portion of his discourse about the human need for an educator by saying that although this teacher necessarily appears in human form, He "must be at once a material, a human, and a spiritual educator, and, soaring above the world of nature, must be possessed of another power, so that He may assume the station of a divine teacher." He continues by noting, "Were He not to wield such a celestial power, He would not be able to educate, for He would be imperfect Himself. How then could He foster perfection? If He were ignorant, how could He make others wise? If He were unjust, how could He make others just? If He were earthly, how could He make others heavenly?[8]

'Abdu'l-Bahá then proceeds to describe the nature, powers, and proofs of the Manifestations as Divine Educators empowered by God to fulfill this task of uplifting and enlightening human civilization by degrees. It is precisely through these means, the Bahá'í writings explain, that human civilization advances, and it is reasonable to assume that it was through such instruction that the rapid increase in the human powers of communication through speech was also advanced.

LEARNING TO SPEAK

Continuing with our analogy of the emergence of *Homo sapiens* to the birth of a child, we can observe that possibly the first thing the newborn wants is to make contact with others in order to understand what is happening to it. Through the sounds and motions associated with certain actions—such as being cuddled, cleaned, soothed, fed—we begin this endless process of trying to communicate, that we might understand and be understood. Later, as we learn how certain combinations of sounds come to represent reality, the language we acquire becomes an extraordinarily sophisticated system whereby the twin aspects of our reality—the spiritual essence and the human temple—interact.

If we accept the Bahá'í theory about human reality, then we must also conclude that when we communicate with another human being, we are effectively speaking soul to soul. That is, we are employing a process that begins in the metaphysical realm of the cognitive or rational mind (a power of the soul), instigating the mind's associative relation with the brain, which in turn directs electrical impulses to the speech center of the brain. The speech center then translates the idea into the symbolic forms of words, which are given material form by the complex relationship among the vocal cords, tongue, teeth, and palate as air is exhaled through this system by the diaphragm compressing the lungs. The vibrations in the air are received into the auditory processes of the outer, mid, and inner ear of the hearer, then transformed from physical vibrations back into electrical impulses, where they are conveyed by the auditory nerve to that portion of the brain capable of translating them into patterns of ideas as understood by the conscious mind of the person to whom we have spoken.

Of course, this cursory explanation purposefully avoids a full analysis of the details of all the parts of the physical systems involved because our purpose here is not so much to understand the miraculous complexity of human physiology. Rather, it is our intent to discern that the apparatus at the heart of distinguishing human communication from that of lesser beings is the rational mind understood as a power of the metaphysical essence that is the soul.

Speaking Soul to Soul

Clearly a more direct route would be for us to speak soul to soul and thought to thought without the need for the complex and sometimes less accurate process of language, which entails the ambiguity of all complex symbolic systems, as well as the fact that we have become a world community without a global language. Additionally, we cannot assume, even within the same language, that everyone has the same depth and breadth of vocabulary and education and can thereby employ this symbolic communication with equal ability.

In the following three crude but possibly useful graphic illustrations of the process of communication, we see the basic process that takes place with ordinary speech. First is a demonstration of the process we have alluded to several times during our study regarding how our essential reality, our "self," is an emanation from the Creator, and how from it derives all our essential "human" powers:

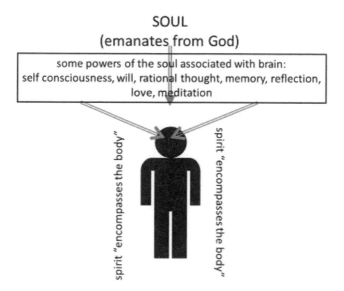

Figure 7. Spiritual Self in Relation to Physical Self

We have not included "speech" in our list because speech is the product of rational thought translated into sound, not a separate capacity of the soul. A second illustration demonstrates the bare outline of this process graphically in a kind of flowchart:

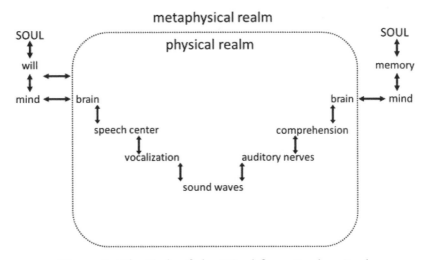

Figure 8. The Path of the Word from Soul to Soul

The third diagram illustrates the same process but with an example of someone saying the word *key* to someone else:

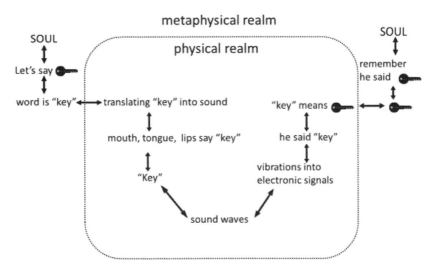

Figure 9. The Path of a Particular Word from Soul to Soul

Again, we have omitted the intricacy of the process whereby the "speech center" of the brain, the so-called "Broca's area" (the posterior inferior frontal gyrus of the brain) combined with "Wernicke's area" (the left posterior section of the superior temporal gyrus) assumes the task of translating one's will or wish that the word *key* become communicated.

One important reason we have done this is because we are still in the very beginning stages of understanding exactly how the brain does what it does. Researchers have mapped the brain to discover what areas are active during specific emotions, actions, and experiences, yet even the inferences we might draw from these general observations are speculative. For example, if Broca's area becomes afflicted gradually—say, by a tumor—the function of speech seems to be taken over by nearby regions. The brain thus seems capable of "rewiring" itself to some extent.

A sudden injury to this same area, however, can result in aphasia, a disorder extremely relevant to what we are discussing about creating and understanding words as the patient thus afflicted must be trained to use the conscious will to rehabilitate the speech center of the brain. Thanks to evolving technology, mapping brain function, combined with the study of injuries to distinct areas of the brain resulting from accidents, strokes, or various forms of dementia, we are acquiring more sophisticated tools wherewith we can learn increasingly more about the complex subsets of aphasia.

It is truly remarkable that our conscious mind can willfully collaborate with a trained therapist to "rewire" our own brain to compensate for some ability that has been lost. To me, the efficacy of this process serves, to a certain degree, as proof of the nonlocality of the conscious mind. Of course, the fact that the neurons of which the brain is composed are not distinct from one another nor specialized in their construction can in part explain the mechanics of how such a restoration of powers might take place. While we may well assume that such "repair" might be confined to a specific location—since various brain functions usually appear to be allocated to particular areas—we are at such an early stage of understanding this amazing creation that we can hardly presume at this point to know to what extent brain function is rigidly segmented.

Where Memory Resides

These considerations relate, importantly, to another major question regarding the brain's capacity as transceiver for our distinctly human powers, namely its retention of conceptual memories.* This question is almost as perplexing to scientists as the nature of self-consciousness, since both capacities are essentially abstract or metaphysical processes.

Memory also relates importantly to discussions of the afterlife experience. Those who have had an NDE confirm what the Bahá'í writings explain about the assessment of our lives that will be one of our first experiences upon entering the spiritual realm: "It is clear and evident that all men shall, after their physical death, estimate the worth of their deeds, and realize all that their hands have wrought."[9]

If the Bahá'í concept of the relationship between the human temple and the essential self is correct, then we can presume that certain functions—particularly memory—that are commonly thought to "reside" in certain parts of the brain are not really "resident" per se. Rather, as we have previously observed, metaphysical powers and capacities of the self (consciousness, will, reflection,

---

* I have discussed this at great length in *Close Connections: The Bridge between Spiritual and Physical Reality* (Wilmette, IL, Bahá'í Publishing Trust, 2005), pp. 251–56.

memory, and so on) are continuously being processed by the soul through the intermediary of the brain. Therefore, a memory is never eternally lost.

And perhaps this is one of the most important conclusions we can derive from exploring the model of the associative relationship between the "self" and the human temple—that while various sorts of injuries or debilitating diseases can impair the ability of the brain to transmit communication well with others or even allow for internal reflection or ideation, as soon as the body-soul associative relation is severed, then all memory and related functions are successfully communicated within the non-compartmentalized and non-material essential self. All memory is accessible. All mental capacities and acquired knowledge and spiritual enlightenment are instantly regained. In brief, all metaphysical powers are intact, and all metaphysical or abstract experiences are regained.

Stated metaphorically, once this fallible and defective intermediary mirror image of ourselves is no longer intervening, we become directly aware of our "true" and total self without any of the impairments, delusions, or misapprehensions we might have had prior to this dissociation. This includes emotional or affective disorders—depression, anxiety, delusions, and so forth.

THE POINT OF DISSOCIATION

Bahá'u'lláh begins a discussion of the relationship of the "rational faculty" as a power of the human soul with the physical powers of the human temple in the following passage:

> Consider the rational faculty with which God hath endowed the essence of man. Examine thine own self, and behold how thy motion and stillness, thy will and purpose, thy sight and hearing, thy sense of smell and power of speech, and whatever else is related to, or transcendeth,

thy physical senses or spiritual perceptions, all proceed from, and owe their existence to, this same faculty. So closely are they related unto it, that if in less than the twinkling of an eye its relationship to the human body be severed, each and every one of these senses will cease immediately to exercise its function, and will be deprived of the power to manifest the evidences of its activity. It is indubitably clear and evident that each of these aforementioned instruments has depended, and will ever continue to depend, for its proper functioning on this rational faculty, which should be regarded as a sign of the revelation of Him Who is the sovereign Lord of all. Through its manifestation all these names and attributes have been revealed, and by the suspension of its action they are all destroyed and perish.[10]

He then continues this explanation by observing that while the severing of this associative relation between the brain as transceiver and the rational faculty as a power of the soul causes all outward or physical manifestations of the powers of vision and other physical senses to cease, the cognitive self and all its powers are in no wise impaired: "It would be wholly untrue to maintain that this faculty [the rational soul] is the same as the power of vision, inasmuch as the power of vision is derived from it and acteth in dependence upon it. It would, likewise, be idle to contend that this faculty can be identified with the sense of hearing, as the sense of hearing receiveth from the rational faculty the requisite energy for performing its functions."[11] He concludes this extremely helpful analysis of the cognitive faculty with a daunting caveat about our ability to understand in this life the subtlety and totality of its foremost function as the power that binds together the essential "self" (the soul) with the human temple (what I sometimes allude to as the "metaphorical self"):

This same relationship bindeth this faculty with whatsoever hath been the recipient of these names and attributes within the human temple. These diverse names and revealed attributes have been generated through the agency of this sign of God. Immeasurably exalted is this sign, in its essence and reality, above all such names and attributes. Nay, all else besides it will, when compared with its glory, fade into utter nothingness and become a thing forgotten.

Wert thou to ponder in thine heart, from now until the end that hath no end, and with all the concentrated intelligence and understanding which the greatest minds have attained in the past or will attain in the future, this divinely ordained and subtle Reality, this sign of the revelation of the All-Abiding, All-Glorious God, thou wilt fail to comprehend its mystery or to appraise its virtue. Having recognized thy powerlessness to attain to an adequate understanding of that Reality which abideth within thee, thou wilt readily admit the futility of such efforts as may be attempted by thee, or by any of the created things, to fathom the mystery of the Living God, the Daystar of unfading glory, the Ancient of everlasting days. This confession of helplessness which mature contemplation must eventually impel every mind to make is in itself the acme of human understanding, and marketh the culmination of man's development.[12]

Nevertheless, these observations, when combined with other related discussions by Bahá'u'lláh and 'Abdu'l-Bahá about the human reality, make it clear that while our knowledge can never encompass the total reality of the soul, we can progressively acquire an endless amount of information *about* it.

In this context, one of the most important statements relating to our present discussion regarding the capacity for communica-

tion during our earthly existence is a previously cited statement*
by Bahá'u'lláh worth repeating here—whatever impairment might
impede the outward manifestation of our inner powers in no way
impairs the source and essence of those powers:

> Know thou that the soul of man is exalted above, and is inde-
> pendent of all infirmities of body or mind. That a sick person
> showeth signs of weakness is due to the hindrances that inter-
> pose themselves between his soul and his body, for the soul
> itself remaineth unaffected by any bodily ailments. Consider
> the light of the lamp. Though an external object may inter-
> fere with its radiance, the light itself continueth to shine with
> undiminished power. In like manner, every malady afflict-
> ing the body of man is an impediment that preventeth the
> soul from manifesting its inherent might and power. When
> it leaveth the body, however, it will evince such ascendancy,
> and reveal such influence as no force on earth can equal.
> Every pure, every refined and sanctified soul will be endowed
> with tremendous power, and shall rejoice with exceeding
> gladness.[13]

---

* See chapter 3, p. 60.

-6-

THE WORD AND THE DIVINE METHODOLOGY

Say: The first and foremost testimony establishing His truth is His own Self. Next to this testimony is His Revelation. For whoso faileth to recognize either the one or the other He hath established the words He hath revealed as proof of His reality and truth. This is, verily, an evidence of His tender mercy unto men. He hath endowed every soul with the capacity to recognize the signs of God. How could He, otherwise, have fulfilled His testimony unto men, if ye be of them that ponder His Cause in their hearts. He will never deal unjustly with anyone, neither will He task a soul beyond its power. He, verily, is the Compassionate, the All-Merciful.

Bahá'u'lláh, *Gleanings,* no. 52.2

It is obvious that an Omnipotent Creator could have fashioned us howsoever He wished. We could have been made perfect, without the need for learning or struggling. And indeed, the Bahá'í writings affirm that those souls who, for whatever reason, have no chance in this life to experience physical reality in such a way as to participate in their own advancement—those who die as infants or children or those who are deprived of education or the basic necessities of life—are cared for and enabled to advance upon attaining the spiritual realm. For God is not legalistic but logical. And as He is entirely aware of all the variables at work in our lives; He is capable of perfectly assessing or evaluating how we have lived our lives and, consequently, what is most appropriate and propitious for our further enlightenment and advancement.

The Value of Physical Experience

Inasmuch as the Creator fashioned us as essentially spiritual beings, He would not have created for us a foundational physical environment and experience wherewith to begin our eternal journey unless He regarded it as the perfect method by which we could begin learning what we need to know about ourselves, about reality as a whole, and, subsequently, about how best to exercise this knowledge in metaphorical physical exercises.

Stated another way, this physical life, though ostensibly contrary to spiritual aspirations, is an ingenious but indirect method for learning about our spiritual nature and purpose. For example, our physical experience forces us to develop spiritual perceptions, spiritual tools and capacities that we might not acquire as well in any other way, and the free will to determine what we will make of this opportunity. That is, this indirect association we have with the underlying spiritual meaning latent in physical reality forces us to utilize judgment in deciding whether or not we will make appropriate choices during this foundational period of our lives.

Of course, from an earthly perspective, we may be understandably dismayed by the inequality of opportunities people are afforded, but the scriptures assure us that there is logic and wisdom in this apparent disparity and that the rationale for distinctions among us will be made apparent once we enter the realm of the spirit.

In this regard, Christ asserts, "Every one to whom much is given, of him will much be required . . ."[1] In short, those of us who have opportunity to utilize this brief span to progress spiritually—and thereby to assist in the collective advancement of humankind—are expected to dedicate our lives unrelentingly to this endeavor, for that is our inherent purpose for this stage of our lives, as well as all those stages that we shall experience hereafter. Thus, the purpose in this initial indirect experience—this physical or associative stage of our existence—derives from the indirect methodology the Creator has determined to be the most efficacious means by which we can be raised up, trained, and prepared for our eternal progress.*

It would seem, then, that independent rational judgment and free will are among the capacities the Creator desires for us to recognize and develop during this initial stage of our life, so as to enable us to make and implement our decisions with a certain degree of autonomy. However, developing these capacities requires assistance from the guidance contained in the explicit texts of the Revealed Word of the Manifestations, combined with our opportunity to study spiritual attributes and practices as exemplified perfectly in the actions and comportment of the Prophets.

In this regard, it is well worth noting that one of the practices ordained by the Manifestations is daily prayer. For were we to rely solely on our own inclination, we would probably commune with the Holy Spirit only when we feel very sad, very happy, or very much in need of help. Consequently, the daily routine prescribed

---

* See John S. Hatcher, *The Purpose of Physical Reality*, for a more expansive treatment of this theme.

by Bahá'u'lláh for humankind in this Day includes prayer, media-tion and reflection, and personal assessment. The Báb's observation about prayer helps us appreciate that without this mandate to pray and commune with God, our progress might become impaired: "O my God! Thou hast inspired my soul to offer its supplication to Thee, and but for Thee, I would not call upon Thee."[2]

Stated succinctly, because the essentially spiritual purpose of physical creation is veiled from us, we need guidance—sometimes direct and obvious and sometimes subtle and indirect—to inspire us to grasp why we have been created and how we can best uti-lize this initial stage of our existence. Consequently, such personal progress cannot rely on merely a single instance of enlightenment. Rather, our spiritual education is a process requiring that we pur-sue our own development on a daily basis. And to assist us in rec-ognizing this purpose and pursuing it methodically, the Creator has devised a world in which our view of the underlying spiritual foundation of reality is veiled by a metaphorical material garb.

This indirect association with spiritual reality during this phys-ical stage of our lives thus challenges us to reject the allure and enticements of less substantive yet more readily perceivable trap-pings—fame, fortune, power, sensual delights. In addition, this teaching methodology requires that we actively participate in our own training by employing our rational minds to become aware that these evanescent distractions are capable of temporarily divert-ing us from our principal objectives—or possibly even deterring us completely—and that we should therefore resist and reject them.

Revelation and "the Word made Flesh"

It is in the context of this indirect methodology that we can begin to appreciate how the primary means by which the Creator's Intermediaries instruct us, other than Their own exemplary char-acter, is Their language—which, while sometimes quite direct and obvious, can at other times be extremely indirect and challenging, attired as it often is in symbol, metaphor, and other analogical rhetorical devices:

> It is evident unto thee that the Birds of Heaven and Doves of Eternity speak a twofold language. One language, the outward language, is devoid of allusions, is unconcealed and unveiled; that it may be a guiding lamp and a beaconing light whereby wayfarers may attain the heights of holiness, and seekers may advance into the realm of eternal reunion. . . . The other language is veiled and concealed, so that whatever lieth hidden in the heart of the malevolent may be made manifest and their innermost being be disclosed. . . . In such utterances, the literal meaning, as generally understood by the people, is not what hath been intended.[3]

In *The Ocean of His Words: The Art of Bahá'u'lláh*, I attempt to explain how Bahá'u'lláh employs various literary devices and styles in the myriad works of His vast Revelation. By means of such literary artistry, the Manifestation coaxes us to become active participants, or cocreators, in our enlightenment, as well as active coworkers in establishing a global commonwealth founded on spiritual principles.

Of course, we should expect no less than an ingenious teaching technique from a Perfect Teacher. And if we are not yet capable of penetrating the sometimes veiled or symbolic and metaphorical language of the Prophet, He employs another indirect but equally effective teaching method—the example of His own actions. For instance, Christ tells His disciples that if they cannot understand what He means when He says that they can behold the Father by seeing Him (His example), then they should simply follow Him because they appreciate (and can thus emulate) His actions:

"Believe me that I am in the Father and the Father in me, or else believe me for the sake of the works themselves."[4]

In this same vein Bahá'u'lláh states that everything the Prophets say and do should be understood to be identical with the will and purpose of God: "The essence of belief in Divine unity consisteth in regarding Him Who is the Manifestation of God and Him Who is the invisible, the inaccessible, the unknowable Essence as one and the same. By this is meant that whatever pertaineth to the former, all His acts and doings, whatever He ordaineth or forbiddeth, should be considered, in all their aspects, and under all circumstances, and without any reservation, as identical with the Will of God Himself."[5]

Thus, the two primary indirect methods employed by the Prophets of God—the "Word" (Their utterances) and Their perfect exemplification of spiritual behavior—both employ the same sort of indirection and challenge that characterize the Creator's overall plan for our enlightenment and advancement. To recognize the spiritual powers and exemplary character manifested by the Prophet—Who does not demonstrate His power or authority through obvious material or sensational means and Whose station is, thus, veiled—we need to discover for ourselves what qualities and behavior are indicative of a "good" or spiritually refined person. And these qualities we derive first from our own early instruction from parents and teachers, coupled with our interaction with other human beings. It is precisely for this reason that teaching virtues to children is so often discussed and is designated as being one of the most meritorious of undertakings. In speaking to women—the first and foremost teachers of their progeny, 'Abdu'l-Bahá exhorts them to "suckle your children from their infancy with the milk of a universal education, and rear them so that from their earliest days, within their inmost heart, their very nature, a way of life will be firmly established that will conform to the divine Teachings in all things."[6]

Clearly this early training provides us with a knowledge of the standards by which we can assess our own character and that of those with whom we associate. But more to the point, by means of our awareness of those standards of goodness as borne out in human behavior, we can subsequently recognize the Manifestation. Indeed, this axiom explains why some people encountered the Manifestations and were unmoved by being in the presence of the Beloved of God.

Christ explains to His followers that the evidence of a Prophet of God is the "fruit" He brings forth—implicitly, His demeanor, comportment, spiritual qualities, teachings, and treatment of others, as well as the actions His followers exemplify. "Beware of false prophets," He begins. "Who come to you in sheep's clothing, but inwardly who are ravenous wolves." He continues with a simple but helpful analogy when He explains, "You will know them by their fruits. Are grapes gathered from thorns, or figs from thistles? So, every sound tree bears good fruit, but the bad tree bears evil fruit. A sound tree cannot bear evil fruit, nor can a bad tree bear good fruit." He concludes, "Every tree that does not bear good fruit is cut down and thrown into the fire. Thus, you will know them by their fruits."[7]

But again, because the generality of people are not raised to recognize and manifest spiritual attributes, far too many become attracted to, swayed by, and obsessed with the outward and obvious expressions of power as characteristics of the rich, the famous, and the celebrated. By contrast, recognition of the Prophet is a challenge because He is humble, seeks no earthly powers or ascendancy, and may not be physically impressive. His "fruits" are discernible only to those who know the qualities of what they seek, whose hearts are pure, or who are not preoccupied with wealth, fame, or worldly possessions. So it is that the simple fishermen were Christ's first followers, even as He Himself was, to outward seeming, but the untutored son of a simple carpenter.

For this reason, another "fruit" of the Manifestations that enables us to distinguish Them from "false prophets" is the humble and spiritual character of Their followers. This sort of indirect attraction to the Prophet is especially applicable and true after His passing, and its effect can be observed in seekers who wish to know the message of the Manifestation not because they read His writings but because they admire the behavior of His followers. In this verity, we readily appreciate the obligation of those who claim to be followers of the Manifestation to constantly evaluate their own character and comportment so as to become an indirect source of attraction for seekers.

'Abdu'l-Bahá emphasizes this concept of the Bahá'ís as being observable "fruit" of Bahá'u'lláh when he exhorts the believers to "conduct yourselves in such a manner that ye may stand out distinguished and brilliant as the sun among other souls." He writes, "Should any one of you enter a city, he should become a center of attraction by reason of his sincerity, his faithfulness and love, his honesty and fidelity, his truthfulness and loving-kindness towards all the peoples of the world, so that the people of that city may cry out and say: 'This man is unquestionably a Bahá'í, for his manners, his behavior, his conduct, his morals, his nature, and disposition reflect the attributes of the Bahá'ís.'"[8] But here again, such souls will be attractive and impressive only to those who are attentive to the qualities that delineate a person who possesses and demonstrates spiritual attributes.

Indirection and the Advent of Spring

Before we examine the most obvious and enduring teaching method of the Manifestation—the Word or the Revelation itself—

we should mention one more indirect evidence of the advent of a new "Day." With the advent of a new Revelation, advancement takes place in every sphere of human enlightenment and learning, whether in social structure and organization or, more particularly, in human relationships themselves. 'Abdu'l-Bahá describes this influence in the symbolic terms of world undergoing a springtime: "The day of the advent of the Holy Manifestations is the spiritual springtime. It is divine splendor and heavenly grace; it is the wafting of the breeze of life and the dawning of the Sun of Truth. Spirits are revived, hearts are refreshed, souls are refined, all existence is stirred into motion, and human realities are rejoiced and grow in attainments and perfections. Universal progress is achieved, the souls are gathered up, and the dead are quickened to life, for it is the day of resurrection, the season of commotion and ferment, the hour of joy and gladness, and the time of rapture and abandon."[9] As we have previously noted, this broad evidence of the influence of past Revelations is most easily observed in hindsight, retrospectively examining the fact that virtually all major progress in human civilization results from the revitalization of human affairs when the influence of a new Manifestation is unleashed, even though the world at large may be totally oblivious to the source of transformation.

Insofar as the Bahá'í Revelation is concerned, the evidence that something earth-shaking and transformative has awakened human civilization since the Declaration of the Báb in 1844 is apparent everywhere. It would be totally accurate to observe that in this relatively brief span of time, more substantive change in human society has occurred than in all the past centuries combined, qualitatively as well as quantitatively.

The earth has become a single, interdependent community—not yet a particularly peaceful and happy community, but a global polity all the same. In every field, the sciences have become totally transformed so that we now understand more about the nature of reality than the wisest of the wise could have imagined prior to the incipience of this Day.

Politically, we have witnessed virtually every empire and kingdom extant during the life of Bahá'u'lláh crumble, a process Shoghi Effendi discusses in detail in *The Promised Day is Come*. Similarly, concepts of justice, equity, and universal suffrage are now accepted as universal standards, even if they have not yet been universally implemented. Instantaneous communication to any part of the planet is now a reality, and we have the means—though not yet the collaboration and collective will—to cure all the major ills that afflict humankind.

During this same period, what began with the late-night conversation and declaration of an unknown Merchant to a young student from Karbilá in the upstairs of a small apartment in Shiraz has become the second most widespread religion in the world.* And the single force behind this movement is nothing other than the impetus set in motion by the Revelation itself. No single resource, no cadre of powerful individuals, no government or armed force had any part to play in the transformation that occurred simultaneously in the rapid expanse of this sacred Cause and in the secular world of peoples and nations.

One might argue that there is no obvious evidence that the advent of the Bahá'í Faith was the direct cause of the discoveries and inventions that brought about the Industrial Revolution or set aflame the democratization of human polity. The simultaneity of the Revelation of Bahá'u'lláh with such change could make this

---

* The declaration of the Báb to Mullá Husayn on May 23, 1844, marks the beginning of the twin Revelations of the Báb and Bahá'u'lláh. Christianity is considered the most widespread faith, though such an assessment necessarily includes the myriad forms of the religion—Catholicism, Protestantism, the Eastern Orthodox Church, as well as thousands of denominations and sects.

assertion seem merely a *post hoc* fallacy. And it is certainly true that such a claim relies primarily on accepting the station of Bahá'u'lláh and the validity of His teachings, which posit the theory that human social history is a spiritually driven phenomenon. The actual proof of this assertion derives from combining the details of this argument in the Bahá'í texts with a retrospective examination of the causes underlying the advancement of civilization. Here again, assessing the "fruit" of the advent of a true Prophet—in this case, the validity of His teachings about human history—relies importantly on first establishing the station of the Prophet through less abstract and theoretical methods.

The Word Made Flesh

The most obvious proof of the station of the Prophet is the Prophet Himself—His character and personhood. And yet, after the Prophet has ascended, we must necessarily rely on a relationship with Him based on His words. Establishing such a relationship with Bahá'u'lláh is no problem because of the vast number and variety of texts that He has bequeathed us. Among these are meditations and prayers through which we can feel empathy and intimacy with the personhood of Bahá'u'lláh. Furthermore, it becomes readily apparent that all He suffered and all He wrote was solely for our own benefit and not to assert His own celebrity as do those "false prophets" or self-proclaimed gurus who seek fame for self-aggrandizement or monetary reward.

In fact, it is valuable for those first establishing a relationship with Bahá'u'lláh to examine His life in order to appreciate the absolute purity of motive in all He did. Likewise, meaningful conversation with Him can also be attained through the abundance of information we have about what He endured, as well as through spiritual communion we can derive by means of reciting or intoning the prayers and other meditative works He revealed.

Once we establish to our satisfaction the authenticity of the Prophet by examining firsthand the "fruits" of His Revelation, we can begin to understand the encompassing sense in which He both reveals the "Word" and is Himself the most perfect expression of the "Word." And indirect though it be, our association with the Manifestation is the "way"[10] for us to know God and attain "the Presence of God Himself"[11]—whether in this world or the world to come:

I am the way, and the truth, and the life; no one comes to the Father, but by me.[12]

The purpose of God in creating man hath been, and will ever be, to enable him to know his Creator and to attain His Presence. To this most excellent aim, this supreme objective, all the heavenly Books and the divinely revealed and weighty Scriptures unequivocally bear witness. Whoso hath recognized the Dayspring of Divine guidance [the Manifestation] and entered His holy court hath drawn nigh unto God and attained His Presence, a Presence which is the real Paradise, and of which the loftiest mansions of heaven are but a symbol.[13]

We cannot know God directly, but only through His Prophets. We can pray to Him, *realizing* that through His Prophets we know Him, or we can address our prayer in thought to Bahá'u'lláh, not as God, but as the Door to our knowing God.[14]

We will have experience of God's spirit through His Prophets in the next world, but God is too great for us to know without this Intermediary.[15]

In sum, the subtlety of the indirection by which God teaches us through the Manifestations is not that They are in any sense "ordinary." They are perfect exemplars of spirituality expressed in a human form—not in Their physical prowess or appearance, but in Their perfect manifestation of Godliness to the extent Godliness can be given human expression. Or put more directly, for us the Manifestations are and will remain the most perfect access to God we can attain, and entering Their "presence" will always be equivalent to entering the presence of God Himself.

Rending the Veils of Words

As we noted early on, words are never truly literal—they are graphic symbols of sounds which themselves are representations of another reality, whether that reality be something physical, such as a rock or tree, or something metaphysical, such as an emotion or an idea. Therefore, it is not surprising that these perfect Teachers—the Manifestations of God—are masterful in Their use of language. And in the same way that access to God is indirect, even as recognition of the Manifestation is itself an exercise in developing our spiritual perception and receptivity, so language as the essential tool of the Prophets also requires effort on our part if we are to penetrate the outer shell of signs and sounds to glimpse the multiple levels of inner intended meaning.

One useful example of how the Manifestation employs rhetorical tools to exhort us to think for ourselves is Christ's use of parables both when teaching His followers and when responding to abstruse questions posed to Him by the Pharisees and Sadducees, who thought their knowledge quite superior to that of the untutored Nazarene. Of particular value for our present discussion is His own answer to His disciples' question, following the parable of the sower, about why He employs this indirect teaching method.

The occasion for the parable occurs as Christ is preaching to a crowd gathered along the shore of the Sea of Galilee. During the course of this sermon, He employs various parables, one of which is the parable of the sower: "Listen! A sower went out to sow. And as he sowed, some seed fell along the path, and the birds came and devoured it. Other seed fell on rocky ground, where it had not much soil, and immediately it sprang up, since it had no depth of soil; and when the sun rose it was scorched, and since it had no root it withered away. Other seed fell among thorns and the thorns grew up and choked it, and it yielded no grain. And other seeds fell into good soil and brought forth grain, growing up and increasing and yielding thirtyfold and sixtyfold and a hundredfold." He then exhorts the crowd, "He who has ears to hear, let them hear," meaning, of course, that whoever is spiritually receptive will, with effort, be capable of deciphering the meaning of the analogy.[16]

Later, when He is alone with His disciples, they ask Him what the parable means, whereupon He explains that while they have been able to recognize Him by virtue of heavenly bestowal, others will have to discern the meaning of His words through their own effort because in them is fulfilled God's revelation to Isaiah: "[Jesus] said to them, 'To you has been given the secret of the kingdom of God, but for those outside everything is in parables; so that they may indeed see but not perceive, and may indeed hear but not understand; lest they should turn again, and be forgiven.'"[17]

Christ first exhorts them to learn how to understand the underlying meaning of the story or else they will be incapable of comprehending His teachings: "And he said to them, 'Do you not understand this parable? How then will you understand all the parables?'"[18] He then demonstrates to them how the parable works by explaining how the seeds represent the Word of God and the various places where the seeds fall represent the variety of spiritual conditions of those who hear the words:

The sower sows the word. And these are the ones along the path, where the word is sown; when they hear, Satan immediately comes and takes away the word which is sown in them. And these in like manner are the ones sown upon rocky ground, who, when they hear the word, immediately receive it with joy; and they have no root in themselves, but endure for a while; then, when tribulation or persecution arises on account of the word, immediately they fall away. And others are the ones sown among thorns; they are those who hear the word, but the cares of the world, and the delight in riches, and the desire for other things, enter in and choke the word, and it proves unfruitful. But those that were sown upon the good soil are the ones who hear the word and accept it and bear fruit, thirtyfold and sixtyfold and a hundredfold.[19]

Christ expects His followers to be capable of discerning the intended meaning of His teachings, while He also is fully aware that the learned but literalistic and legalistic Pharisees and Sadducees are likely to be baffled by His indirect answers to their taunting inquiries. Indeed, the persistence of this pattern of rejection of the new Manifestation by the most influential religious leaders of the previous Revelation is the initial proposition Bahá'u'lláh articulates in His principal doctrinal work, the Kitáb-i-Íqán: "Consider the past. How many, both high and low, have, at all times, yearningly awaited the advent of the Manifestations of God in the sanctified persons of His chosen Ones. . . . And whensoever the portals of grace did open, and the clouds of divine bounty did rain upon mankind, and the light of the Unseen did shine above the horizon of celestial might, they all denied Him, and turned away from His face—the face of God Himself. Refer ye, to verify this truth, to that which hath been recorded in every sacred Book." In this context, Bahá'u'lláh explains that one condition of receptivity in the individual is that each person pursue knowledge independently, as opposed to relying on the learning passed down from others, for only in this manner can one be said to have justly attained true understanding: "O Son of Spirit! The best beloved of all things in My sight is Justice; turn not away therefrom if thou desirest Me, and neglect it not that I may confide in thee. By its aid thou shalt see with thine own eyes and not through the eyes of others, and shalt know of thine own knowledge and not through the knowledge of thy neighbor. Ponder this in thy heart; how it behooveth thee to be. Verily justice is My gift to thee and the sign of My loving-kindness. Set it then before thine eyes."[20]

This exhortation is similar in purport to a passage we have already cited in which Bahá'u'lláh says that some believers have recited the verses of the Qur'án for over a thousand years, and yet still fail to understand the intended, or hidden, meaning: "Again and again they read those verses which clearly testify to the reality of these holy themes, and bear witness to the truth of the Manifestations of eternal Glory, and still apprehend not their purpose. They have even failed to realize, all this time, that, in every age, the reading of the scriptures and holy books is for no other purpose except to enable the reader to *apprehend their meaning and unravel their innermost mysteries. Otherwise reading, without understanding, is of no abiding profit unto man.*"[21] [italics added]

Unto Every Nation Sent We a Prophet

Another useful exercise we can undertake prior to examining some of the indirect techniques employed by Bahá'u'lláh in His own revealed texts is to study the explicit relationship of language to the condition of the peoples to whom the Manifestation appears.

As we have noted, the theme and substance of the Word inevitably deals with the social and spiritual conditions that exist at the

time and place in which the Manifestation appears. More particularly, the Word sets forth goals and the methods for implementing them for a particular "Day" or Dispensation—the reasonable
objectives and social tools that will enable the spiritual and social
advancement of the peoples.

We find that the more obvious and direct discussions of this
concept of progressive Revelation can be found in the revealed
words of the Abrahamic line of Prophets. For example, Muhammad states, "Unto every people (was sent) a Messenger. When their
Messenger comes (before them), the matter will be judged between
them with justice, and they will not be wronged."[22] The Arabic
word *ummah* translated here as "people" can also sometimes be
translated as "nation," "tribe," or "community."

Muhammad's observation about progressive Revelation is particularly interesting when we examine even cursorily the chronological sequence in relation to the geographical dispersal of the
various revealed world religions. I use the term "revealed" here to
distinguish them from syncretic religions, sects, variants of existing
religions, and religious movements invented by ordinary human
beings who believe themselves to be divinely inspired.

For example, the Bahá'í texts distinguish between the religions
of the Manifestations and the subsequent furtherance or invigo-
ration of those religions by minor prophets or spiritually inspired
leaders. Thus, the Jewish religion revealed by Moses also includes
the minor Old Testament Prophets such as Isaiah, Ezekiel, and
Daniel. Likewise, regarding the Dharmic line of Manifestations,
the Bahá'í texts allude to the Buddha as a Manifestation, while
Confucius is considered a renowned teacher and moral reformer,
but not a Manifestation. Along these same lines, Martin Luther
set in motion the events that led to the establishment of the Protestant Movement, resulting in a succession of Christian religious

denominations, but these are all subsets of the religion instituted by Christ, even as are the Eastern Churches resulting from the early schism with Roman Catholicism, such as the Greek and Russian Orthodox Churches. The Bahá'í writings similarly reject the assertions of those individuals who have claimed to be Manifestations and who have instigated religious movements but who do not possess the requisite proofs for such a station.

Thus, when we examine a rough chronology of the more widespread and influential religions throughout history, we see that in addition to the well-known Dharmic ones, other religions had an important influence on specific peoples or cultures in various parts of the world.

For the sake of brevity and clarity, I have arranged in Table 1 some of the religions which known Manifestations have mentioned in their writings as being founded by authentic Prophets. The purpose is to demonstrate the following four points. First is the fact that there is no single line of Prophets in religious history, even though those intended to unify this process come from the Abrahamic line, perhaps because They are the most recent. Second, at various periods in human history, there were more than one Manifestation at work in the world at the same time, and the various religions emanating from these Manifestations were characterized by teachings appropriate to the people and cultures to whom They appeared. Third, while evidence of some of the beliefs and practices of ancient religions remains, the only authentic and authoritative texts that exist in anything similar to a complete and reliable form are those from the Abrahamic line of Prophets. Fourth, 'Abdu'l-Bahá notes that while historians may theorize about the accuracy of extant scripture, most of the scriptural accounts are thoroughly reliable when understood appropriately:

Our purpose is to show that even in Scriptural history, the most outstanding of all histories, there are contradictions as to the time when the great ones lived, let alone as to the dates related to others. And furthermore, learned societies in Europe are continually revising the existing records, both of East and West. In spite of this, how can the confused accounts of peoples dating from before Alexander be compared with the Holy Text of God? If any scholar expresses astonishment, let him be surprised at the discrepancies in Scriptural history.

Nevertheless, Holy Writ is authoritative, and with it no history of the world can compare, for experience hath shown that after investigation of the facts and a thorough study of ancient records and corroborative evidence, all establish the validity of God's universal Manifestation; once His claim proveth true, then whatsoever He may choose to say is right and correct.[23]

There are other Manifestations mentioned in the Old Testament, the Qur'án, and the Bahá'í texts, but as 'Abdu'l-Bahá notes, entire cycles of Manifestations have been lost forever to our collective memory because no recorded evidence of their history or their revealed texts survive: "When a cycle comes to a close, a new one is inaugurated, and the previous cycle, on account of the momentous events which transpire, vanishes so entirely from memory as to leave behind no record or trace."[24] However, because the Bahá'í teachings assert that all major advances in civilization ultimately derive from the appearance of these Divine Emissaries, we can reasonably infer where some of the forgotten Manifestations likely appeared.

Table 1. Chronological Chart of Some Revealed Religions

Origin	Religion	Manifestation	Place of Origin	Texts
4000 BCE	Day of Adam	Adam		Story in Torah and Qur'án
2000–1000	Hinduism	Krishna	Indian Subcontinent	Rig-Veda, Vedanta, Bhagavad Gita
2300	Day of Noah	Noah		Story in Torah and Qur'án
	Day of Húd	Húd*	People of 'Ád: Southern Arabian Peninsula	Story in Qur'án and Bahá'í texts.
	Day of Sálih	Sálih	People of Thamud: Southern Arabian Peninsula	Story in Qur'án and Bahá'í texts.
	Sabean		Chaldea	
2000–1850	Day of Abraham	Abraham	Ur and Canaan	Story in Torah and Qur'án
1700	Judaism	Moses	Eastern Mediterranean	Pentateuch
1000	Zoroastrianism	Zoroaster	Eastern Persia	Gathas, Avesta
563	Buddhism	The Buddha	Indian Subcontinent	Dhammapada
33 CE	Christianity	Jesus the Christ	Palestine	Four Gospels
622	Islam	Muhammad	Medina in Arabia	Qur'án
1844	Bábí Faith	The Báb	Persia	Persian Bayán and many others.
1853	Bahá'í Faith	Bahá'u'lláh	Persia, Ottoman Empire	Kitáb-i-Íqán, Kitáb-i-Aqdas, and many others.

* "The people of 'Ad and Thamud inhabited a large tract of country in Southern Arabia. Tradition has it that 'Ad was a fourth-generation descendant of Noah. His people, who are said to be of a tall race, were idolaters and aggressive people. In the Qur'án it is stated that the People of both 'Ad and Thamud were fine builders, gifted with intelligence and skills, but that they were guided by the Evil One, Satan" (Adib Taherzadeh, *The Revelation of Bahá'u'lláh*, vol. 4, p. 425).

The Authority of Early Religious Texts

Clearly, an important concern in the evaluation the influence of a religion in the advancement of civilization is determining in retrospect when and to what extent the religion became outdated or replaced by more advanced guidance in the form of a new Revelation. While we often lack sufficiently reliable historical information to determine exactly when such a process of corruption of the texts or misapplication of the teachings of the Prophet occur, it may prove a useful exercise for us to examine how religious practices stray from what we can infer was the original intent of the teachings of the Founder of the religion.

Naturally, the problem with even a broad overview of the progress of the history of revealed religions is the lack of access we have to the original utterances of the Manifestation. Only in a few instances do we have what we can reliably assume to be the authoritative Word as taught and disseminated by the Manifestation, though in some cases we have texts that purport to represent His core teachings. To understand more fully the relevance of this problem to the abiding theme of our discussion about how language advances civilization by binding together our essentially spiritual nature and impulses with our daily physical life, we will review several examples of what are widely accepted to be the authoritative texts of several revealed religions.

A further problem is that the teachings derived from works within the canon of a religion often result from later interpretations and commentaries by clerical leaders and other self-proclaimed religious scholars.

For example, most contemporaries who consider themselves Buddhists affirm that Buddha did not believe in God but instead was advocating a spiritually based humanism. However, there are no authoritative texts by the Buddha to confirm this notion. Likewise, a large portion of Hindus believe that their religion authoritatively advocates a belief in various deities and in reincarnation, though the most reliable Hindu literature seems to allude to "rebirth" as a spiritual awakening and the various iconic deities are seen as the "names" of various spiritual attributes available to the human aspiration to become a "good" person.

But in both cases, there are no authentic texts by Buddha or Krishna supporting those beliefs or contradicting the description of reality and the divine process of progressive Revelation that—the Bahá'í texts assert—all the Manifestations clearly understand and confirm in Their teachings. And if all the Manifestations are aware of Each Other and share the same goal of teaching us about the same reality, then beliefs incongruent with it must derive from literalist readings of figurative teachings or other forms of distorted interpretation. Indeed, we presently bear witness to this same process in the warped understanding of teachings and in the application of literalism and fanaticism that afflict so many religions and have become the source of so much current religious contention and bloodshed.

THE HINDU RELIGION

The primary texts associated with the Hindu religion were composed during the Vedic period (between 1700 and 500 BCE), the Rig-Veda having been composed over several centuries. The most well-known Hindu work is the Bhagavad-Gita, part of the Mahabharata epic composed around the eighth or ninth century BCE, though not written down in Sanskrit until around the fifth century BCE, more than two thousand years after the Avatar*

---

* The term *Avatar* employed in the Hindu religion is more or less synonymous with the concept of the Manifestation as defined in the Bahá'í texts, a Messenger from God come with new teachings for a more advanced unfolding of the Eternal Plan of God.

Krishna is presumed to have lived. Nevertheless, translations of and commentaries on the Gita reveal a very sophisticated theology and an explicit path by which the human soul can progress, both in the physical realm and in the realm of the spirit.

ZOROASTRIANISM

The Gathas within the collection of the Avesta are purported to have been composed by Zoroaster Himself, and other works in this same collection are derived from His teachings. While His influence was not as widespread geographically as that of Krishna and the Buddha, His religion still has followers, and it is likely that the Zoroastrian texts more authentically represent the teachings of the Prophet than the works purporting to represent Hindu or Buddhist teachings.

BUDDHISM

There are no texts presumed to have been written by the Buddha, but the Dhammapada is considered to be one of the most authentic and complete collections of the sayings and teachings attributed to the Buddha. Expressed in verse form, these verses are not so much in a logical order; rather, they are each independent moral or spiritual teachings that take their complete meaning from the context of the sermons in which they were originally delivered. Though Buddhism is a religion, it is often considered a humanistic philosophy because its teachings focus primarily on those practices and axioms that define human goodness as borne out in daily life, rather than on an explicit relationship with God. However, inasmuch as the practices include meditation, the study of scriptures, the renunciation of passions and materialism, and finding solace in a spiritual relationship with the Buddha—all of which culminate in the attainment of contentment or a sublime spiritual condition (Nirvana)—Buddhist teachings accord with the Christian, Islamic,

Bábí, and Bahá'í belief that it is only through a relationship with the Manifestation and the study of His example and guidance that human development is achieved. In short, the scarcity of explicit theological discourse in no way diminishes the essentially religious nature of the spiritual practices and objectives contained in the teachings attributed to the Buddha.

JUDAISM

The Pentateuch, presumed by some to have been composed by Moses, may well be the wisdom of the Prophet—including history, laws, and sermons—as passed down by oral tradition from tribal poet to poet until written down, several hundred years later, possibly by several different authors. Its worldwide circulation occurred because it was included in the final assemblage of the Christian canon around the fourth century CE when St. Jerome had the original Hebrew and Greek texts of the Old and New Testaments translated into Latin. Importantly, the accounts of many of the major events in the Pentateuch are retold or alluded to in the Qur'án, but with some minor changes that, we might presume, are more authentic or authoritative if we accept the Bahá'í premise that the Manifestation pre-exists and has authoritative access to both human history and whatever texts He desires to examine: "Thou knowest full well that We perused not the books which men possess and We acquired not the learning current amongst them, and yet whenever We desire to quote the sayings of the learned and of the wise, presently there will appear before the face of thy Lord in the form of a tablet all that which hath appeared in the world and is revealed in the Holy Books and Scriptures."[25]

CHRISTIANITY

The New Testament contains the four gospels (the teachings of Christ as recalled by four of His followers), together with "Acts of the Apostles," their letters to various early Christian congregations, and the Book of Revelation. It was originally written in Koine or "common" Greek, the language most commonly used in the Mediterranean region during the time of Christ and for a period of time thereafter.

Christianity spread among the provinces of the Roman Empire, but with overthrow of the empire during the great tribal migrations that took place between the third and the seventh centuries, it was often suppressed by the tribal religions of the invaders. For the most part, the polytheistic religions of the tribal invaders had diminished to something more akin to cultural traditions rather than carefully considered and deeply held systems of belief. Nevertheless, in the wake of the barbarian invasion of the Roman Empire, Christianity became temporarily separated from its alliance with the governing authority.

After this long period of virtually ceaseless conflict, Christianity was reintroduced, most especially with the rapid conversion of strong tribal kings, such as Alfred the Great in England and Charlemagne in France. The advancing secular power of the papacy was instrumental in the establishment of the Holy Roman Empire, and in this milieu, the Christian teachings and texts, together with the Judaic texts that were included as the "Old Testament," were spread first in Latin, then gradually translated into other languages. Notable milestones in this process were the translation of the Bible into Old French by Guyart des Moulins in the thirteenth century and into Middle English by John Wycliffe in 1383.

In the succeeding centuries, there were various efforts to render the most accurate translations of the Bible possible, especially in English. One such endeavor is the Revised Standard version of the King James Bible (with its sometimes difficult Elizabethan dialect). The New International Version Study Bible project, updated as recently as 2011, includes scholarly references to the original Greek text. Every new translation returns to the original Greek text in an attempt to offer accurate renditions that could facilitate alternative and possibly more accurate interpretations. But the fact remains that it is still left to the individual to decide what the text ultimately means, because the only "authoritative" or binding interpretations would have had to be authorized by Christ or an intermediary designated by Him as having such capacity and authority. Neither of these conditions occurred.

ISLAM

The Qur'án records much more reliably the words of the Prophet Muhammad, since Muslims consider the text to be the Word of God as delivered to Muhammad through the intermediary of the archangel Gabriel. This belief seems confirmed by the fact that whenever Muhammad was in the process of revealing "the Word," He would enter a trancelike condition and speak as if He were merely reciting what He was being guided to reveal. According to tradition, when these revelatory moments would occur, someone would record the words by any available means, whether by inscribing them on parchment, carving them on the shoulder blade of a camel, or simply having them memorized by a believer.

These separate instances or outpourings, now known as Súrihs, were later assembled and arranged in order from longest to shortest, rather than according to theme or according to the chronological order in which they were revealed. The result is that each Súrih is complete unto itself, and the traditional layout of the Qur'án, while containing many related themes and historical accounts, has no significant overriding structure.

However, there is one important interjection that I think is relevant to include here regarding the relationship between the Revelation of Muhammad and the central schism that irreparably fractured Islam and diminished the extent to which the light the Prophet shed its brilliance in the world. In a previous citation from the words of Bahá'u'lláh, we noted His assertion that everything the Manifestations do and say is identical with the will of God: "His acts and doings, whatever He ordaineth or forbiddeth, should be considered, in all their aspects, and under all circumstances, and without any reservation, as identical with the Will of God Himself."[26]

In light of this axiom, we necessarily conclude that even though Muslim clerics and scholars regard only the Súrih of the Qur'án as being unquestionably the authentic and authoritative Word of God, there are a number of critical hadiths that both Shí'ih and Sunní agree are authentic. Among these are two that relate importantly to the succession of Muhammad's lineal descendants as authoritatively designated leaders of the religion (Imams).

The most important of these are two hadíth that derive from a sermon the Prophet gave at the Pond of Khumm on 10 AH.* On this occasion Muhammad is recorded as having affirmed, "O people, Allah is my Lord and I am the lord of the believers. I am worthier of believers than themselves. Of whomsoever I had been Master (*Mawla*), Ali here is to be his Master. O Allah, be a supporter of whoever supports him (Ali) and an enemy of whoever opposes him and divert the Truth to Ali."[27]

The second of these two hadith is usually referred to as the "Hadíth of the Two Weighty Things." After alluding to His impending ascension, Muhammad is reported to have said, "Indeed, I am leaving among you, that which if you hold fast to them, you shall not be misguided after me. One of them is greater than the other: (First is) The book of Allah is a rope extended from the sky to the earth, and (the second is) my family, the people of my house (*ahlul bait*), and they shall not split until they meet me at the *hawd*, so look at how you deal with them after me."[28]

---

* Sunday, March 15, 632 CE of the Julian calendar.

In her brief but useful book *Six Lessons on Islam*, Marzieh Gail describes both hadíth very simply and clearly:

> When the Prophet was returning from His Farewell Pilgrimage to Mecca, He had the caravan halt; He told the concourse of people to gather in the shade of some thorn trees, and had them build a pulpit of saddles, near the Pool of Khumm. Then He raised 'Ali up and said, "Whoever hath Me as his Master, hath 'Ali as his Master . . . I have been summoned to the gate of God, and I shall soon depart . . . to be concealed from you." Then He spoke of two treasures He would leave them: "The greatest treasure is the Book of God . . . Hold fast to it and do not lose it and do not change it. The other treasure is the line of My descendants."
>
> The great tragedy of Islam is that three men, one after the other, took over the headship of the Faith for a period of twenty-four years, and that all this time the Imam 'Ali was forced to stand aside. He must have suffered untold agonies as He watched the irreparable damage being done, knowing all the time in His heart that He was the intended of God—the Imam, the one who stands before the people, the divinely ordained, divinely inspired.[29]

How the Manifestations Advance Civilization

To summarize this point, it seems to be clear that all the Manifestations intend that the advancement of civilization be accomplished by two central sources—the example of Their own comportment and character and the "Word" and all that it ordains. In short, as the previous passage from Bahá'u'lláh indicates, all that They do and say should be received as being identical with the will of God for that age.

What is equally apparent is that contained within the revealed Word (whether it be written, dictated, or recollected) are updated laws, updated spiritual guidance, and some form of succession—whether individuals or institutions—whereby the Revelation as a whole can be conveyed to the populace, the laws can be implemented, and the teachings can be protected from distortion and corruption by unenlightened or self-seeking individuals.

Thus, the revealed spiritual teachings, exemplary character, and explicit laws revealed by Moses are sustained by the tribal polity He also designed; we cannot separate one from the other. While the teachings of Christ regarding succession are left vague or ambiguous, His laws and guidance to His disciples about their mission is not. Christ bade His eleven disciples, "Go therefore and make disciples of all nations, baptizing them in the name of the Father and of the Son and of the Holy Spirit, teaching them to observe all that I have commanded you; and lo, I am with you always, to the close of the age."[30] And we can infer that the "age" in this context refers to the time when the next Manifestation—the Paraclete (i.e., Muhammad)—would appear.

Similarly, Muhammad bequeaths to His followers the example of His own life, the Book (which consists not only of the Qur'án but also the authenticated hadíth) and His family as successors to Him, beginning with His son-in-law 'Alí. In addition—again in the context of the axiomatic statement by Bahá'u'lláh about all that the Manifestations do being a form of guidance—we can well accept the Constitution of Medina as being His model for a multi-religious, constitutionally based *ummah* or community.

This model can be regarded as an obvious advancement from the tribal state Moses had devised and a departure from Christ's ambiguous instructions about how the community of believers should be governed. Possibly Christ foreknew that by the time

His teachings had spread throughout the Roman Empire and had become incorporated into the Roman state (which had its own polity), the age or Dispensation of Christianity would have accomplished all that was possible in breaking with the rigidity of the Judaic theocracy and introducing the concept of a personal God (Father), together with the idea of a personal relationship with the Creator through the Intermediary of Christ as His "Son."

This assumption regarding Muhammad's idea of a governmental structure more advanced and broader in scope than tribal governance is confirmed by Shoghi Effendi's assertion that Islam introduced the concept of a nation-state. "The Faith of Islam," he begins, "the succeeding link in the chain of Divine Revelation, introduced, as Bahá'u'lláh Himself testifies, the conception of the nation as a unit and a vital stage in the organization of human society, and embodied it in its teaching." He continues, "This indeed is what is meant by this brief yet highly significant and illuminating pronouncement of Bahá'u'lláh: 'Of old (Islamic Dispensation) it hath been revealed: "Love of one's country is an element of the Faith of God."'" Shoghi Effendi concludes by noting that this concept of the autonomy of nationhood was in effect until the advent of Bahá'u'lláh's ordination of a global commonwealth:

This principle was established and stressed by the Apostle of God [Muhammad], inasmuch as the evolution of human society required it at that time. Nor could any stage above and beyond it have been envisaged, as world conditions preliminary to the establishment of a superior form of organization were as yet unobtainable. The conception of nationality, the attainment to the state of nationhood, may, therefore, be said to be the distinguishing characteristics of the Muhammadan Dispensation, in the course of which the nations and races of the world, and particularly in Europe and America, were unified and achieved political independence.[31]

Because of the early schism in Islam, by the end of the Islamic era (1844), the religion had become thoroughly remote from the pluralism and concept of progressive Revelation that Muhammad had taught. At that point in time, the Báb revealed Himself as the next Manifestation of God and, similar to Christ, created a vast update of the Word of God by creating new laws. Perhaps most relevant in the continuity of the Divine Plan of God, He interpreted some of the most important, abstruse, and misunderstood Súrihs of the Qur'án. One of the most weighty of these authoritative interpretations is found in the Qayyúmu'l-Asmá' in which the Báb explains the symbolism of the Súrih of Joseph as a prophecy foretelling the life of Bahá'u'lláh Who, like Joseph, would be horribly betrayed by His brother.

Of course, as noted early in our discussion, historically and theologically, it is particularly noteworthy that in His authoritative texts, the Báb implicitly and explicitly alludes to the imminent advent of "Him Whom God shall make manifest," Bahá'u'lláh. Indeed, in the *Persian Bayán*, the Báb states specifically that the people should become attentive to "the Order of Bahá'u'lláh":

It should be noted, in this connection, that in the third Váhid of this Book [the Persian Bayán] there occurs a passage which, alike in its explicit reference to the name of the Promised One, and in its anticipation of the Order which, in a later age, was to be identified with His Revelation, deserves to rank as one of the most significant statements recorded in any of the Báb's writings. "Well is it with him," is His prophetic announcement, "who fixeth his gaze upon the Order of Bahá'u'lláh, and rendereth thanks unto his Lord. For He will assuredly be made manifest. God hath indeed irrevocably ordained it in the Bayán."[32]

Thus, while the religious laws and institutions devised by the Báb were never implemented before the time came for the unfolding the second Revelation from these "Twin Manifestations," the Revelation of Bahá'u'lláh and all the authoritative institutions devised within His Covenant can be correctly portrayed as the fulfillment of the divine process begun by the Báb in 1844.

These twin Revelations, then, designate a singular milestone in the religious history of our planet for a number of fairly obvious reasons. Foremost among these is the fact that this is the first time that the mission of the Manifestation has been to create world peace through the establishment of a global polity; prior religions were focused on bringing about unity and peace to as much of the world as they could reasonably be expected to reach during the age for which they were revealed. Bahá'u'lláh's Dispensation marks the beginning of the era in which the Manifestation is able to establish an inviolable Covenant whereby His teachings would bring about the reformation of the entire planet.

For global peace and unity to occur, it was necessary that the material wherewithal would become available, that human experience would make obvious the need for a global commonwealth of nations, and that the Manifestation would have the opportunity to reveal the panoply of teachings sufficient to provide all necessary spiritual and material guidance for such an edifice, including detailed written instructions for the succession of authority until the appearance of the next Manifestation.

In conclusion, while some of the previous religions have now spread worldwide, they did so by exceeding the duration of time for which they had been designed, and long after the clarity of the Prophet's words, or access to His words, had become distorted and misinterpreted. Consequently, these religions became subject to schisms, dysfunction, and corruption—the perverse effects wrought by the very human race they were intended to serve. But with the advent of the Bahá'í era, it is now possible for the Manifestation to construct a global edifice capable of unifying the peoples of the world under the shelter of a single, undivided faith, thereby fulfilling the long-awaited promise of an enduring world peace.

Some Conclusions about the "Authoritative" Word

Having glimpsed briefly the breadth of the influence of those material and spiritual powers that emanate from the advent of the Word, and how it is intended to entwine human existence with the fabric of reality, let us provide further clarity about what is implied by the term *Word* as we will apply it.

While in many religions someone (an individual, an institution, or a collective) whom the followers consider to express trustworthy and definitive opinions decides what constitute its authoritative texts ("scripture"), these writings may not necessarily be just the words revealed by God through the Manifestation.

The most obvious distinction between what constitutes authoritative texts and "the Word of God" or "the Book" would be the difference between those words presumably revealed by God through the Manifestations as opposed to traditions (hadíth),* interpretations, commentaries, and additional guidance that believers may consider divinely guided or authoritatively binding, and yet that obviously do not have the same station or status as the "revealed"

---

* Words attributed to the Manifestation. However, in the sense this term is employed in Islam, all of the words attributed to Christ in the four gospels of the New Testament would befit this criterion.

utterances of the Manifestation or those words He has explicitly designated as having the same authority as the Holy text.

For example, Christ left no written texts, but as we have noted, there are four different accounts of what He was recalled to have said. Three of these accounts (Matthew, Mark, and Luke) are categorized as "synoptic" gospels because they are only slightly different accounts of more or less the same information. The gospel of John, however, is peculiar, in that it leaves out some important events, adds others, and incorporates a distinct theological and philosophical orientation regarding the station of Christ and the Second Coming.

The problem thus arises as to what the Christians should consider infallible guidance. Some accept only the words actually spoken by Christ as the "Word of God." Others accept the totality of the New Testament, even though the decision about which works should constitute the "New Testament" was not finalized until more than three hundred years after the crucifixion of Christ. Still others accept both the Old and New Testaments as authoritative—the Word or the Book. But the fact is that the Qur'án is the first scripture that can be reliably said to be the authentic words of the Manifestation.

And yet, as we have noted, we find a similar problem in Islam. The Qur'án, though revealed episodically, then collected and arranged according to length, is considered to report the actual words uttered by Muhammad when He would recite the words God conveyed to Him through the archangel Gabriel. And yet other statements made by Muhammad were also recollected and recorded when He was not in this "revelatory" state. These utterances are considered hadíth (traditions) and possess varying degrees of authority but are certainly regarded as less reliably authoritative than the Qur'án, even though many hadíth were recollected and recorded at least as faithfully as were the gospels of the New Testament. And while the meaning of these statements is subject to various interpretations, so are the Súrihs of the Qur'án.

The same problem of authority holds true for the words written or recorded by the Imams. For Shí'ih Muslims, the Imams, as lineal descendants of Muhammad, are considered appointed by the Prophet in the hadíth of the Two Weighty Things, and their utterances are thus considered authoritative and infallible. For Sunní Muslims—who, instead, accept the elected polity of the Caliphate—the Imams possessed no such authority. Indeed, according to Shí'ih sources, the Imams were murdered by order of the Caliph specifically to prevent them from utilizing their inherited authority to strengthen the Shí'ih following.

Thus, from a Shí'ih (and Bahá'í) perspective of Islamic history, the schism that began at the death of the Prophet and persists to this day effectively deprived Islam of the intended guidance it would have received through the leadership of the twelve Imams. Consequently, though the influence of the advent and teachings of Muhammad produced great advances in civilization and learning, as well as a mighty empire, Islam was prevented from attaining the heights it could have achieved had the Covenant of Muhammad not been shattered at His death.

The central point here is that while various sects of Islam regard a variety of texts as having authority, the only Islamic text uniformly regarded by all Muslims as the revealed Word of God is the Qur'án itself. But throughout the Qur'án, when Muhammad refers to the "Book" or the "people of the Book," He is alluding to the successively revealed authoritative utterances of previous emissaries from God—Whom He designates by the term *Rasúl* (Messenger) or *Nabí* (prophet) depending on Their station—making no distinction about what the followers of those previous Prophets consider "scripture." Returning to our earlier observations regarding the first verses in the Gospel of John about the Word becoming flesh (John

1:14) and being synonymous with God Himself, we can reasonably conclude that if these distinctive, immaculate, and infallible Beings are—as the Bahá'í texts attest—the highest expression of God we can know and if everything they say and do accords with His Will, then the meaning of the passage from John makes total sense. True, the "Word" represents the utterances of the Prophets, but it also alludes to Their character and comportment, to the power emanating from Their appearance, and to the guidance They give regarding succession of authority and continuity of the religion They establish.

The Bahá'í Concept of "Authoritative Texts"

In the Bahá'í Faith, various terms are used to distinguish between the forms that the "Word" will assume in this era. First, of course, there are the weighty texts revealed by the Báb and Bahá'u'lláh, whether written in Their own hand or dictated by Them to an amanuensis and then reviewed by Them. These texts constitute the "revealed Word," and Their authority is binding, subject only to authoritative interpretation by 'Abdu'l-Bahá and Shoghi Effendi, and elucidation and implementation by the Universal House of Justice.

The texts of the Báb and Bahá'u'lláh constitute what Bahá'u'lláh refers to as a "Revelation direct from God" and what Shoghi Effendi has poetically described as the "creative Word of God." The authenticated words of 'Abdu'l-Bahá and Shoghi Effendi, as well as the guidance by the Universal House of Justice, although not the "revealed Word," are also considered authoritative and no less binding. For while the creative power emanates from the Word of God as revealed by the Manifestation, 'Abdu'l-Bahá confirms that all authoritative guidance has "the same effect as the Text itself." It is therefore considered as binding and infallible as the "creative

Word," and thus an integral and inseparable part of the Revelation itself.[33]

This power—from which also derive the power and authority of the institutions created by Bahá'u'lláh, 'Abdu'l-Bahá, Shoghi Effendi, and the Universal House of Justice—is the direct result of the critical documents that delineate the succession of authority in the Covenant of Bahá'u'lláh. In previous Dispensations, any guidance regarding succession was, alas, ignored or intentionally evaded and destroyed by perverse opposition. And it is from reflecting on the coherence and inviolable links in the Covenant that the student of the Bahá'í Faith comes to appreciate how the "Word" designates the totality of these ingredients integrated into the outpouring of the appearance of a Manifestation at this critical turning point in human history. In this "Day," the unity of the human race is no longer a choice but an inescapable fact, no longer merely a desired outcome but the only source of the salvation of humankind.

In the simplest of terms, our planet has, in the course of a single century, become contracted into one interdependent political and social entity whose diverse communities, cultures, languages, and beliefs are now forced to accept the reality that the global commonwealth ordained by Bahá'u'lláh is not one among several possible solutions to the percolating global crises, but the sole rational resolution available.

-7-

INDIRECTION IN THE LANGUAGE OF THE MANIFESTATIONS

None apprehendeth the meaning of these utterances except them whose hearts are assured, whose souls have found favor with God, and whose minds are detached from all else but Him. In such utterances, the literal meaning, as generally understood by the people, is not what hath been intended. Thus it is recorded: "Every knowledge hath seventy meanings, of which one only is known amongst the people. And when the Qá'im shall arise, He shall reveal unto men all that which remaineth." He also saith: "We speak one word, and by it we intend one and seventy meanings; each one of these meanings we can explain."

Bahá'u'lláh, Kitáb-i-Íqán, ¶283

If we understand the overall context and abiding theme and purpose for a poetic work, we obviously have a head start in trying to interpret the verses. In the study and understanding of scripture from the various religious traditions, knowing the unfolding religious history underlying the revealed Word allows us to figure out what might otherwise be obscure or indecipherable. Because we do know that history, we can appreciate that the Manifestations often employ forms of indirection such as symbolism and other poetic and figurative devices. Once we appreciate that this indirection is purposeful and is meant to require thoughtful reflection on our part, we have a much greater chance of discerning the intended meaning of the Word. Of course, once we realize that this is an ongoing process rather than a single point of insight, then we also come to accept the fact that we never complete this process, that the Word is inexhaustible in its meanings and applications, and that, consequently, we must humbly pursue on a daily basis our lifelong study of God's will.

Some Background

If we are assured ahead of time that nothing about this process is haphazard, illogical, or merely a cultural invention, we can then be confident that our efforts to discern what God's Emissary is trying to teach us will be fruitful. I have always given the same assurance to my students when I was teaching them poetry, especially if it was particularly imagistic or the sometimes challenging work of symbolist poets. It was important that they understood that the works they were studying were not arbitrarily selected to be included in the anthology and, further, that from among all the poems in their textbook, I had carefully selected those I felt best demonstrated the strengths of indirection as a teaching technique so that their quest for understanding would not be in vain, as long as they invested sufficient time and effort and were attentive to the clues the poet had provided.

I also give this same assurance in my lectures and courses on the poetry of the Prophets: the choice of language, symbols, and various figurative devices is very purposefully devised by them to involve us in the process of learning and to awaken and challenge our inmost thoughts and loftiest capacities. Good poetry says what is otherwise unsayable. The pains the Prophet (or good poet) has taken to translate ideas into symbols, images, or parables is not for the purpose of being coy or clever; obscurantism has no greater value than a difficult crossword puzzle.

No, the indirection draws us in, exhorts us to reflect and meditate on meaning, to examine the similarity between two essentially distinct and often contrary realities, for therein lies the linchpin of meaning. Take for example, a common thread of imagery employed by Christ, Who not only challenged the literalism and legalisms of the Pharisaic scholars with His parables, but also employed imagery and symbolism in almost everything He said. Obviously He could have said in a straightforward manner, "I am the Promised One, the Messiah, and if you follow my words and my example, you will become spiritually awakened and revitalized!" Instead, He repeatedly employed the parallel between spiritual enlightenment and revitalization and physical nourishment. "I am the bread of life," He told His followers, after explaining to them that the manna received by the Hebrews in the desert was not a miracle performed by Moses, but rather spiritual nourishment bestowed by God Himself: "Truly, truly, I say to you, it was not Moses who gave you the bread from heaven, but my Father gives you the true bread from heaven."[1]

Knowing that they do not understand the meaning of this symbolism, He explains, "For the bread of God is he who comes down from heaven and gives life to the world." Still not grasping what He means—that the Manifestation, whether Moses or Christ Himself, is the source of spiritual nourishment for the peoples of the world, the people ask Him to "give us this bread." Whereupon Christ responds a bit more clearly, but still challenging them to understand the symbolic or metaphorical nature of what He is saying, "I am the bread of life; whoever comes to me shall not hunger, and whoever believes in me shall never thirst."[2]

Christ goes on to explain the concept to them in somewhat plainer language, though even at the Last Supper, He employs this same symbolism: "Now as they were eating, Jesus took bread, and after blessing it broke it and gave it to the disciples, and said, 'Take, eat; this is my body.' And he took a cup, and when he had given thanks he gave it to them, saying, 'Drink of it, all of you, for this is my blood of the covenant, which is poured out for many for the forgiveness of sins.'"[3] Thus it is that the Prophet, like the good and thoughtful poet, does not think His readers merely vessels needing to be filled with His thoughts. Rather He desires more than aught else to have the seekers discover for themselves the truth underlying the sometimes veiled language or perplexing analogies. For unlike pure abstraction, images, parables, and examples stay with us. God is the ultimate source of nourishment, the Bestower of the bread of life, and that bread of life is none other than the Prophet Himself. His utterances and the example of His sacrificial life are indispensable sources of substance for all humankind.

Thus, through these brief examples, we come to appreciate that this indirection, this subtlety and divine poetry give a concrete referent, something memorable to remind us on a daily basis of precisely what gift God has bestowed, how He has bestowed it, and how essential that gift is to our daily existence. He nourishes our soul and quenches our thirst for life and love and meaning.

But the challenge of deciphering the meaning of the "Word" and the indirection with which the term is employed in scripture is not confined to the utterances of the Prophets. As we observe in the book of John, the Prophets Themselves are poetic expressions of God—perfect Manifestations of all the divine attributes of God. Recognizing God as expressed indirectly through the appearance of One Who, to outward seeming, is but an ordinary human being also represents a challenge that involves our relationship with "the Word": "In the beginning was the Word, and the Word was with God, and the Word was God" and "the Word was made flesh and dwelt among us."[4]

The same verity is demonstrated in many of the allusions in the Qur'án in which Muhammad refers to Himself as fulfilling Christ's prophecies about the "Comforter," and, most prominently, Muhammad several times chastises the Christian clerics who have vitiated a central theological reality by claiming that Christ was God incarnate. Sometimes Muhammad alludes to this perversion of Christ's teachings by directly reproaching the Christian doctrine of the trinity, and other times He criticizes the idea that Christ was literally the Son of God.[5] Muhammad also focuses much of His ministry on preparing His followers for the long-awaited "Day of Days," or "Day of Resurrection."

These are but a few of the examples of the indirect method God's Intermediaries employ to teach us. The efficacy of this methodology also underlies the poetic or rhetorical devices in their utterances, a concealing or veiling of meaning by which we are tested as to whether we can discern the spiritual significance underlying the literal or surface meaning of the Word. Through this indirection and testing, the Manifestations also ensure that we become increasingly self-reliant and enlightened in our understanding of Their Revelation, that by degrees we may become self-assured in our adherence to Their teachings, and stalwart in the confirmation of our belief. Indeed, one of the definitions of justice Bahá'u'lláh provides pertains to our obligation to investigate truth for ourselves: "The best beloved of all things in My sight is Justice; turn not away therefrom if thou desirest Me, and neglect it not that I may confide in thee. By its aid thou shalt see with thine own eyes and not through the eyes of others, and shalt know of thine own knowledge and not through the knowledge of thy neighbor."[6]

The point is that while the underlying concepts that unify all the Revelations may be apparent to anyone who is sincerely seeking spiritual guidance, we also can discover continuity of the Word in all its various expressions from Dispensation to Dispensation—whether in scripture, in the example of the Prophet's life, or in the influence manifest in the advancement of society with the advent of a new Revelation. In this sense, the reappearance and continuity of the Word with each successive "Day" or Revelation constitute an ongoing narrative, the continuous story of the ascent of society. But this coherence becomes apparent only if one is capable of discerning in each successive appearance of the Word the motive force of the overarching plan devised by the Creator to educate humankind by degrees.

Of course, here I am referring to the Word in its authentic pure form, not what becomes of the Revelation from the manmade institutions or interpretations that unfortunately derail its original intentions, an unfortunate but predictable result that appears most prominently when the Revelation is extended long beyond the time for which its teachings were intended. Thus, the inflexible and often spurious legalism of Jewish law and clergy had, by the time of Christ, not only become dictatorial and constraining rather than spiritual and enlightening, but it had in many cases also contrived traditions, superstitions, and practices that had neither scriptural basis nor spiritual efficacy.

The very same thing can be said of the intransigent stance of the Christian Church by the time of Muhammad's appearance and of the Sharia law of Islam, most of which is a spurious interpretation or application of concepts, rather than law derived explicitly from the Prophet. By the time of the advent of the Báb in 1844 (the appearance of the Qá'im for the Muslims, the "end of days" for the Christians), the deterioration of both Christianity and Islam was so pronounced as to rapidly emerge as possibly one of the central causes of global conflict. Indeed, for the Bahá'ís, it comes as no surprise that the principal focus of world attention as a result of the distorted remnants of Islam are the very places where Bahá'u'lláh was imprisoned by Islamic authorities, whether Shí'ih or Sunní: Iran (Tehran), Iraq (Baghdad), Turkey (Constantinople), and Israel (Akká).

In light of this abiding unity of purpose and continuity of narrative and guidance, and with the goal of coming to discover and appreciate how the Word weaves together human purpose into the tapestry of human history, we will proceed to consider some hermeneutical principles that are designed for more intensive study of the process whereby the "creative word" accomplishes by degrees God's intended goal for humankind. These principles about how we should approach the revealed Word will help us to discern its intended meaning rather than the one that has since been imposed by clerics and scholars. For while they may be well-trained in discrete areas of learning, they generally fail to appreciate the most basic and fundamental precepts regarding the station of the Prophets, namely, the twofold nature of Their teachings (spiritual insight translated into individual and collective action) combined with the underlying essential unity that binds together all Their Revelations.

Hermeneutical Principles

In a very general sense, hermeneutics is the study, or art, of interpreting the written word. The term has become associated most frequently with the study of religious scripture for purposes of deciphering or "decoding" the various layers of meaning cloaked by the surface or literal meaning of the text. For example, in his extremely useful study of how the authoritative texts of the Bahá'í Faith can be translated into patterns of social practice, Paul Lample sets forth what he describes as "Hermeneutical Principles in Bahá'í Teachings."[7]

While he affirms that these are only "some" of the principles that might be applied, we would do well to review them prior to examining some of the rhetorical devices that in past Revelations were so often intentionally misconstrued or applied literally by those who wished to pervert or "corrupt"* the text for the self-serving purpose of gaining and maintaining power over others:

1. The Book has an intended meaning.
2. Judgments about meaning should be made from the perspective of the Revelation.
3. There is no contradiction between authoritative passages.
4. Meaning is sometimes explicit and sometimes veiled.
5. The meaning of the Book cannot be exhausted.
6. Truth unfolds progressively within the dispensation.
7. Understanding is influenced by the stages of the Faith's organic development.
8. Personal interpretations of the meaning of the Text should be weighed in the light of science and reason.
9. History and context have implications for understanding the meaning of the Text.

Let me give a few obvious but hardly simple examples of how these principles come into play in the examination of the Bahá'í authoritative texts and those of the previous Revelations. In his explanation of the allegorical meaning of the myth of Adam and Eve, 'Abdu'l-Bahá first establishes that the story is clearly symbolic

---

* ". . . by corruption of the text is meant that in which all Muslim divines are engaged today, that is the interpretation of God's holy Book in accordance with their idle imaginings and vain desires" (Bahá'u'lláh, Kitáb-i-Íqán, ¶93).

because any literal meaning would be patently illogical and therefore untenable. He then asserts that the story has a variety of valid interpretations or applications (hermeneutic principle no. 5): "The account of Adam and Eve, their eating from the tree, and their expulsion from Paradise are therefore symbols and divine mysteries. They have all-embracing meanings and marvelous interpretations, but only the intimates of the divine mysteries and the well-favored of the all-sufficing Lord are aware of the true significance of these symbols."[8]

This notion of "mysteries" is similar to Bahá'u'lláh's use of the term "húrís of inner meaning that are as yet concealed within the chambers of divine wisdom."[9] The concept of purposefully concealed meaning represents an example of Lample's fourth hermeneutic principle about verses that are purposefully veiled to require the reader to solve the mystery in order to obtain the "inner meaning." 'Abdu'l-Bahá then proposes what He describes as one of the "numerous meanings" of the Adamic myth by establishing the symbolic values of the central figures:

> These verses of the Torah have therefore numerous meanings. We will explain one of them and will say that by "Adam" is meant the spirit of Adam and by "Eve" is meant His self. For in certain passages of the Sacred Scriptures where women are mentioned, the intended meaning is the human self. By "the tree of good and evil" is meant the material world, for the heavenly realm of the spirit is pure goodness and absolute radiance, but in the material world light and darkness, good and evil, and all manner of opposing realities are to be found.[10]

He goes on to introduce how the temptation and fall of Adam play out in terms of these symbols, especially in light of the fact that, according to both Islamic and Bahá'í belief, Adam was the first Manifestation in the Prophetic or Adamic universal cycle of Manifestations:*

> The meaning of the serpent is attachment to the material world. This attachment of the spirit to the material world led to the banishment of the self and spirit of Adam from the realm of freedom to the world of bondage and caused Him to turn from the kingdom of Divine Unity to the world of human existence. When once the self and spirit of Adam entered the material world, He departed from the paradise of freedom and descended into the realm of bondage. He had abided in the heights of sanctity and absolute goodness, and set foot thereafter the world of good and evil.[11]

In other words, inasmuch as the Manifestations preexist in the spiritual realm, Their acquiescence to the Will of God that They become incarnate in the physical world in order to teach humankind is a willingness to undergo the severe tests and ordeals that ordinary human beings must endure.

There is much more to 'Abdu'l-Bahá's authoritative explication of this text and solution to this "mystery," but for our purposes, it

---

* "Each of the Manifestations of God has likewise a cycle wherein His religion and His law are in full force and effect. When His cycle is ended through the advent of a new Manifestation, a new cycle begins. Thus, cycles are inaugurated, concluded, and renewed, until a universal cycle is completed in the world of existence and momentous events transpire which efface every record and trace of the past; then a new universal cycle begins in the world, for the realm of existence has no beginning. We have previously presented proofs and arguments concerning this subject, and there is no need for repetition" ('Abdu'l-Bahá, *Some Answered Questions*, no. 41.4).

is sufficient that we see in this veiled example (principle no. 4), the indirection and challenge that scripture often employs. By coaxing and challenging us to unravel these literary / spiritual puzzles, the Manifestations teach us to appreciate the hermeneutical principles that are necessary to our independent study and understanding of the Word. However—and this is extremely important to emphasize—we should not infer from this process that meaning or enlightenment is reserved for experts in literature, for scholars, or for those who consider themselves "learned"—at least according to most traditional applications of the term.

In fact, when Christ clothes His own teachings in the garb of parables, it is the "learned" but legalistic and literalist Pharisees who have the greatest difficulty in discerning His intended meaning (principles no. 1, 2, 4, and 5). In expounding the principle by which we distinguish between possession of an understanding heart versus academic learning—"those veils of idle learning that are current amongst men"—Bahá'u'lláh makes the following powerful statement about access to the inner meaning of the revealed Word:

> Heed not the idle contention of those who maintain that the Book and verses thereof can never be a testimony unto the *common* people, inasmuch as they neither grasp their meaning nor appreciate their value. And yet, the unfailing testimony of God to both the East and the West is none other than the Qur'án. Were it beyond the comprehension of men, how could it have been declared as a universal testimony unto all people? If their contention be true, none would therefore be required, nor would it be necessary for them to know God, inasmuch as the knowledge of the divine Being transcendeth the knowledge of His Book, and the common people would not possess the capacity to comprehend it.[12] (Italics added)

Continuing this theme, Bahá'u'lláh says that the lowly but pure-hearted are most often the first to recognize the Manifestation and comprehend the inner meaning of what is so often confusing to their own religious leaders: "And yet, in the sight of God, these *common people* are infinitely superior and exalted above their religious leaders who have turned away from the one true God. The understanding of His words and the comprehension of the utterances of the Birds of Heaven are in no wise dependent upon human learning. They depend solely upon purity of heart, chastity of soul, and freedom of spirit."[13]

The term *hermeneutics* and the literary and philosophical theories it encompasses may sound intimidating, but when viewed carefully with an open mind the principles of understanding the sacred texts are, in fact, the application of common sense. For example, taking a single passage out of context and imagining we could determine its meaning would be tantamount to having someone judge us by a single sentence we may have said about ourselves when we were ten years old. Thus, returning once again to the passage where Christ says "I am the bread of life," He is obviously speaking metaphorically and in a particular context.[14] It is only outside the proper context that this statement can be taken literally and with ridiculous consequences. Its inner meaning is made clear when viewed in the historical context (principle no. 10). Christ made this declaration after He performed the miracle of feeding the masses by multiplying the bread and fish.* He is explaining to those present that they should not follow Him for what they regard as His power to perform this miraculous act, but rather because He can provide them with lasting and perdurable spiritual nourishment of which He is the source; He is the "bread

---

* The feeding of the multitude is recorded in all four canonical Gospels: Matthew 14:13–21, Mark 6:31–44, Luke 9:10–17, and John 6:5–15.

of life." And as we have already noted, this passage comes in the larger context of Christ's repeated use of this same nourishment theme throughout His ministry, most notably at the Last Supper.

A Doorway to the Inner Mysteries

It would be presumptuous to assume that in a single chapter we can meaningfully encompass the entirety of the rhetorical devices employed by the Manifestations. But we can at the very least get a general sense that this indirect literary method They employ is made up of various rhetorical devices. Hopefully, the reader will be tempted to extend this sort of study (applying hermetical principles and rhetorical devices) independently; such an exercise can bring forth pearls of wisdom that are the source of unending delight. For once we grasp the sense of how these literary devices work, we discover that we begin to spot them everywhere in the Word, whether in the utterances of the Prophets or in the symbolic actions They perform. Furthermore, once we have invested this energy into decoding the sacred text, these treasured pearls are never lost to us; they remain in our consciousness so that we eagerly return to them again and again.

MYTHS

Let us begin with the myth, a rhetorical device that is usually employed in scripture as an allegorical story. We need to be clear that by "myth" we do not mean that the story has no basis in history or fact, though most often when myth is derived from history, the events are translated into some analogical or symbolic fiction. Since we have already alluded to it, let us begin by examining how this device (or genre) is employed in the important story of Adam and Eve.

Clearly we could also categorize this story as a fable, analogy, or an allegory, but considering the weight it has been given as a literal account, whether in art or in exegesis, the term *myth* works well to convey the mythic characteristics of this fascinating creation story that appears in the Old Testament, is mentioned in the New Testament, and is retold in the Qur'án. Likely, the Adamic myth emerged in the same way as many ancient stories from cultures that were traversing the tribal stage of social evolution. As previously noted, the myth may have a factual basis and derive from an actual historical figure, though the stories surrounding the character are typically hyperbolic as over the course of time the legendary qualities of the central or heroic figure evolve from one telling to the next through what is called the oral formulaic tradition.

The oral tradition—now understood to be a shared characteristic among all tribal cultures—most often involves the intoning or chanting of legends during a social gathering wherein stories and heroes that portray the highest values and ideals of the people are rehearsed, most often in some rhythmic or formulaic meter or verse. This common practice, especially among preliterate peoples, can be amazingly accurate in transmitting history; and the principal narrator—the bard or singer—holds a highly esteemed position as the human repository of genealogies and sacred myths, though all members of the community are expected to acquire this skill so that they might instill familial history in the hearts and minds of their progeny down through successive generations.

Another point worth noting is that a myth will usually retain its central meaning or theme, though each reciting by each successive narrator will be an original work with slight changes. We can observe this phenomenon in the three synoptic gospels of Matthew, Mark, and Luke. We have some idea of when the story of Christ was finally written down, but until that point, the stories were recollected, possibly by the authors of these books but possibly passed to them from several witnesses. Thus, we can observe distinctions among these three narratives about the same events, both in the recounting of the specific words of Christ and in the addition or elimination of various details. And yet the fundamental story remains the same, as does the underlying truth that the teachings and life of Christ represent.

The relative accuracy of the story of Christ is thus demonstrated by the fact that what was originally told as stories by followers was written down, perhaps by oral dictation, relatively soon after the events took place. Likewise, the fact that three different narrations tell more or less the same story further substantiates the reliability of the story so that we can more aptly classify these works as history rather than myth.

When the distance in time between the events and the ultimate transcription of an orally transmitted story is vast, however, then it is probably more accurate to classify the final version of the story as myth, although it does not necessarily have less importance just because it has taken on the trappings of fact translated into fiction. For example, such is the case with the myths of Adam and Eve or Noah because this oral tradition among tribal peoples is likely the manner in which most of the Pentateuch (and possibly much of the rest of the Old Testament canon) was recorded.

So how much of these stories is an accurate portrait of history and how much is shaped by the teller to convey a timely message or, in retrospect, to speculate *post hoc* about God's hand in the course of events? Did Jonah really live inside the belly of a whale? Did God and Satan actually wager on whether or not Job would retain his faith? Did Joshua crumble the walls of Jericho by having his men circle the city and blow their horns? Did God actually turn Lot's wife into a pillar of salt?

Thus, the story of Adam and Eve is clearly a symbolic version of a creation myth, not a record of human history. We notice, for example, that it is the Evian aspect of the self (the soul) that is tempted by the serpent (representing worldliness), not the Adamic self, which might represent the physical temple. While this may seem contradictory, we should take note that the Evian mind is in charge of the "lower," physical self, and thus, having free will, is culpable for giving in to this temptation.

The myth of Abraham and Isaac is similarly symbolic. According to the Torah, it is Isaac whom Abraham binds and is ready to sacrifice in compliance with the command of God. And yet, according to the more recently revealed and more authentic Qur'án, it is Ishmael, the firstborn son, whom Abraham was about to sacrifice. Lample refers to this story as an example of "intended meaning." The story as myth symbolizes the concept of sacrifice, regardless of which son was involved, and one important theme of the myth is that it effectively prefigures God's sacrifice of "his only Son" with the crucifixion of Christ, though this can also be confused if taken in a strictly literal sense, the way clerics did as they shaped and interpreted Christian theology and history and turned myth into fact. Consequently, Muhammad was obliged to remind His followers that God, a metaphysical reality, would hardly literally father a physical offspring: "for Allah is One Allah—glory be to Him—Exalted is He above having a son."[15]

The myth of Noah is similarly more symbol and myth than historical fact. For while Noah was a Manifestation and there was indeed a flood over large portions of the earth, scholars believe that most of the flood myths derive from the Mesopotamian texts of the epics of *Gilgamesh* and of *Atra-Hasis*. But regardless the source of the myth, the point is that the concept of the Ark as a source of salvation is, according to the Bahá'í interpretation, an entirely symbolic allusion to Noah's Covenant, not a literal account of the Prophet constructing a boat.

And what about the details concerning the boat and the gathering of the animals? The Bahá'í authoritative texts confirm that there was no actual Ark or Flood,* but one possible interpretation might be that these various animals, both the male (active or outer) and female (passive or inner), represent various human virtues—both the inner or female understanding of the virtue and the outer or male implementation of the virtue into action. Thus, even as Bahá'u'lláh asserts that human beings potentially possess all the divine virtues, so He also affirms that the Manifestation not only actively possesses all the divine virtues but manifests them perfectly (hence the term "Manifestation").

In short, the myth of Noah illustrates that when the waters of strife and tests arrive, none are secure unless they abide within the Covenant of God where all virtues can be learned and practiced. More particularly, the story highlights how those who believed and followed Noah's teachings were spiritually saved, while those who rejected Him were not so fortunate.

As we have mentioned previously, other good examples of scriptural myths devised to teach valuable symbolic spiritual meanings are the story of the Tower of Babel, the story of Job, the story of the manna bestowed on the Hebrews in the wilderness, and the story of David and Goliath, which has also assumed mythical heroic proportions in numerous kinds of artistic representations.[16] Again we might ponder if there is any factual historical allusions in these stories, and the answer is that we do not know, other than what the Manifestations have to tell us. But we do not question the moral lessons that the myths represent, even as do the parables told by Christ.

---

* "The Ark and the Flood we believe are symbolical" (From a letter written on behalf of Shoghi Effendi to an individual believer, cited in *Light of Guidance*, p. 509).

ALLUSIONS

An allusion is a rhetorical device in which a term or phrase constructs an indirect reference to something. For example, if we were to employ the terms "Founding Father" while speaking to Americans, we might expect them to know we are alluding to individuals such as Thomas Jefferson, John Adams, Benjamin Franklin, and George Washington, who were instrumental in the formation of the governmental institutions of the United States of America.

But allusions can be varied. They can be very simple and obvious, or subtle, complex, and understood only by those who are as learned as their creator—the allusions in T. S. Eliot's *The Wasteland* come to mind—or else who have shared experiences. For example, if I speak about the "elixir of life," the hearer might understand that I am referring to something beneficial. Someone more learned might infer a deeper meaning by knowing that "elixir," for the ancient alchemist, was that unknown substance capable of transmuting base metals (like lead) into gold. Consequently, someone coming across this same allusion in scripture might well conclude that this term is alluding to some spiritual experience or force capable of rejuvenating or transforming us, possibly through teachings with sufficient redemptive powers to make us spiritually refined.

Let us look at a couple of specific examples of allusions from scripture that provide us with insights that might otherwise be misunderstood or veiled in their meaning. One of my favorite examples relates to Christ's last words as He was dying on the cross. He seems to be lamenting the fact that God, the Father, has abandoned Him to grievous affliction: "Now from the sixth hour there was darkness over all the land until the ninth hour. And about the ninth hour Jesus cried with a loud voice, *"Eli, Eli, la'ma sabach-tha'ni?"* that is, 'My God, my God, why hast thou forsaken me?'" As a Christian youth, I had always been troubled by this plaint because it seemed to denote some lack of faith or some weakness on Christ's part. But in my later studies with a Bible that had footnotes, I discovered that Christ was with His dying breath still trying to break through the obstinacy of those He had tried so hard to teach by alluding to a passage from Psalm 22, their own scripture: "My God, my God, why hast thou forsaken me? Why art thou so far from helping me, from the words of my groaning? O my God, I cry by day, but thou dost not answer; and by night, but find no rest."[17] In short, Christ is not lamenting or doubting. He is with his last breath alluding to Jewish scripture that effectively prophesies His crucifixion, demonstrating to those who, unfortunately, were "hard of hearing" that He was the Messiah, that He can cite any verse from their own scripture at will, and that, if they knew the spiritual or inner meaning of their own scripture, they would have recognized His station instead of killing Him.

Obviously there is much more we could say about this single allusion. For example, we might ponder why He was not more direct, why He did not directly remind them about prophecies from their own Book. But here again we witness the indirection in the teaching methods of the Manifestations; They employ rhetorical devices to instruct, not to chastise or berate. What is more, the Manifestations are Each aware that what They do and say will have its greatest impact *after* Their mortal lives have ended.

Another favorite allusion of mine occurs in the Qur'án when Muhammad laments what the Christian hierarchy had done by way of creating the Trinitarian doctrine—that is, the literalist interpretation that Christ was not a Prophet or Messenger of God but, according to the Nicene Creed, God in the flesh. Correcting this misunderstanding is a major theme of the Qur'án—that there is only one God and that all else (including Manifestations such as Muhammad) are but His creation.

Thus, in one of His several discussions of this misperception and its pernicious impact on the concept of God and of the succession of Prophets as His Emissaries, Muhammad quite emphatically and directly calls such corruption of Christ's teachings blasphemy, stating that Christ Himself would never have presumed to be coequal with God: "They do blaspheme who say: 'Allah is Christ the son of Mary.' But Christ said: 'O children of Israel! Worship Allah, my Lord and your Lord.' . . . They do blaspheme who say, 'Allah is one of three in a Trinity, for there is no god except One God.'"[18]

The point is that allusions abound throughout scripture, in virtually every verse. Sometimes these are culturally based; sometimes they refer to previous scripture. But fortunately for us, modern texts containing scripture have useful notes to assist the reader in recovering or uncovering the concealed meaning of the allusions. And yet, far too often, the followers of the religion are content to accept the words at face value or else rely on what others (including clerics and other religious authorities) might assert the allusions to mean.

Here again, the value of the Bahá'í axiom about the need for independent investigation of the truth becomes evident. But whether the allusion is to some event associated with past history or scripture, or to the Manifestation's own history and experiences, or to some culturally based poetic tradition, it is obvious that the concealment is never intended to obfuscate meaning but rather to enhance it and to exhort the reader to think creatively about the inner or spiritual concepts contained within the shell of language.

Symbols and Metaphors

The most pervasive rhetorical devices that characterize scripture are symbols and metaphors, whether simple and direct or veiled and elusive, whether expressed in a single word or in a more elaborate conceit.* Though a frequently used metaphor can become

---

* See John Hatcher, *The Purpose of Physical Reality*, chapters 6 and 7, and *The Ocean of His Words*, chapter 5, for more expansive discussion of these figurative devices.

a symbol, and many symbols work metaphorically, there is an important—if at times somewhat nebulous—distinction between the two. It is worthwhile to briefly note it to appreciate how symbols and metaphors operate so that we can become better able to discern the levels of meaning beneath the surface of words.

For example, as we have mentioned, Christ often uses nutritional imagery in alluding to His purpose and mission. Thus, when He states that He is the "bread of life," He is employing a metaphor. He is implicitly comparing His function as intermediary between God and humankind as providing spiritual nourishment in the same way that bread provides nourishment for the body. Had He said, "I am like bread," we would say He is employing a simile, because the comparison is explicit.

At the heart of these two devices—metaphor and simile—is a comparison, but, importantly, the comparison is between essentially different things. For example, if Christ had said, "I am a Prophet like Moses," this would be a comparison, but not a simile or metaphor because They were both Prophets—essentially the same category of being. But in a metaphor or a simile, the comparison between two fundamentally different things focuses on some shared or common qualities.

Every simile and metaphor thus possesses three distinct parts: the thing that is being described (the tenor), the thing compared to it (the vehicle), and the attributes they have in common (the meaning). A simple Venn chart demonstrates the relationship among these three components of a metaphor or simile:

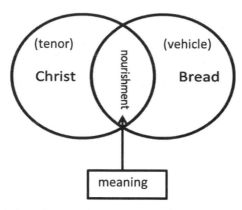

Figure 10. The Three Components of a Metaphor or Simile

In this metaphor, Christ is the tenor, bread is the vehicle, and the concept of nourishment is what these two different categories of existence share in common—this is the meaning of the metaphor. All analogical rhetorical devices work more or less this same way, whether they are a single word employed as a metaphor or a complex parable.

Understanding the basics of these rhetorical devices does not make figuring out the meaning always simple or easy, but it does mean that we are more likely to know how to go about discovering it.

This same sort of approach holds true for decoding a symbol, even though a symbol is usually constructed somewhat differently. For while a symbol also has three parts, it does not necessarily form a comparison, even though it will sometimes derive from one. For example, when we are driving and we see a traffic light turn red, we know immediately that we are to stop. Red is a symbol for "Stop!" But this relationship between symbol and meaning is not a comparison; there is no implication that red is like stopping.

With most symbols, there originally was some inherent relationship or comparison. For example, the cross symbolizes Christianity because obviously it alludes to the crucifixion of Christ.

This process of uncovering the rationale underlying the symbolic relationship has been called "discovering" (also "uncovering" or "recovering") the allusion—how the symbol came to represent something else, whether a concrete object or an abstract idea. Our chart representing the structure of a symbol demonstrates how the three parts relate to each other:

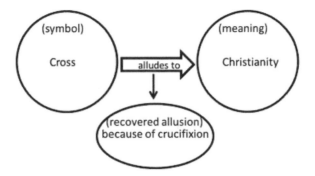

Figure 11. The Three Components of a Symbol

In this case, the cross is the symbol, Christianity is the referent or meaning, and knowing that Christ was crucified enables us to uncover or recover how the symbol came to refer to the religion as a whole.

In some cases, recovering the allusion is easy, and in other cases it is hard and unnecessary. For example, the earliest symbol for Christianity was a fish drawn with two arcs intersecting in the following manner:

Figure 12. Fish as Symbol for Christianity

In part, this symbol derives from the various allusions to fishing in the New Testament. Christ feeds the masses by multiplying the bread and fish. His first disciples were fishermen to whom Christ said, "Follow me and I will make you fishers of men." The Greek word for fish is "*Ichthys,*" and the Greek letters spelling the word are "ΙΧΘΥΣ." From this word the early Christians created the acrostic "*Iesous Christos Theou Yios Soter,*" which translates into English as "Jesus Christ, God's Son (and) Savior."[19]

Complicated and contrived perhaps, but this symbol nevertheless became an easily inscribed secret sign Christians could use to identify one another. Furthermore, although made simply with two lines, it is replete with various levels of meaning. Indeed, one finds this symbol still being employed by Christians everywhere. As we have noted previously, the use of Greek derives from the fact that the Apostle Paul was Greek, that many of the stronger Christian congregations were in Greece, and—as we have also mentioned—that the Gospel itself was first written down in Koine Greek.

Of course, we have already examined extensively the Bahá'í calligraphic symbol for the "Greatest Name" (Bahá) in chapter 3. Certainly it is equally complex and layered in meaning. This is not to say that a believer or follower of a religion needs to recover all the allusions of a particular symbol for it to have depth of meaning. The context of usage will often provide an existential meaning that ultimately may have more impact than knowing how the symbol came about.

Parable, Fable, or Allegorical Tale

Like the myth, a parable is a story, but unlike the myth, the parable is entirely fictional and pointedly devised by the author to explain or illustrate a moral concept. As the etymology of the word itself indicates—it comes from the Greek word *parabole*, meaning "comparison"—this rhetorical device is also analogical. It is usually an allegory and thus constructs a narrative in which characters, objects, or situations have a one-to-one correlation in representing an abstraction, such as a virtue, power, or attitude.

While each of these components of the parable are usually analogical rather than symbolic—at least in the original usage—the parable or its components can, after a history of frequent usage, take on symbolic value. For example, in the previous chapter, we examined Christ's parable of the Sower. Because this parable is so well-known and so applicable to every culture, the Manifestation as a Sower and His words as seeds planted in the heart of the hearer might well be considered as symbols, even though they started out as metaphors.

But let us try to make distinctions that are possibly more lucid with some other examples. In my graduate training many years ago, there used to be a simplistic but somewhat effective way of distinguishing between symbol and allegory. The play *Everyman* (1500), a medieval morality play, is allegorical, as is Bunyan's *The Pilgrim's Progress* (1678). In these works, we need not wonder what the characters represent—their names indicate a one-to-one relationship. Everyman represents all human beings. Likewise, when Death comes to visit him unexpectedly, we need not wonder what this represents, yet the situation is sufficiently dramatic and well-written that we may empathize with the emotional tension all the same. We identify with his lack of readiness and his frantic desire to have some companion accompany him on this unexpected journey he must suddenly undertake.

The same holds true for Bunyan's character of Christian and his journey to the Celestial City—we need not wonder what this character represents or what his life's journey is all about. While entirely didactic in purpose, the work holds our interest. Regardless of whether or not we agree with the moral message it conveys, we become emotionally engaged in the trials and tests this "everyman" figure must encounter in his spiritual journey through life.

In scripture, we find this same rhetorical literary device being employed—most prominently by Christ, but also by other Manifestations. Indeed, as we have already noted, the story of Adam and Eve, while mythic, could also be considered allegorical. Likewise, our discussion of Christ's story of the Sower is a perfect example of how a parable works, primarily because after narrating it, Christ Himself explains the one-to-one correlation between the different soils (the hearts of men) where the seeds (the Word of God) of the Sower (the Manifestation of God) fall. Thus, we come to understand the value of our receptivity to the Word of God. But for our present purposes, let us examine the parts of the parable as it functions rhetorically to teach through this indirect method. First, let us review Christ's explication:

> And he taught them many things in parables, and in his teaching he said to them: "Listen! A sower went out to sow. And as he sowed, some seed fell along the path, and the birds came and devoured it. Other seed fell on rocky ground, where it had not much soil, and immediately it sprang up, since it had no depth of soil; and when the sun rose it was scorched, and since it had no root it withered away. Other seed fell among thorns and the thorns grew up and choked it, and it yielded no grain. And other seeds fell into good soil and brought forth grain, growing up and increasing and yielding thirtyfold and sixtyfold and a hundredfold." And he said, "He who has ears to hear, let him hear."[20]

Using the same sort of Venn chart we devised for explaining metaphor and simile, we can create a similar illustration for the overall meaning of the story:

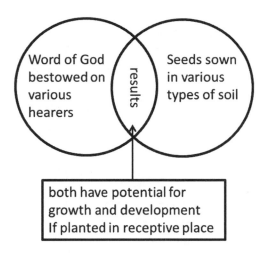

Figure 13. Venn Chart for Parable of Sower

But while this chart conveys the general sense of what Christ intends with this parable, we could also create a more elaborate and complete analysis of the parts of the allegory. This we can do by first listing all the literal or surface components of the parable. Since these are the items that represent the real meaning, these would all be vehicles:

Table 2. Vehicles

Tenor	Vehicle	Meaning
	Sower	
	Sows	
	Seeds	
	Soil	
	Path	
	Birds devouring seeds	
	Rocky ground with no depth of soil	
	Sun rises	
	Plants are scorched	
	Thorns	
	Thorns choke plants	
	Good soil	
	Fruit	

With a second step in this process of demonstrating how the parable works, we can now insert the tenors, the objects that are being represented by each vehicle:

Table 3. Tenors and Vehicles

Tenor	Vehicle	Meaning
Manifestation	Sower	
Teaches everyone	Sows	
Words	Seeds	
Heart of hearer	Soil	
Those who do not understand	Path	
"Evil one" (insistent self)* snatching away the words in the heart of the hearer	Birds devouring seeds	
A hearer who receives the Word eagerly but who has no depth of understanding	Rocky ground with no depth of soil	
The Revelation intensifies as more believers become attracted	Sun rises	
The hearer with no depth of understanding cannot withstand the tests and demands of belief	Plants are scorched	
The cares and enticements of worldly concerns	Thorns	
These affections overcome the effects of the Word in the believer's heart	Thorns choke plants	
A believer who receives the Word, studies it, nourishes it, and produces good works	Good soil	
The good deeds and noble character resulting from firm belief	Fruit	

* In the Bahá'í writings, as we have previously noted, the concept of Satan or the Satanic is a symbol for self-centeredness or what 'Abdu'l-Bahá calls the "insistent self" ('Abdu'l-Bahá, *Selections from the Writings of 'Abdu'l-Bahá,* no. 206.9).

Finally, we can fill in the meaning—that which the vehicle and the tenor share in common in the context of the parable:

Table 4. Tenors, Vehicles, and Meanings

Tenor	Vehicle	Meaning
Manifestation	Sower	Christ
Teaches everyone	Sows	Brings new Revelation
Words	Seeds	The Sacred Word from God is delivered to everyone
Heart of hearer	Soil	The nature of our receptivity depends on our spiritual attitude or condition
Those who do not understand	Pathway	The Words are lost (spilled) for those who do not or cannot understand the Word
"Evil one" (insistent self) snatching away the words in the heart of the hearer	Birds devour seeds	We have a choice whether to heed the Word or to allow our worldly desires to "devour" our desire for spiritual ascent.
A hearer who receives the word eagerly but who has no depth of understanding	Rocky ground with no depth of soil	Though having some receptivity, a person with no depth of understanding will not withstand tests
The Revelation intensifies as more believers become attracted	Sun rises	The number of followers rapidly increases as does the unfolding of the message
The hearer with no depth of understanding cannot withstand the tests and demands of belief	Plants are scorched	The followers with no grasp of Who the Manifestation is or what His message means will fall away as tests increase

Tenor	Vehicle	Meaning
The cares and enticements of worldly concerns	Thorns	The desire for earthly delights one refuses to abandon
These affections overcome the effects of the Word in his heart	Thorns choke plants	If the believer does not rid himself of attachment to worldly attraction, these will soon overtake belief
A believer who receives the Word, studies it, nourishes it, and produces good works	Good soil	One with a receptive heart, hearing ears, and clear vision about the truth of reality
The good deeds and noble character resulting from firm belief	Fruit	The results of those actions by one who understands the Word and acts on that understanding

At this point, we seem to have charted how the parable works indirectly to teach those who are attentive and creative in studying the utterances of the Manifestation. Certainly we have paraphrased most of what Christ explains by way of interpreting the tenor for these vehicles. And yet, to a large extent, in this parable the meaning seems more or less to replicate the tenor. Consequently, when interpreting a parable, we may not always need to be so elaborate or precise in distinguishing between what the two things have in common. In short, once we have figured out the tenor, we may already have discerned the veiled or concealed meaning.

In this sense, the parts of the parable or allegory might well be considered to be more symbolic than metaphorical in that they allude directly to what they mean. But this directness is not always there—parables and allegories can be more or less complex. But we have at least accomplished the task of appreciating how the parable works to create a parallel narrative on the figurative level while telling an interesting story on the literal or surface level. We have also discovered why the Prophets find these devices so useful in conveying sometimes very complex spiritual concepts, if for no other reason than the fact that because the stories are memorable, the spiritual insight or message will likewise be easily recalled.

IMAGERY

The term *imagery* can refer to a variety of rhetorical or poetic effects. In some scholarly discussions, imagery alludes to metaphors and similes, but sometimes the term refers to the richness of visual or sensual description, whether this be through literal or figurative means. And because imagery concerns the extent to which the depiction of reality evokes our sensual response, it most often indicates the degree to which the writer has been able to provide us with sufficient detail that our imagination creates mental pictures of what is in his mind.

Direct imagery is most often the process of adding adjectives to nouns. We can have the writer tell us that we are in a meadow, and we may immediately be pleased because the word *meadow* itself evokes a pleasant feeling. Or the writer can expand on the image by making the meadow verdant, dotted with flowers of various hues, perfumed with the scent of jasmine, delightsome with the sound of larks nesting in the shade of leafy elms amid the soft melody of a bubbling spring, and so on.

Indirect imagery might employ various analogical devices, perhaps comparing the meadow to a quilted paradise whereupon we might recline and rest, as we might upon a sumptuous bed while musicians play panpipes and we inhale in the perfumed air a scent reminiscent of the fragrant locks of our beloved.

I still remember, when I first read *Paradise Lost* so many years ago, being struck by the care Milton took in building the paradise of Eden in his mind. I am sure he thought to himself that this pastoral scene, so rich with nature's beauty, could so easily be ruined if there were bugs and biting insects. So Milton wisely banished the bugs in the following lustrous image of the couple's "blissful bower":

> Thus talking, hand in hand along they passed
> On to their blissful bower. It was a place
> Chosen by the sovran Planter, when he framed
> All things to Man's delightful use. The roof
> Of thickest covert was inwoven shade,
> Laurel and myrtle, and what higher grew
> Of firm and fragrant leaf; on either side
> Acanthus, and each odorous bushy shrub,
> Fenced up the verdant wall; each beauteous flower,
> Iris all hues, roses, and gessamin,
> Reared high their flourished heads between, and wrought
> Mosaic; under foot the violet,
> Crocus, and hyacinth, with rich inlay
> Broidered the ground, more coloured than with stone
> Of costliest emblem. Other creature here,
> Beast, bird, insect, or worm, durst enter none;
> Such was their awe of Man.[21]

In scripture, we find images of equal power, particularly in poetically rendered works such as the Psalms of David, the beatitudes of Christ, or the Persian Hidden Words of Bahá'u'lláh. Perhaps the prayers of the Bahá'í Revelation are some of the richest repositories of evocative and stirring imagery.

One of my favorites is part of a prayer of 'Abdu'l-Bahá where he supplicates God to make the believers dutiful teachers and servants of humankind: "Heroes are they, O my Lord, lead them to the field of battle. Guides are they, make them to speak out with arguments and proofs. Ministering servants are they, cause them to pass round the cup that brimmeth with the wine of certitude. O my God, make them to be songsters that carol in fair gardens, make them lions that couch in the thickets, whales that plunge in the vasty deep."[22]

Certainly one of the supplications most well-known among Bahá'ís for its rich imagery is the following prayer by Bahá'u'lláh:

From the sweet-scented streams of Thine eternity give me to drink, O my God, and of the fruits of the tree of Thy being enable me to taste, O my Hope! From the crystal springs of Thy love suffer me to quaff, O my Glory, and beneath the shadow of Thine everlasting providence let me abide, O my Light! Within the meadows of Thy nearness, before Thy presence, make me able to roam, O my Beloved, and at the right hand of the throne of Thy mercy, seat me, O my Desire! From the fragrant breezes of Thy joy let a breath pass over me, O my Goal, and into the heights of the paradise of Thy reality let me gain admission, O my Adored One! To the melodies of the dove of Thy oneness suffer me to hearken, O Resplendent One, and through the spirit of Thy power and Thy might quicken me, O my Provider! In the spirit of Thy love keep me steadfast, O my Succorer, and in the path of Thy good-pleasure set firm my steps, O my Maker! Within the garden of Thine immortality, before Thy countenance, let me abide for ever, O Thou Who art merciful unto me, and upon the seat of Thy glory stablish me, O Thou Who art my Possessor! To the heaven of Thy loving-kindness lift me up, O my Quickener, and unto the Daystar of Thy guidance lead me, O Thou my Attractor! Before the revelations of Thine invisible spirit summon me to be present, O Thou Who art my Origin and my Highest Wish, and unto the essence of the fragrance of Thy beauty, which Thou wilt manifest, cause me to return, O Thou Who art my God!

Potent art Thou to do what pleasest Thee. Thou art, verily, the Most Exalted, the All-Glorious, the All-Highest.[23]

In another of my favorite imagistic passages revealed by Bahá'u'lláh, the imagery focuses on the theme of how all created things bear witness to the Creator:

Within every blade of grass are enshrined the mysteries of an inscrutable Wisdom, and upon every rosebush a myriad nightingales pour out, in blissful rapture, their melody. Its wondrous tulips unfold the mystery of the undying Fire in the Burning Bush, and its sweet savors of holiness breathe the perfume of the Messianic Spirit. It bestoweth wealth without gold, and conferreth immortality without death. In each one of its leaves ineffable delights are treasured, and within every chamber unnumbered mysteries lie hidden.[24]

PERSONIFICATIONS AND EPITHETS

One of the simplest and most succinct forms of rhetorical indirection consists of the abundance of personifications and epithets used by the Manifestations to convey spiritual status or attributes or else to personify abstract powers or concepts. Of course, to call these "simple" does not mean they are easily understood. Often they have been the source of vehement disputes among believers within a religion or between various systems of belief.

I group these together (personifications and epithets) because in both cases a single word or phrase is used to represent a personage, whether this be the Manifestation, some other historical figure, a representation of a mythic figure, or possibly an important concept. And, in fact, in many cases, an epithet will be a personification, and vice-versa.

One of the best examples of the importance of this device is the personification of the "insistent self" as Satan, a mythic figure who tempts us to violate the laws of God. The basis for the myth of Satan, while scriptural, is in every instance intended to be symbolic, as Bahá'u'lláh notes when explaining that this personification represents the negative aspects of the self—our base instincts and our appetitive drives. Likewise, symbolic are the epithets representing spiritual states of being as physical abodes. So it was that the Manifestations described spiritual states as being a literal heaven or hell, though these epithets were utilized for educational purposes, not to mislead Their followers: "Even the materialists have testified in their writings to the wisdom of these divinely-appointed Messengers, and have regarded the references made by the Prophets to Paradise, to hell fire, to future reward and punishment, to have been actuated by a desire to educate and uplift the souls of men."[25]

In fact, even though Bahá'u'lláh and 'Abdu'l-Bahá explain that "Satan" and the "satanic" allude to forces within us, such as base sensual desires and or the urge to exalt ourselves above others, They still find it useful to employ these epithets and personifications Themselves: "The Evil One hath stirred up mischief in their hearts, and they are afflicted with a torment that none can avert"; "The Evil One is he that hindereth the rise and obstructeth the spiritual progress of the children of men"; "A world in which naught can be perceived save strife, quarrels and corruption is bound to become the seat of the throne, the very metropolis, of Satan."[26]

Sometimes Bahá'u'lláh makes it clear that this is a symbolic epithet, as in the following passage from the Kitáb-i-Íqán: "Observe, how those in whose midst the Satan of self had for years sown the seeds of malice and hate became so fused and blended through their allegiance to this wondrous and transcendent Revelation that it seemed as if they had sprung from the same loins."[27] Some might think these allusions confusing because some of the terms are capitalized, but the capitalization of personifications is purely a traditional mechanical device in grammar and not an indication that the figure is an actual being.

Like other metaphors or images, taking certain poetic epithets at face value can lead to confusion or erroneous assumptions by the reader. Two that most readily come to mind are the epithet "the Son of God" for Christ and "the Seal of the Prophets" for Muhammad. In both instances, these terms, which were intended as poetic and symbolic, have led followers and clerics alike to conclude that these titles are literal—that Christ was the physical son of God and that Muhammad was the final Prophet from God.

THE PERSONA DEVICE

The "persona device" is distinct from personification. Where personification gives human characteristics to an inanimate object or some force or power, the persona device is a narrative technique whereby the first-person speaker is a character other than the actual author of the words. By this means, the author can portray reality from another point of view. One of the most famous examples of this technique in English literature is *Gulliver's Travels* by Johnathan Swift, a work in which the narrator / author is Lemuel Gulliver, a somewhat naïve and "gullible" character created by Swift to make the adventures to fictional lands all the more credible for the reader.

Of course, the Manifestations are not writing fiction, but They do often veil Their true identity and powers in the guise of an ordinary human persona, especially before revealing or declaring Their station and purpose. Thus, Moses has a transformed appearance and bearing when He descends Mount Sinai with the Ten

Commandments—which He asserts have been inscribed by God, even though He was fully aware of His station prior to what He reports as a transformative experience—and the commandments, while divinely inspired, were written down by Moses Himself: "Briefly, the Manifestations of God have ever been and will ever be Luminous Realities, and no change or alteration ever takes place in Their essence. At most, before Their revelation They are still and silent, like one who is asleep, and after Their revelation They are eloquent and effulgent, like one who is awake."[28]

Similarly—as we have previously noted—Muhammad goes into a trancelike state during which times He recites what He purports to be words conveyed to Him from God through the intermediary of the archangel Gabriel. Likewise, Bahá'u'lláh in the Súriy-i-Haykal reiterates what He says are the words the Maiden Who appeared to Him in the Siyáh-Chál:

> In His Súratu'l-Haykal (the Súrih of the Temple) He thus describes those breathless moments when the Maiden, symbolizing the "Most Great Spirit" proclaimed His mission to the entire creation: "While engulfed in tribulations I heard a most wondrous, a most sweet voice, calling above My head. Turning My face, I beheld a Maiden—the embodiment of the remembrance of the name of My Lord—suspended in the air before Me. So rejoiced was she in her very soul that her countenance shone with the ornament of the good-pleasure of God, and her cheeks glowed with the brightness of the All-Merciful."[29]

Thus it is that the Manifestation will speak or write in the guise of whatever form best befits the audience and age He has come to teach and reform. In this context, Bahá'u'lláh acknowledges how

He assumes these various personae or points of view in His works: "At one time We spoke in the language of the lawgiver; at another in that of the truth-seeker and the mystic, and yet Our supreme purpose and highest wish hath always been to disclose the glory and sublimity of this station. God, verily, is a sufficient witness!"[30] This same passage is itself a good example of the Manifestation speaking frankly as God's Intermediary. In fact, the entirety of this work—a survey of His ministry and the last major work of His life—is a review of both His personal experiences and a chronicle of the highlights from the major works of His ministry.

One of the first major works of Bahá'u'lláh, the Hidden Words, is written almost entirely from the point of view of divine authority. This is the voice of God revealing the sum total of spiritual guidance that has been revealed heretofore: "This is that which hath descended from the realm of glory, uttered by the tongue of power and might, and revealed unto the Prophets of old. We have taken the inner essence thereof and clothed it in the garment of brevity, as a token of grace unto the righteous, that they may stand faithful unto the Covenant of God, may fulfill in their lives His trust, and in the realm of spirit obtain the gem of divine virtue." Almost without exception, the antecedent for the personal pronouns (the person or thing referred to) in both the Arabic and Persian sections of this collection of spiritual axioms is the voice of God, even though Bahá'u'lláh is the fashioner of these remarkable verses: "O Son of Man! I loved thy creation, hence I created thee. Wherefore, do thou love Me, that I may name thy name and fill thy soul with the spirit of life."[31]

Among these passages, any allusion to Bahá'u'lláh is in the third person. For example, note Bahá'u'lláh's expression of concern about how His followers will fare once He is no longer in their midst: "O My Children! I fear lest, bereft of the melody of the dove of heaven, ye will sink back to the shades of utter loss, and, never having gazed upon the beauty of the rose, return to water and clay."[32]

In His various epistles to the kings, rulers, and religious leaders of the world, Bahá'u'lláh uses a variable point of view or persona. In some parts of these powerful and carefully fashioned documents, He speaks as a human prisoner and exile Who has no interest in undermining Their power or authority. To the shah of Persia, He famously observes, "O King! I was but a man like others, asleep upon My couch, when lo, the breezes of the All-Glorious were wafted over Me, and taught Me the knowledge of all that hath been. This thing is not from Me, but from One Who is Almighty and All-Knowing. And He bade Me lift up My voice between earth and heaven, and for this there befell Me what hath caused the tears of every man of understanding to flow."[33]

But in the opening passage of His epistle to the sultan of the Ottoman Empire, He speaks with power and authority; He is God's Emissary reminding the king that it is his duty to serve justly and wisely those over whom God has allowed him to be a guardian: "Hearken, O King, to the speech of Him that speaketh the truth, Him that doth not ask thee to recompense Him with the things God hath chosen to bestow upon thee, Him Who unerringly treadeth the straight Path. He it is Who summoneth thee unto God, thy Lord, Who showeth thee the right course, the way that leadeth to true felicity, that haply thou mayest be of them with whom it shall be well."[34]

One of the more interesting uses of this variable persona or point of view in the works of Bahá'u'lláh can be found in the prayers He revealed. Since these prayers are generally meant for us to recite, the first person is obviously the suppliant who may be in a variety of spiritual conditions. Consequently, sometimes the persona is a sinner seeking forgiveness: "I am a sinner, O my Lord, and Thou art the Ever-Forgiving. As soon as I recognized Thee, I hastened to attain the exalted court of Thy loving-kindness. Forgive me, O my Lord, my sins which have hindered me from walking in the ways of Thy good-pleasure, and from attaining the shores of the ocean of Thy oneness."[35] Bahá'u'lláh thus imaginatively devised prayers to befit every sort of human perspective, condition, and appropriate orison: prayers pleading for assistance or healing, prayers of praise and thanksgiving, prayers for steadfastness, and so on.

Regarding Bahá'u'lláh's use of the persona device, perhaps most striking of all the prayers are those in which He speaks as the Manifestation beseeching God for assistance in enduring the tribulations that have befallen Him—tribulations that we, the people He has come to assist, have brought upon Him. Interestingly, in each of these same factual recitations of what He has endured, Bahá'u'lláh praises God and expresses gratitude for the privilege of functioning on His behalf:

> Thou beholdest, therefore, O my God, how this wronged one hath fallen into the hands of such as have denied Thy right, and broken off from Thy sovereignty. He, round whose person circleth Thy proof, and in whose name and on behalf of whose sovereignty Thy testimony crieth out unto all created things, hath suffered more grievously in his days than any pen can recount, and been so harassed that He Who is Thy Spirit (Jesus) lamented, and all the denizens of Thy Kingdom and all the inmates of Thy Tabernacle in the realms above cried with a great and bitter lamentation . . .
>
> Should any one consider Thy Books which Thou didst name the Bayán, and ponder in his heart what hath been revealed therein, he would discover that each of these Books announceth my Revelation, and declareth my Name, and testifieth to my Self, and proclaimeth my Cause, and my Praise,

and my Rising, and the radiance of my Glory. And yet, not-withstanding Thy proclamation, O my God, and in spite of the words Thou didst utter, O my Beloved, Thou hast seen and heard their calumnies against me, and their evil doings in my days.[36]

Before we leave our examination of this fascinating rhetorical device, let us delight in what is possibly one of the best known and more effective uses the persona device. In the twenty-third Psalm of David, a poem or hymn in praise of God, the persona is a sheep speaking about the guardianship of God as the Eternal Shepherd who looks over it and provides it with whatsoever it needs:

> The Lord is my shepherd, I shall not want;
> he makes me lie down in green pastures;
> He leads me beside still waters;
> he restores my soul.
> He leads me in paths of righteousness for his name's sake.
> Even though I walk through the valley of the shadow of death,
> I fear no evil, for thou art with me;
> thy rod and thy staff,
> they comfort me.[37]

Without delving too deeply into the ample portrait of this pastoral image, we can note that the poet has stated the persona device at the beginning. He then notes that the Lord as Shepherd provides for all his needs (the green pastures and the still waters). He also feels safe even when passing through a dangerous or treacherous valley, as the Lord has two implements with which to protect him—the staff (or shepherd crook) to save him from peril, and the rod to chastise him, when necessary, so that he will take the right path.

Clearly, we could analyze at great length how these two tools—reward and punishment or staff and rod—function to teach humankind. Indeed, the Bahá'í writings discuss at length these pillars of human enlightenment and education. But the point at hand is sufficiently made—that by employing the persona device, the poet / prophet has given to the traditional epithet of the spiritual leader as "pastor" a very wonderful image of how safe we can feel if we are cognizant of the bounty and sufficiency that God has bestowed for our safety and enlightenment.

Perhaps the rod represents the law and the concept of the consequences for a breach of the law, and perhaps the staff represents both the love and guidance that are capable of rescuing us from our own waywardness. By thinking of ourselves as being entirely at the mercy of the Shepherd / Lord but also entirely in His care and protection if we have the wisdom to discern how to be submissive in the path He has devised for us, we need not think of being His "sheep" and being obeisant to His will as a form of weakness or mindlessness but as the greatest strength we can attain. Bahá'u'lláh notes so pointedly: "Say: True liberty consisteth in man's submission unto My commandments, little as ye know it. Were men to observe that which We have sent down unto them from the Heaven of Revelation, they would, of a certainty, attain unto perfect liberty. Happy is the man that hath apprehended the Purpose of God in whatever He hath revealed from the Heaven of His Will, that pervadeth all created things. Say: The liberty that profiteth you is to be found nowhere except in complete servitude unto God, the Eternal Truth. Whoso hath tasted of its sweetness will refuse to barter it for all the dominion of earth and heaven."[38]

To conclude our survey of some of the rhetorical devices the Manifestations use in Their indirect method of conveying the Word to us, we can infer one overriding lesson: the motive behind this teaching methodology is never to obfuscate or conceal Their message or to prevent us from gaining admission to the inner meaning of the Word. Neither is it Their purpose to force us to rely on scholars or religious leaders for understanding. Quite the opposite is true.

The Manifestations have placed us, the ordinary believer or reader, in the position of being responsible for discovering the truth of Their teachings; and what we discover is that Their meaning is logically consistent, personally satisfying, and accessible to everyone. We also come to realize that often we can discover the various levels of meaning of the Word by means of our own sincere efforts when we apply the aforementioned hermeneutical principles. And to repeat the axiom we have already noted above, if we merely accept the explication someone else has devised—even someone whom we feel has capacity—we may be assisted temporarily. But unless we ourselves are active participants in the art of discovery—as the language of the Word requires of us—we are not learning; instead, we are merely committing to memory the learning someone else has retrieved through their study. Furthermore, inasmuch as the meaning of the Word is inexhaustible, the pearls of wisdom someone else has discovered can never be the only or complete meaning. Thus, it is probably correct to conclude that whatever insights we discover on our own may be ultimately more valuable and meaningful to us than those adopted from someone else.

After all, our objective in trying to attain spiritual and intellectual development is not to learn a certain quantity of information but to acquire the tools for spiritual development that will help us both in this life and hereafter. Unlike studying for exams in school, we are not being tested to demonstrate we have found the correct answers, but rather we are being challenged to see if we have been transformed by developing those capacities with which the Creator has endowed us.

- 8 -

WEAVING REALITY TOGETHER

The spiritual world is like unto the phenomenal world. They are the exact counterpart of each other. Whatever objects appear in this world of existence are the outer pictures of the world of heaven.

'Abdu'l-Bahá, *The Promulgation of Universal Peace*, p. 12

The title of this chapter is somewhat deceiving, especially when juxtaposed with the head quote about the two dimensions of reality already being "the exact counterpart of each other." Apparently reality already is "together." So, what remains for us to do other than recognize this counterpart relationship and discover that objects and relationships in this world are intended to demonstrate to us the reality we are destined to experience when our earthly existence is completed?

In sampling some of the kinds of rhetorical devices employed by the Manifestations in teaching humankind, we have emphasized the manner in which this indirect method forces the recipient to participate in the process of arriving at the intended meanings. As we noted at the outset, every experienced teacher knows the value of this indirect methodology. In fact, as we also noted, if the teacher-student relationship is merely that of a fountain of information to an empty receptacle waiting to be filled, not much learning is likely to take place. Authentic education requires that the teacher help the student acquire the tools for systematic, self-actuated inquiry, reflection, and implementation of the acquired knowledge.

Later we will examine more closely some further examples of how critical it is that the reader of scripture appreciate this obligation to become an active participant in discerning what the Manifestation is conveying. The importance of this concept becomes apparent when we realize that what we are being taught is not a certain quantity of facts, but transformative practices and life-altering skills—that we are obliged to transmute those ephemeral symbols that are words into plans and patterns of behavior. For as we have already noted, learning to comprehend meaning has no value if the learning remains merely a cerebral exercise. Indeed, it is precisely in this sense that the chapter title takes its most important meaning. There is an inherent wisdom in the Divine Plan whereby the spiritual realm is concealed from us while we dwell in the physical dimension, even as the Teacher for this Day, Bahá'u'lláh, confirms that there is a wisdom in His temporary physical presence among us, and another wisdom in His absence: "Let not your hearts be perturbed, O people, when the glory of My Presence is withdrawn, and the ocean of My utterance is stilled. In My presence amongst you there is a wisdom, and in My absence there is yet another, inscrutable to all but God, the Incomparable, the All-Knowing. Verily, We behold you from Our realm of glory, and shall aid whosoever will arise for the triumph of Our Cause with the hosts of the Concourse on high and a company of Our favored angels."[1] In light of our observation about the student-teacher relationship in this process, we might conclude that one wisdom in the absence of the Manifestation is that the long-term goal of His Revelation is to have us put into practice the patterns of behavior and the social structures that He has prescribed.

This conclusion should not be taken to mean that we should disdain the study of scripture for its own benefit and bounty, but it does imply that the end result of all such study is personal and collective transformation and action. Here again, Lample's book *Revelation and Social Reality* is a good source for examining how this process can occur and is, in fact, presently occurring in the global efforts of the Bahá'í Faith to uplift humankind from the ground up, one community at a time.

Rhetoric and Reality

Now that we have examined some of the methods by which the Manifestation instigates this process of empowering us to translate language into action, we are better able in this chapter to see how the twofold nature of these rhetorical devices effectively weaves reality together for humankind. Therefore, let us attempt to discern how language empowers us individually and collectively to become proficient weavers.

Whether we are discussing symbol, metaphor, parable, myth, or any of the other devices we examined in the previous chapter, we observe that all have at least one thing in common—an outer surface meaning, or literal value, and an inner significance that is sometimes obvious but often concealed. Regardless of the difficulty of solving the mystery to get at the inner meaning, the value of obtaining this meaning has the additional benefit of teaching us to participate in acquiring what Lample, in his first hermeneutical principle, calls the "intended meaning."

Needless to say, it is this inner meaning that the Manifestation intends for us to discover, hopefully by a process of meditation and reflection rather than by accepting someone else's interpretation.

And it is for this reason that the term *conceit* is sometimes used to allude to these devices, because it is the abstract "concept" that is most often at the heart of meaning.*

On the charts in the previous chapter illustrating how the metaphor, symbol, and parable work, we could easily discern their components as well as the meaning or explanation for the relationship between the two ostensibly or essentially dissimilar realities. But what was not made completely clear is that in scripture, this process is most often a means by which the Manifestation links together in our minds and in our actions the relationship between the twin expressions of reality—the physical and the spiritual.

The Crucial Importance of this Relationship

There are several ways of explaining exactly what is so important about this relationship. One is the axiomatic passage that serves as the epigram for this chapter, 'Abdu'l-Bahá's statement that there is an intended parallelism between these two expressions of reality: "The spiritual world is like unto the phenomenal world. They are the exact counterpart of each other. Whatever objects appear in this world of existence are the outer pictures of the world of heaven."[2] In other words, knowledge of one aspect of reality helps us comprehend the nature of the corresponding expression of that knowledge expressed as its counterpart in the other aspect.

However, this passage should not be taken to imply that these two expressions of reality are coequal. Here we confront Lample's second hermeneutical principle that "Judgments about meaning should be made from the perspective of the Revelation." That is to say, from the perspective of virtually all religions and religious

---

* The term *conceit* in this context derives from the Italian word *concetto* (concept, notion). It was adopted into English when the Italian sonnet became such a popular poetic form throughout the sixteenth century among English poets.

scripture, the spiritual realm is the "real" world, and this physical realm is a metaphorical or outer expression of that reality. Stated even more directly, the metaphysical world has primacy in this relationship. Or, stated in terms of how language weaves these two realities together, the physical world and our experience in it provide the means by which we begin to learn about and gain access to the spiritual realm.

But the fact that there is a hierarchy in this counterpart relationship does not mean the process cannot work both ways—that we cannot learn about the metaphysical realm by our study of physics or, conversely, learn about the nature of the physical realm through an examination of the logical principles of metaphysics. For example, if we know that the Creator has no beginning, then we can deduce He has always been creating—the idea of creating something was not a sudden impulse for Him. From the fact that the human being is the fruit of creation, we can then deduce that human life has always existed, at least potentially, somewhere in the created universe. And if an inalienable attribute of the Creator is the act of creating, then we must conclude He never ceases to do so. And if He never ceases, then we must further conclude that celestial bodies are "countless."* We can further conclude that there may well have been more than one Big Bang, that this point of beginning from which our galaxy seems to have emanated could hardly have been the first such event. Additionally, we can also infer that while we do not presently possess the capacity to view beyond the outer edges of this expanding universe, we can be sure that an infinite universe has no limits, that outside the province of our Big Bang, there are others that we will, in the course of time, discover.

---

* "As to thy question concerning the worlds of God. Know thou of a truth that the worlds of God are countless in their number, and infinite in their range" (Bahá'u'lláh, *Gleanings*, no. 79.1).

Similarly, if we know from scriptural authority that the spiritual dimension of the human reality (the soul) is the source of all our human powers, including our self-consciousness, then we can study the human brain already aware that it functions as a transceiver or intermediary from our spiritual essence and not as the primary source of our personal reality. Or if we accept the assertion we have already examined that the planned intervention of the Manifestations is part of an organic and integrating plan for the advancement of human civilization on our planet, then as historians or anthropologists, we can be miles ahead if we come to comprehend the "end" result in the "beginning" of our research—that underlying all apparent physical causes is a metaphysical force at work impelling human history forward and without which there would be no human progress.

The importance of this "head start" for students of history or anthropology or sociology cannot be overemphasized. For example, the realization of the metaphysical dimension of reality that underlies and becomes manifest in the physical dimension prevents us from the most common *post hoc** fallacies in our examination of human history. To use but one of a multitude of possible analogies about how this advanced understanding helps us know how the two dimensions of reality are woven together, let us imag-

---

* *Post hoc, ergo, propter hoc* is a Latin phrase meaning "after this, therefore, because of this." It describes the common logical fallacy of assuming that temporal sequence is all that is necessary to determine whether one event is causative of another. For example, if our car malfunctions after we have broken a mirror, we might incorrectly assume that breaking a mirror automatically brings about bad fortune.

ine we are unearthing the remnants of an ancient village. Over the course of years of careful digging, brushing, and sifting through remnants of the past, we might by degrees discover the layout of the town. From the various fragments, we might begin to discover how we think each building was used. But how much more rapidly our study would progress if, prior to our digging, we discovered the blueprint for the city in which each building was labeled and described. In other words, if we knew the "end" in the "beginning" of our efforts, we could proceed at a greatly accelerated pace.

This design, whether it applies to the study of human evolution, the advancement of civilization, or the manner in which creation comes into being and takes part in the entire process of the living infinite universe, is precisely what the Bahá'í teachings affirm that the writings of the Manifestations provide. This hypothesis is especially applicable to the authoritative texts of the Bahá'í teachings, inasmuch as Bahá'u'lláh is able to distill and clarify all the detailed information about reality to which previous Revelations had only been able to allude. According to His own assertion, He thus provides sufficient new information for our learning and advancement until the advent of the next Manifestation, whereupon we will be provided with even more enlightenment about the intricacies regarding how the two dimensions are conjoined—an even more detailed blueprint.

But as we noted at the end of the previous chapter, enlightenment is not the only intended result of this process which is, in essence, a process of creative action, whether by the individual or by the body politic. The intended result is a progressive reciprocity between knowledge and action, in which spirituality is implemented or "dramatized" in its physical expressions. This is the ongoing and endlessly rewarding objective for each successive Dispensation.

Sewing the Spiritual Blueprint to the Fabric of Social Order

In previous books,* I have discussed in some detail how this reciprocal relationship between knowledge and action—a conceit I termed the "pendulum theory"—applies to the advancement of civilization over the course of human history, a process that is at the heart of the Divine Plan of God and to which Bahá'u'lláh alludes as "an ever-advancing civilization."[3]

The central idea in this analogy is that the more knowledge we gain, the more empowered we become to express it in creative action. Subsequently, as we experiment with dramatizing spiritual principles in action, the action itself further informs us about the nature and efficacy of the underlying spiritual principle, as well as the various pragmatic corollaries related to acting out what we have learned. Once we have accomplished this implementation of knowledge in action, we are then ready to return to further study of the principle itself. This back and forth process in which knowledge begets action, and action begets further knowledge, can be visually portrayed in the following manner:

---

* See *The Arc of Ascent* and *The Ascent of Society: The Social Imperative in Personal Salvation*.

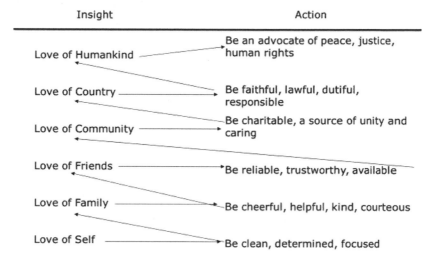

Figure 14. Reciprocity between Knowledge and Action

Here we observe an ascending graph of how the knowledge of love results in a corresponding outcome or action. We also observe that each expression of that knowledge in action can lead to a more encompassing understanding of the attribute, force, or principle being practiced—in this case, the power and concept of love. Of course, the ascending knowledge and practice should not be inferred to mean that we should abandon the "lesser" concepts and actions as we ascend, nor that we should deem them diminished by our more encompassing insights and their corresponding articulations.

In this sense, we need to monitor constantly how all expressions of this virtue or power are working as we expand our understanding and manifest that knowledge in more encompassing and sophisticated practices. For while we might consider the nature of love to be ever more complete or selfless, its understanding and continued practice at every level remains essential to our individual and collective health.

Returning to the heart of our present theme, we can observe, implicit in this analogy, how it is the power of language enables us to proceed back from knowledge to action and to ascend to the heights of understanding and refinement. It is language, whether in the form of personal meditation and reflection or in collective consultation with others, that is responsible for weaving together the guidance from the realm of the spirit to the fabric of social organization and action.

After all, while the Manifestations receive the will or wish of God directly through a revelatory process, we receive that same information in the form of the revealed words through which the Manifestations translate divine guidance and concepts into terms we can comprehend. And it is thus through our study of the language They employ at each stage of the evolution of human society that we acquire instruction about the course of action that will allow us to manifest this knowledge in action.

Therefore, while spiritual and physical reality are inherently conjoined in the counterpart relationship mentioned earlier, our task is to participate in making this inherent organic relationship manifest in our lives, as an ongoing spiritual exercise for our individual and collective development. This imperative may take the form of simply forming friendships and practicing neighborliness, or it may take the more encompassing and complex expression of reforming and refining the entire infrastructure of human society.

As in the graphic illustration below, then, instead of considering the lines going from one expression of reality to the other as a process of action and reaction, let us imagine these lines as threads of rational thought and reflection with which we strive to weave the fabric of society into a pattern that emulates the nature and qualities of the spiritual realm:

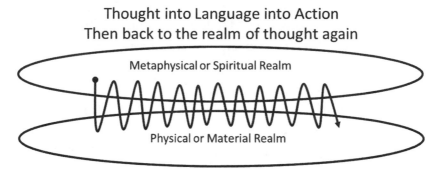

Figure 15. The Counterpart Realities Stitched Together

In this diagram, the idea, wish, or will of the Creator originates in the realm of the spirit, is conveyed directly to the conscious mind of the Manifestation, Who then translates the idea as guidance in the form of language understandable to humankind at a given period of human development.

It is precisely in this context that the Manifestation is designated in the Gospel of John as "the Word made flesh," appearing among us as He does in human form. The Manifestation thereby translates information into language while simultaneously manifesting perfectly how these ideas can be expressed in practices capable of lending social form and structure to a metaphysical vision of a "heavenly kingdom." It is likewise through this process by which ideas become audible sounds and visible words that metaphysics is translated into physics, so that the two counterpart realms are sewn together. Of course, the process does not end with words or action. As we have previously noted, the process never "ends," inasmuch as human perfectibility and the advancement or refinement of human society are without limits.

Both of these charts can also be used to convey the essential value of the dual nature of the figurative or rhetorical devices employed by the Manifestations to convey spiritual concepts. As we have noted, because the Manifestations must utilize a means of conveying abstract or metaphysical concepts into terms we can comprehend, They rely heavily on these linguistic devices to explain one reality in terms of the other, and, by employing the collective task of creating a spiritually based social order, They demonstrate with language how physical actions can exemplify these same principles. This "class project," if you will, while inherently valuable, also constructs an increasingly powerful and supportive educational environment for humankind.

To appreciate the long-term benefits of this social project, we need only imagine how it might be to live in a society in which everyone managed to manifest even merely one of the spiritual attributes we are exhorted to understand and then acquire. Take the virtue of truthfulness, for example, a virtue that 'Abdu'l-Bahá asserts "is the foundation of all human virtues": "Without truthfulness progress and success, in all the worlds of God, are impossible for any soul. When this holy attribute is established in man, all the divine qualities will also be acquired."[4]

If we allow ourselves to envision for a moment living in a society where we could rely on everyone being honest with one another, we can immediately sense how utterly transformed daily life would become. After having contemplated the dramatic effects that would result from the embodiment of a single virtue by the body politic, let us reflect on how much time, money, and energy we spend protecting ourselves from the fact that in our present society we cannot assume that everyone is trustworthy. This brief reflection on the transformation in our lives that would instantly occur were this single virtue to be understood and practiced allows us to quickly appreciate that this "exercise" of creating a spiritually based society is not an arbitrary practice but a profound goal well worth the dedicated effort of every citizen in our global community.

But let us switch from these broad-based assumptions to the specific requisites for transforming our lives on a daily basis. After all, it is pointless to exhort people to be "good" without laying out for them a specific regimen that models what constitutes being "good." This is not a matter of pulling a switch. Transformation of society, like personal refinement, will never be the instantaneous product of some profession of faith. This process of stitching the two dimensions of reality together requires daily vigilance in every aspect of our individual lives:

> Such a chaste and holy life, with its implications of modesty, purity, temperance, decency, and clean-mindedness, involves no less than the exercise of moderation in all that pertains to dress, language, amusements, and all artistic and literary avocations. It demands daily vigilance in the control of one's carnal desires and corrupt inclinations. It calls for the abandonment of a frivolous conduct, with its excessive attachment to trivial and often misdirected pleasures. It requires total abstinence from all alcoholic drinks, from opium, and from similar habit-forming drugs. It condemns the prostitution of art and of literature, the practices of nudism and of companionate marriage, infidelity in marital relationships, and all manner of promiscuity, of easy familiarity, and of sexual vices. It can tolerate no compromise with the theories, the standards, the habits, and the excesses of a decadent age. Nay rather it seeks to demonstrate, through the dynamic force of its example, the pernicious character of such theories, the falsity of such standards, the hollowness of such claims, the perversity of such habits, and the sacrilegious character of such excesses.[5]

The Personal Experience of Willfully Conjoining Reality

Our personal participation in this process of knitting together the ostensibly disconnected dimensions of reality takes place early on. At first, perhaps, it begins on an unconscious level. As we develop and mature, however, it becomes the province of conscious choices and relentless challenges confronted on a daily basis.

We start this process as infants and toddlers, acquiring experiences, seeing how categories of objects and experiences can be meaningfully grouped or assembled. Over time, we begin inferring generalizations about reality. This inferential process, so much like the approach to solving algebraic equations, is an inherent faculty of the rational soul, even though it needs to be nourished, encouraged, and trained to fulfill its nascent capacity.

In infancy, for example, we may infer similitude among shapes— roundness or squareness—or between situations and facial expressions—pain with a sad face, happiness with a smile. Because our mind is inherently logical, it will flourish (unless it is abused or constrained), and our capacity to participate in this process will evolve accordingly. Unless we are trained (explicitly or subtly) to respond otherwise, we will embrace people of different colors even as we would the various hues of flowers, birds, fragrances, songs, and voices.

In all we learn as we begin to experience reality, we are solving these equations, discovering the slightly concealed shared ingredient among the diverse expressions of reality. A person can be kind and loving, regardless of shape, size, or color. An animal may respond to love and caring even as do we. And the more we are encouraged and assisted in this learning process, the more rapidly we acquire these fundamentally human skills of conjoining groups of objects, relating situations to emotional states, or practicing and developing spiritual powers of prayer and reflection, of kindness and love for others.

This metaphorical relationship permeates our physical experience of existence because this stage of our life is specifically designed by the Creator for our moral and spiritual instruction. Physical reality is, as it were, an exquisitely designed classroom for beginning our eternal education and enlightenment.* More specifically, our earthly beginning is a period of training in which we learn indirectly about the nature of that unseen realm in which we will spend the vast majority of our eternal existence. Gradually, we come to realize the value of spiritual perception and acquire the power to manifest those insights and confirm them in preparation for navigating a world that transcends physical limitations of time and space, of composition and decomposition.

The Wisdom of Concealing the Unseen Realm

Perhaps the most obvious way in which the limitations imposed on our perspective during our physical lives encourage our study of reality is our desire to understand self-consciousness and willful thought. Is the sense of "self" an illusion accidentally created by the mechanisms of the human brain, or is it we ourselves—some "self" and mind independent of that miraculous organ—who employ the brain as our connection to physical reality to do our bidding?

This area of interest is especially important because it relates directly to whether we should apply ourselves to preparing for an existence in which we no longer need this indirect relationship with reality, or whether we should enjoy life in whatever manner seems most expedient because this is all there is. Since this is such a pivotal factor in determining our approach to the way we live our

---

* For a more expansive treatment of this idea, see John S. Hatcher, *The Purpose of Physical Reality*.

lives, we might understandably wonder why, if it is God's intention that we focus our attention on preparing for a metaphysical existence, we are not given more access to some assurance that such an afterlife actually exists.

According to the Bahá'í texts, a major reason the exact nature of our existence beyond this life is concealed from us—in addition to the need for us to focus our attention on learning about our essential nature and the inherent purpose of physical life—is that were we to be completely aware of the nature of the destiny that awaits us, we would not be able to restrain ourselves from trying to attain it:

> If any man be told that which hath been ordained for such a soul in the worlds of God, the Lord of the throne on high and of earth below, his whole being will instantly blaze out in his great longing to attain that most exalted, that sanctified and resplendent station. . . . The nature of the soul after death can never be described, nor is it meet and permissible to reveal its whole character to the eyes of men. The Prophets and Messengers of God have been sent down for the sole purpose of guiding mankind to the straight Path of Truth. The purpose underlying Their revelation hath been to educate all men, that they may, at the hour of death, ascend, in the utmost purity and sanctity and with absolute detachment, to the throne of the Most High.[6]

Since it is neither possible nor "meet and permissible" to reveal the "whole character" of the spiritual realm or what our experience in it will be, the Manifestations employ comparisons to our experiences and conditions in the physical world to explain that portion of information about the spiritual realm that is permissible and helpful for us to understand. Such comparisons, constructed with the rhetorical devices discussed in the previous chapter, effectively link the two realms and the two sorts of experiences together by describing the one in terms of the other.

To cite but one example of the effectiveness of these rhetorical devices, we have only to see how succinctly Bahá'u'lláh is able to convey the importance and function of this life in relation to the afterlife by employing the analogy of our life in the womb as preparation for this life: "If ye be seekers after this life and the vanities thereof, ye should have sought them while ye were still enclosed in your mothers' wombs, for at that time ye were continually approaching them, could ye but perceive it. Ye have, on the other hand, ever since ye were born and attained maturity, been all the while receding from the world and drawing closer to dust. Why, then, exhibit such greed in amassing the treasures of the earth, when your days are numbered and your chance is well-nigh lost?"[7]

It is worth noting, however, that the language of the Manifestations is not always indirect, nor is it necessary that we be consciously aware of how the indirect language works before we can understand it. In this regard, it has been my own experience in teaching poetry that those who are most capable of deciphering the meaning of poetic language are not necessarily the brightest students in terms of ordinary standards, nor are they necessarily aware of how they "get it." Since the objective is always to attain understanding, it ultimately does not matter whether or not we become formally trained in how language works.

For example, Bahá'u'lláh makes the following statement about the fact that there is an inherent value in simply reciting the revealed verses (the Word) because the inherent power and creative influence of these words often transcends a definable intellectual process:

Intone, O My servants, the verses of God that have been received by thee, as intoned by them who have drawn nigh unto Him, that the sweetness of thy melody may kindle thine own soul, and attract the hearts of all men. Whoso reciteth, in the privacy of his chamber, the verses revealed by God, the scattering angels of the Almighty shall scatter abroad the fragrance of the words uttered by his mouth, and shall cause the heart of every righteous man to throb. Though he may, at first, remain unaware of its effect, yet the virtue of the grace vouchsafed unto him must needs sooner or later exercise its influence upon his soul. Thus have the mysteries of the Revelation of God been decreed by virtue of the Will of Him Who is the Source of power and wisdom.[8]

The point is that the Word has an effect regardless of the precise method we employ in our personal relationship with the language of the Manifestation. Some of us may be instinctively adept at understanding poetic language. Others may become proficient by learning how to penetrate the logic underlying poetic devices. Still others may simply recite the words because we understand the sense of them and, more importantly, because they have a therapeutic effect on our inmost self.

But regardless of our distinct personal abilities or level of learning, it is our God-given duty and inherent capacity to become active participants in this process. It is likewise obvious that while reciting verses repeatedly might enable us to grasp more fully the meaning of the Word, the more we come to grasp how the revealed words convey meaning, the more rapidly we can improve our ability "to apprehend their meaning and unravel their innermost mysteries."[9]

For example, once we understand how the Manifestations employ rhetorical or figurative language—particularly symbols

and various analogical devices—we become better able to understand that which is unfamiliar, abstruse, and abstract when it is
expressed in concrete terms or physical experiences that are familiar
and ordinary. We become less likely to "corrupt the text"* by taking
passages out of context or by failing to appreciate the metaphorical
or symbolic meanings underlying the literal passages.

Guidance on Weaving the Word

While reality is inherently woven together into a single fabric,
and though the revealed texts of all religions stress the ultimately
objective of creating a social order that manifests the attributes of
the divine realm, this social process begins with and ultimately
depends upon the efforts of each individual, not upon a pervasive
top-down system of governance. Shoghi Effendi stresses this axiom
in the following passage, which employs the weaving metaphor—
the abiding analogy for our overall discourse—though he also usefully compares the individual believer to links in a chain and bricks
in the foundation of a building:

> This challenge, so severe and insistent, and yet so glorious,
> faces no doubt primarily the individual believer on whom, in
> the last resort, depends the fate of the entire community. He
> it is who constitutes the warp and woof on which the quality

---

* According to some Islamic scholars, Christians did not recognize Muhammad because their texts had been corrupted. In the Kitáb-i-Íqán, Bahá'u'lláh
explains that the corruption of the texts pointed to by Muhammad (See Qur'án
2:75 and 2:79) alludes to misinterpretation due to the inability of the so-called
learned divines to understand the symbolism in Christ's prophecies about His
return: "Nay, rather, by corruption of the text is meant that in which all Muslim
divines are engaged today, that is the interpretation of God's holy Book in accordance with their idle imaginings and vain desires" (Bahá'u'lláh, Kitáb-i-Íqán,
¶93).

and pattern of the whole fabric must depend. He it is who acts as one of the countless links in the mighty chain that now girdles the globe. He it is who serves as one of the multitude of bricks which support the structure and insure the stability of the administrative edifice now being raised in every part of the world. Without his support, at once whole-hearted, continuous and generous, every measure adopted, and every plan formulated, by the body which acts as the national representative of the community to which he belongs, is foredoomed to failure.[10]

This concept of the various forms the emanation of the will of God takes as it nurtures and advances human knowledge and social development is, as we mentioned at the outset of our discussion, a foundational premise of the Bahá'í view of reality, the concept of progressive Revelation. And this attempt to discern how this force eventually reaches us indirectly through the Intermediaries Who are the Manifestations helps us further appreciate the indirect teaching techniques these Teachers use to assist us. Hopefully this illustration also explains how the Word becomes flesh, as both the exemplary character of the Prophets and Their words help us give material expression to Their guidance, whether in our individual or collective responses to Their Revelation.

In this regard, let us now "follow the thread" as it weaves its way into our daily lives by virtue of the explicit instruction given us by Bahá'u'lláh for this turning point in the advancement of human society. As we do so, let us consider how this "thread" of influence and empowerment works to knit the fabric of our personal lives to the divine purpose that is our goal in this life, as well as in our preparation for the life to come.

We have already explained how our personal goals cannot be considered distinct from our collective goal as part of the human body politic. We are exhorted to work collaboratively with others to transform our environment for ourselves, here and now, and to establish the foundation to assist the generations to come. Here again a visual demonstration can help us appreciate how this process works at the level of individual belief in fashioning a program of personal action.

First, let us begin with a simple diagram of the process of expressing spiritual guidance and insight in a personal program of daily practices.

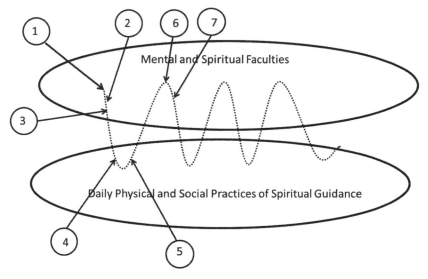

Figure 16. Daily Process of Expressing Spiritual Guidance in Action

Here we see how the thread of our activity begins in the realm of thought with our decision (1) that we believe that the Manifestation is Who He claims to be, and that we are going to follow His guidance for our lives. We then advance through a process that can be analyzed and described in any number of ways because we each respond to this realization in our own particular way. But certainly among the processes that will subsequently follow this "recognition" of the station of the Manifestation are the specific spiritual exercises mandated by Bahá'u'lláh.*

As we set out on our daily routine, we may begin the new day by following Bahá'u'lláh's commandment that we (2) "Recite . . . the verses of God every morn and eventide." Bahá'u'lláh does not designate which verses or how many, but He does caution, "Whoso faileth to recite them hath not been faithful to the Covenant of God and His Testament . . ." In this same vein, Bahá'u'lláh notes that what matters is the quality of attention and attitude with which one recites the words: "Pride not yourselves on much reading of the verses or on a multitude of pious acts by night and day; for were a man to read a single verse with joy and radiance it would be better for him than to read with lassitude all the Holy Books of God . . ."[11]

Another spiritual activity commanded by Bahá'u'lláh is daily prayer, one of the most immediate and powerful means by which we weave our spiritual and mental intention into the fabric of daily action. Here again, while one is free to pray as much and as often as one chooses, Bahá'u'lláh designates that, at the very least, we recite one of three obligatory prayers. Among these, the so-called medium prayer (because of its length compared to the other two obligatory prayers) is to be recited in the morning, at noon, and in the evening. Thus, most Bahá'ís pray before setting out on their daily tasks, but only this one prayer—the medium obligatory prayer—is required to be recited in the morning.**

---

* Previous Manifestations also established mandatory spiritual practices according to the needs and capacities of the age in which They revealed Themselves. While these regimens may differ, their abiding purpose remains constant and changeless.

** Morning is defined as the period between sunrise and noon. (Bahá'u'lláh, Kitáb-i-Aqdas, p. 129)

A third mental or spiritual activity (3) might be the process of goal-setting or planning for the day, though we might have accomplished this in the prior evening as we read and reflected on the Word.* Obviously we do well to be constantly involved in the process of planning and reflecting on our plans as to how we can best spend the brief time that is ours during our earthly existence. It would thus seem beneficial, prior to setting out on our daily routine, to reflect on the course of action we should take with regard to our immediate, intermediary, and long-term plans for ensuring that all we do, however mundane the task, will bear a relationship to our effort to weave a spiritual motive into our actions.

Even work performed primarily to provide physical sustenance for ourselves and our family is portrayed by Bahá'u'lláh as being a noble undertaking imbued with spiritual purpose. It is in this sense that our daily occupation (4) is the most obvious activity or practice in which we weave overt and dramatic expression into the fabric of our inner spiritual condition: "The best of men are they that earn a livelihood by their calling and spend upon themselves and upon their kindred for the love of God, the Lord of all worlds."[12]

In addition to praising every sort of daily labor, Bahá'u'lláh commands all people to engage in some occupation, even if one has sufficient wealth that no further income is needed. This is a related but additional practice of weaving the Word into daily life: "It is incumbent upon each one of you to engage in some occupation—such as a craft, a trade or the like. We have exalted your engagement in such work to the rank of worship of the one true God."[13]

Clearly we might feel ourselves thrice blessed if we are able to engage in an occupation that provides sustenance for our family, is inherently enjoyable, and seems to be a direct service to others (for

---

* I will get back to this when we discuss the sixth daily exercise.

example, teaching, medicine, social work, and so on), but society benefits from and depends upon all work at every level. Furthermore, the Bahá'í writings state that whatever occupation we undertake becomes a form of worship, most especially when we do so with a motive of service to others: "Every individual, no matter how handicapped and limited he may be, is under the obligation of engaging in some work or profession, for work, especially when performed in the spirit of service, is according to Bahá'u'lláh a form of worship."[14]

A fifth pursuit that gives spiritual significance to our daily physical and social practices has to do with our (5) participation in forging spiritually anchored relationships among our neighbors for the explicit purpose of knitting together what we might regard as the "God particle" of any social order, the harmonious family functioning in concert with others to fashion an harmonious neighborhood. For no matter how organized, efficient, and just the infrastructure and superstructure of governance may be, whether at the national or global level, we live our lives locally. In this sense, it matters not how finely devised world polity may be if life is not secure, just, loving, and collaborative within our homes and local communities.

The completion of this cycle—or, to employ the appropriate term from physics, this "period"—results the beginning of a new cycle when (6) we reflect on what we have learned from the experience of attempting to implement a spiritual concept into various personal and interpersonal or collective forms of action, even as we are admonished by Bahá'u'lláh, "Bring thyself to account each day ere thou art summoned to a reckoning; for death, unheralded, shall come upon thee and thou shalt be called to give account for thy deeds."[15] Part of this process of "accounting" necessarily involves reflecting on our actions, which should result in a determination about how we can do better, if we feel we have fallen short of the goals we established the previous day. Additionally, (7) we should establish a plan for becoming even more proficient or expansive in our expression of spiritual attributes in physical actions the following day.

The Calendar as Framework and Loom

If we are discussing the fabric of Bahá'í community life, then we might well consider the Bahá'í calendar as the loom or framework upon which that life is secured and displayed for all to see. Related to this concept is the fact that we start counting time anew with the appearance of each successive Manifestation. For example, when I began work on this book, it was the year 5773 AM (*Anno Mundi*, year of the world) on the Hebrew calendar, 2013 AD (*Anno Domini*, the year of our Lord) on the Christian or Gregorian calendar, 1434 AH (*Anno Hegirae*, year of the Hegira) on the Muslim calendar, and 170 BE (Bahá'í Era) on the Bahá'í calendar.

There are other calendars as well, also based on religious history, but the point is that each of these calendars not only begins counting anew with the advent of a new Messenger from God but that each calendar organizes community life according to the commemorations and structure ordained by the Founder. Consequently, since Bahá'ís believe Bahá'u'lláh is the most recent Manifestation from God, let us examine how the Badí' calendar instituted by the Báb and confirmed and refined by Bahá'u'lláh serves as the loom upon which the Bahá'í tapestry of community life is woven.

To begin with, the Bahá'í year consists of nineteen months, each named after an attribute of God. On the first day of each month, every Bahá'ís community worldwide holds a "feast"—a tripartite meeting consisting of devotions, consultation on community matters, and socializing with fellow believers. The consultative portion (sometimes called the administrative portion) is also a time when the Local Spiritual Assembly gives formal reports about actions it has taken, reviews the fiscal status of the community, and receives recommendations from the community at large about any matters that individuals feel the Local Spiritual Assembly should consider.

The calendar also includes several Holy Days, on nine of which work is to be suspended. These days commemorate important events from Bahá'í religious history, and for some of these, specific times are designated for gatherings, prayers, and whatever other appropriate commemorative activities the community might desire to hold. Since there are very few rituals or rites in the Bahá'í Faith, creativity regarding most activities is encouraged, whether the occasion be a wedding, a funeral, or a holy day. In addition, it is important to note that all community activities are culturally neutral so that they can be adapted to the predilections of the community and cultural milieu in which the people live.

The organization and running of the administrative institutions is likewise an integral part of the religious calendar, inasmuch as the Bahá'í writings affirm that the spiritual and administrative life of the community are also woven together: "To dissociate the administrative principles of the Cause from the purely spiritual and humanitarian teachings would be tantamount to a mutilation of the body of the Cause, a separation that can only result in the disintegration of its component parts, and the extinction of the Faith itself."[16]

Let us briefly review a few more examples of how the sacred and the secular aspects of Bahá'í life are entwined by the calendar. The last month of the Bahá'í year ('Alá) is preceded by the commemoration of *Ayyám-i-Há*, a four- or five-day period of gift-giving, acts of service to others, and spiritual preparation for the fast that occurs during the following month. During the fast, which is ordained in the Kitáb-i-Aqdas by Bahá'u'lláh, adult Bahá'ís do not eat or drink from sunrise to sunset. This spiritual exercise in restraint and reflection culminates in the commemoration of

Naw-Rúz (new year), which takes place on the day of the vernal equinox (the 20th, 21st, or 22nd of March).

The most sacred festival in the Bahá'í calendar is the twelve-day period of *Ridván*, the commemoration of the time in 1863 when Bahá'u'lláh formally announced to His followers that He was the One promised by scripture to fulfill the long-awaited "Day of Days"—what the Báb refers to as the "Latter Resurrection." On the first of these days, Bahá'í communities throughout the world elect their Local Spiritual Assemblies.

There is much more we could discuss about the way in which the Bahá'í calendar organizes and gives spiritual meaning to the individual and collective life of the community, but clearly this device designed by the Manifestation is a crucial and effective tool for symbolizing and actuating the convergence of secular life with the foundational spiritual underpinning which weaves the fabric of an entirely holistic approach to the well-lived life.

Meditation and Reflection

From a Bahá'í perspective, the heart of our spiritual development, though expressed and assisted by community life, is the personal and private attention to our inner life. There is neither confession of sins nor public testimony of one's salvation in the Bahá'í Faith. Rather, quite the reverse is true. There is no clergy, and we are responsible for own spiritual development. And while we are encouraged to share prayers with others, our private periods of prayer and reflection constitute the most critical period in the forging of a spiritually centered life: "One thing and only one thing will unfailingly and alone secure the undoubted triumph of this sacred Cause, namely, the extent to which our own inner life and private character mirror forth in their manifold aspects the splendor of those eternal principles proclaimed by Bahá'u'lláh."[17]

There is no obligatory congregational prayer (except for the prayer for the departed), and there is no specific technique by which Bahá'ís are required to carry out this personal and private maintenance of our "inner life and private character" (except for certain motions that are prescribed for the medium and long obligatory prayers).* Prayer, reflection, and meditation are mandated, but there is no recommended process or regulations for these valuable activities, nor will any be imposed. What is essential is that the believer appreciate the weight ascribed to these practices in the sacred writings.

'Abdu'l-Bahá provides an informative description of how reflection, contemplation, and meditation are uniquely human powers that should be approached with the realization of what insights such periods of quietude and focus can help us attain:

> Bahá'u'lláh says there is a sign (from God) in every phenomenon: the sign of the intellect is contemplation and the sign of contemplation is silence, because it is impossible for

---

* "Congregational prayer, in the sense of formal obligatory prayer which is to be recited in accordance with a prescribed ritual as, for example, is the custom in Islám where Friday prayer in the mosque is led by an imám, has been annulled in the Bahá'í Dispensation. The Prayer for the Dead (see note 10) is the only congregational prayer prescribed by Bahá'í law. It is to be recited by one of those present while the remainder of the party stands in silence; the reader has no special status. The congregation is not required to face the Qiblih (Q and A 85).

The three daily Obligatory Prayers are to be recited individually, not in congregation.

There is no prescribed way for the recital of the many other Bahá'í prayers, and all are free to use such non-obligatory prayers in gatherings or individually as they please. In this regard, Shoghi Effendi states that . . . although the friends are thus left free to follow their own inclination . . . they should take the utmost care that any manner they practice should not acquire too rigid a character, and thus develop into an institution. This is a point which the friends should always bear in mind, lest they deviate from the clear path indicated by the Teachings." (Bahá'u'lláh, Kitáb-i-Aqdas, note 19)

a man to do two things at one time—he cannot both speak and meditate.

It is an axiomatic fact that while you meditate you are speaking with your own spirit. In that state of mind you put certain questions to your spirit and the spirit answers: the light breaks forth and the reality is revealed.

You cannot apply the name "man" to any being void of this faculty of meditation; without it he would be a mere animal, lower than the beasts.

Through the faculty of meditation man attains to eternal life; through it he receives the breath of the Holy Spirit—the bestowal of the Spirit is given in reflection and meditation.

The spirit of man is itself informed and strengthened during meditation; through it affairs of which man knew nothing are unfolded before his view. Through it he receives Divine inspiration, through it he receives heavenly food.

Meditation is the key for opening the doors of mysteries. In that state man abstracts himself: in that state man withdraws himself from all outside objects; in that subjective mood he is immersed in the ocean of spiritual life and can unfold the secrets of things-in-themselves. To illustrate this, think of man as endowed with two kinds of sight; when the power of insight is being used the outward power of vision does not see.[18]

Since the Bahá'í teachings do not mandate or recommend any specific form for this exquisite process, it becomes the task of each person to discover when to engage in this valuable and refined activity and what ancillary practices might help us pursue it.

The Medicinal Sound of the Word

Let us conclude this survey of how the Word knits together the sacred and secular aspects of our personal lives by noting the central function of prayer and, in particular, the vocalization of the prayers in melodious tones as exhorted by Bahá'u'lláh. This does not imply that we cannot recite them to ourselves, but it reminds us that He does place importance on the beauty and musicality of the revealed verses. The most explicit benefit cited by Bahá'u'lláh regarding intoning the verses is that these revealed words vibrating in the air have an effect on our soul, even though we may not be consciously aware of their influence.

Certainly no one who has recited the verses aloud or listened to others do so, especially when the verses are chanted in the original Arabic or Persian, can deny the remarkable impact this recitation of the sacred verses has on the spirit. Many years ago in the depth of an agonizing medical condition, I took profound comfort when a dear Persian friend came to visit and, at my request, intoned the verses with such a marvelous melodic voice that my spirit immediately became uplifted, and waves of hope eased my heart and soothed my pain.

I have also found that personally, when I recite the verses out loud, I tend to focus on their meaning, whereas when I read prayers silently my thoughts can more easily become distracted so that the words do not have the same penetrating influence as when intoned. But perhaps my own susceptibility to distraction derives from having taught more or less the same courses at university for forty-three years where, while seemingly lecturing full steam, I would internally be reflecting on what I might have for supper.

A Regimen without Regimentation

To conclude this brief analysis of how the Word weaves together our daily material life with our spiritual purposes, we might do well to set aside what might seem to some a formulaic approach to spiritual exercises that derive from the influence of the revealed Word, or as we noted in chapter 6, what Shoghi Effendi wisely calls the "creative Word." That is, it might be perceived as a disservice to compartmentalize the day into these practices that obviously can take place throughout the twenty-four hour cycle. After all, we should thank God that no two days are the same—what a boring life that would be.

Furthermore, if we are really aware that in everything we do there lies the possibility of spiritual lessons to be learned or spiritual practices to be exercised, then we might best conclude our overview with a diagram that looks something more like the action of a sewing machine as it rapidly weaves back and forth. Perhaps this is a useful image to illustrate how our lives should be lived, where we are in constant and unrelenting dialogue with God through the Word He has provided us as the firm cord by which we are secured to His Covenant:

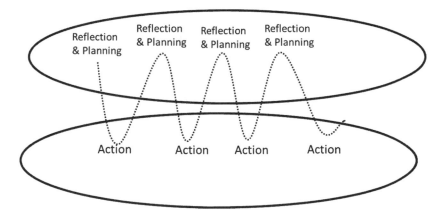

Figure 17. Constant Interplay between the Two Realms

The obvious value of the routinization of the "Bahá'í life" is, well, obvious—at no point during any given day is the conscientious believer very far removed from some spiritual exercise or from planning and evaluating daily activities in terms of their relevance to one's everlasting destiny as a spiritual being.

And yet the fact that prayer, reflection, study, and service take place on a daily basis does not mean that any of these practices need ever be boring or mindless. Therefore, let us review some examples of these practices to understand why the Bahá'í life need never impose homogeneity of thought or actions.

First of all, even with the obligatory prayers, there is choice, and each of the three choices is significantly different from the others in length and form. For example, the short obligatory prayer to be said at noon is exactly three sentences (fifty words) long and can be said any time between noon and sunset. Second, it is completely the responsibility of each individual to oversee his or her own compliance with this guidance. Third, as we already mentioned, there is no congregational prayer, no ritualized format. Prayers can be shared with others, but the obligatory prayers are a private matter: "Whoso reciteth, in the *privacy of his chamber*, the verses revealed by God, the scattering angels of the Almighty shall scatter abroad the fragrance of the words uttered by his mouth, and shall cause the heart of every righteous man to throb."[19]

This same latitude about how one carries out this guidance that the Manifestation has bequeathed us through the Word as a gift for our spiritual nourishment and well-being applies to all of the Bahá'í practices and activities mentioned above. Even as the foundation of a global polity is established upon the integrity, strength, and vitality of local communities, each community is free to decide in what manner it will carry out the guidance it receives.

The logic of the daily routinization of one's personal spiritual life is comparable to the logic regarding our treatment of the physical apparatus with which we carry out these activities—our human temple. Though our body is only a composition of "water and clay," we are exhorted in this same revealed guidance to attend to a regimen of cleanliness and refined conduct as another part of our daily lives, including particulars such as washing our bodies and clothes and monitoring the propriety of our speech and manners as we interact with others.[20]

Thus, in the same way we maintain the physical aspect of our "self" by eating nutritional food on a regular basis or consulting with a competent physician should we become ill, so we are exhorted to use the same sort of wisdom in training ourselves spiritually. A simple analogy explains this comparison well.

Were we to eat the most nutritional meal anyone could devise, and were we to consume in a day three meals of such wonderfully prepared food and drink, our body would still require more food the next day, regardless of how carefully selected and prepared that exquisite nourishment was. For no matter how rigorously we exert ourselves to becoming healthy on a single day, all that effort suffices for only a brief duration.

We might do fairly well were we to follow this fulfilling day with successive days of consuming partially nourishing food, or possibly one slightly nourishing meal a day. But we would not prosper. We would not develop. We would not progress from our present condition unless we make proper nourishment an ongoing routine as part of a holistic regimen, including other healthy activities—*mens sana in corpore sano* (a healthy mind in a healthy body).

The same principle holds true for physical conditioning. We might follow a carefully devised training program calculated to exercise our body at its present capacity. This same program, if intelligently designed, would then gradually increase activity in order to strengthen our body by degrees. By contrast, it would be impossible to transform our physical condition in a single day of rigorous exercise, and if we simply worked out once in a while, we would fare only slightly better than if we were not to exercise at all.

All of these principles are comparable to the wisdom with which Bahá'u'lláh has devised for us a program of spiritual enlightenment and character strengthening. Were we to experience one amazing day of spiritual education in which we felt exalted beyond words and inspired to change our lives, that single episode, while possibly providing a strategic starting point, would not suffice to transform us. Likewise, were someone to recognize the station of Bahá'u'lláh and decide to become a Bahá'í, he or she might find it overwhelming to suddenly attempt to carry out all the parts of the daily spiritual regimen. Being a Bahá'í is a process, not a point in time; it is the acceptance of a goal, not an instantaneous transformation. Thus, it is a beginning, but it is a beginning in which the "end" is always in sight and where there is a clear path that betokens ceaseless and ever more exhilarating rewards.

It is also important to note that this process does not entail competition—we should never gauge our success by what we believe to be the success of others, even as we should never think we can judge someone else's progress. As Bahá'u'lláh states with unmistakable clarity, each of us is a unique being with a special blend of capacities and opportunities: "Unto each one hath been prescribed a preordained measure, as decreed in God's mighty and guarded Tablets. All that which ye potentially possess can, however, be manifested only as a result of your own volition."[21]

Finally, we should consider that in the revealed Word of Bahá'u'lláh there is no important distinction between those writings that exhort us to carry out spiritual exercises and those that are part of revealed laws. The guidance set forth in the Kitáb-i-Aqdas, the book containing the laws of Bahá'u'lláh, makes no difference between obedience to personal spiritual guidance and the manifestation of spiritual refinement in social comportment and interaction, even as the well-trained athlete should not distinguish between the importance of the nourishment of his internal well-being and the exercise of his external self. The Kitáb-i-Aqdas weaves together poetically a tapestry of the well-lived life in which the individual, the family, and community collaborate to create a pattern of life that maximizes personal freedom and ingenuity, while safeguarding the rights and privileges of all and upholding the pillars of the administrative institutions:

> O people of God! That which traineth the world is Justice, for it is upheld by two pillars, reward and punishment. These two pillars are the sources of life to the world. Inasmuch as for each day there is a new problem and for every problem an expedient solution, such affairs should be referred to the Ministers of the House of Justice that they may act according to the needs and requirements of the time. They that, for the sake of God, arise to serve His Cause, are the recipients of divine inspiration from the unseen Kingdom. It is incumbent upon all to be obedient unto them. All matters of State should be referred to the House of Justice, but acts of worship must be observed according to that which God hath revealed in His Book.[22]

-9-

HOW THE WORD STITCHES DISPENSATIONS TOGETHER

Among these teachings was the independent investigation of reality so that the world of humanity may be saved from the darkness of imitation and attain to the truth; may tear off and cast away this ragged and outgrown garment of a thousand years ago and may put on the robe woven in the utmost purity and holiness in the loom of reality. As reality is one and cannot admit of multiplicity, therefore different opinions must ultimately become fused into one.

'Abdu'l-Bahá, *Selections from the Writings of
'Abdu'l-Bahá*, no. 227.7

'Abdu'l-Bahá asserts that the advent of the Manifestations is the force underlying the advancement of human civilization, that without Their influence, all would be "darkness upon darkness."*

---

* "Were it not for the grace of the revelation and instruction of those sanctified Beings, the world of souls and the realm of thought would become darkness upon darkness" ('Abdu'l-Bahá, *Some Answered Questions*, no. 42.3).

Consequently, the knitting together of the successive Revelations in the religion of God is what secures the panoramic tapestry that is the unfolding of human history itself.

The Kitáb-i-Íqán, Bahá'u'lláh's principal doctrinal work, offers, among other things, a superb analysis of the Word in history, as well as an exacting explanation of how misunderstanding and abusing scripture has thereby hindered human progress. Bahá'u'lláh also makes clear that the Word constitutes one continuous Book, and misconstruing its meaning has deterred humankind from recognizing that all the revealed religions throughout human history are really one religion revealed in progressive and successive stages.

Toward the end of His explication of how the Manifestations employ language and how every Prophet comes with signs and proofs of His station, Bahá'u'lláh affirms that the proofs explored in the Kitáb-i-Íqán can be applied to authenticate the appearance of every Manifestation: "[T]he things We have already mentioned suffice the world and all that is therein. In fact, all the Scriptures and the mysteries thereof are condensed into this brief account. So much so, that were a person to ponder it a while in his heart, he would discover from all that hath been said the mysteries of the Words of God, and would apprehend the meaning of whatever hath been manifested by that ideal King."[1]

For our purposes, the Kitáb-i-Íqán functions as a virtual textbook on how the Word is employed by the Manifestations to test and teach the peoples of the world. It answers the question about the "clarity" of the Word through a lengthy and multilayered examination and authoritative elucidation of three verses from Matthew (24:29–31) that contain Christ's prophecy about the advent of Muhammad. In the course of this illuminating examination of the Word, Bahá'u'lláh observes that the indirection and poetic nature of these sacred verses has the purpose of challenging the peoples of the world to perceive, with their heart, the spirit of what is intended. He explains that this challenge is not capricious but rather an exhortation to think for ourselves and to discover the nature of what we seek—even as Christ noted that if we are looking for a Prophet, we first need to figure out what comportment, demeanor, actions, and words would characterize a Prophet.

The most obvious proofs of a Prophet, Bahá'u'lláh concludes, are the immaculate character of the Manifestations, Their rejection of temporal authority and material riches, and Their capacity to reveal the Word spontaneously, without revision and without having been trained in any school or having studied under any scholars. In addition, Bahá'u'lláh notes, are the proofs of the quality and character of the individuals who arise to follow Them and the constancy of the Manifestations in the face of tribulation, torture, or execution. Lastly, each Manifestation acknowledges the veracity and is able to explain the verses of the previous Manifestation, and He elucidates and fulfills the specific prophecies regarding His own advent.

The linking together of each Revelation to the next might thus be viewed metaphorically as the process of "stitching" one "Day" to the next. By this means, human civilization and behavior become ever more refined so that this tapestry of the history of our planet becomes increasingly more complex and beauteous. Indeed, the brilliant threads woven through the fabric of this Divine Plan of God for planet Earth (and for every other planet on which human life exists) constitute the Eternal Covenant with which the Creator fashions every system in the created universe.

Stated another way, the educational plan we have portrayed throughout this discussion in terms of the concept of "progressive Revelation" is not designed solely for planet Earth. Each planet inhabited by human life might be compared to a cell in the universal body that is the infinite physical dimension of creation: ". . . this endless universe is like the human body, and that all its parts are connected one with another and are linked together in the utmost perfection. That is, in the same way that the parts, members, and organs of the human body are interconnected, and that they mutually assist, reinforce, and influence each other, so too are the parts and members of this endless universe connected with, and spiritually and materially influenced by, one another."[2] And like cells, each planet so endowed comes into being and develops through successive stages whereby it gradually achieves its inherent destiny of manifesting divine attributes in social structures.

The planet, like a cell, thus contributes to the physical and spiritual life of the universal body, even as it receives life from it, until the life cycle of the planet is completed and it ultimately goes out of being: "It is likewise clear and evident that this terrestrial globe came to exist, grow, and develop in the matrix of the universe and assumed different forms and conditions until it gradually attained its present completeness . . ."[3]

Consequently, we can observe that while the infinite universal body itself has no beginning and no end, it is in a constant state of change and transformation as the outward expression of a celestial realm that is also constantly changing and evolving. Physical reality might thus correctly be studied as the sensibly perceptible, or artistic, expression of the mind and will of the Creator.

Returning to planet Earth, where our vision is presently focused, we might understandably ponder why, if it is the plan of the Creator that human civilization be progressively transformed and refined, do we not seem a great deal nicer, or more just, or closer to a permanent and lasting peace than we are? The answer is that progress has occurred—and substantial progress at that—even if we have a very long way to go to achieve our collective destiny of a just and peaceful global community.

Of course, the fact that we possess such a vision and aspiration is in itself one important sign of our progress—that we have a collective global view of ourselves, that we are universally aware of our shortcomings, and, in addition, that we have a collective sense of what changes need to occur. For however distant these objectives may presently seem, in our hearts we share the dream of justice, peace, and universal suffrage, of providing sustenance, education, shelter, and all the other essentials that should be the inherent and inalienable right of all who inhabit our planetary neighborhood.

Returning to the subject at hand—the intended connection and binding together of the sequence of the religions of God—we need to respond head-on to what is probably the most obvious problem that this theory of religions calls into question. If it is the plan of the Creator that the followers of each religion accept the advent of the successive Manifestation, why has this never yet occurred? The Jews have never collectively acknowledged Christ as the Messiah. The Christians have never collectively recognized Muhammad as the promised Comforter. The Muslims have vehemently persecuted and slaughtered the Bábís and the Bahá'ís. Most of the Bábís followed Bahá'u'lláh, but a few became some of His most inveterate enemies.

Ultimately, each Revelation does succeed in transforming society in spite of resistance by the very ones we would expect to be the first followers—those who are guardians of the Word of the previous Manifestation. But instead of recognizing the religion of God as a single Faith, a unified and ceaseless transformative teaching process, the followers of each successive religion put their utmost effort into trying to maintain the supremacy and independence of their own Manifestation and the changelessness of the beliefs He revealed.

Some of these religions do recognize a revelatory process and the Manifestation they follow as a part of that Divine Plan, but with the caveat that He was the ultimate educator of humankind and that His is, therefore, the only Revelation that presently matters.

The Pattern of a Dispensation

Here again the explanation for this ostensible glitch is, in fact, that the difficulty lies not in the Divine Plan of God but rather in the sometimes problematic human response to His guidance. As we have noted throughout this study, these instructions are expressed indirectly through the rhetorical devices of the Word as a challenge to those who hear it. We are thereby judged and tested, and, according to the writing on the wall, most of us have been found wanting.

I am referring here primarily to the symbolic language of prophecy employed both in the revealed Word and in the clues bestowed in the divinely-inspired guidance of precursors who forewarn us that the time of the new Day is at hand. But to understand the critical nature of this transition and the "test" or "judgment" that the Word imposes on the believers, we need first to make clear the distinction between the authoritative Word and the commentaries or insights of those who, while perhaps believing themselves spiritually inspired, are not direct, infallible, revelatory sources themselves. This distinction represents the difference between the knowledge bequeathed solely to the Manifestations and the beliefs or conclusions proffered by those who—though sometimes animated by the best of intentions—neither partake of the "Most Great Infallibility" (a power exclusive to the Manifestations) nor are endowed with "conferred infallibility" (a power the Manifestation can bestow upon His named successors).

Second, we need to understand that there is a specific pattern of proofs related to the advent of a new Manifestation alluded to in previous Revelations but made explicit by Bahá'u'lláh in the Kitáb-i-Íqán. Such is the clarity and the extent of this discourse about proofs that Bahá'u'lláh affirms it constitutes the standard for investigating the claims of all Manifestations, not solely the Báb's or His own. And here I am not referring exclusively to the proofs manifest in the Messenger Himself but rather those transitional events that connect the past with the present, and each "Day" or Revelation with the next.

To understand the steps in this process, we first need to examine the general pattern that each Revelation follows. That is, the progress of a Dispensation traces a sort of bell curve rather than a flat line of advancement. It has a beginning or dawning, then a gradual growth followed by a period of efflorescence when it attains its noonday splendor. As its teachings become distorted or out of step with the needs and capacities of humanity, its influence begins to decline until society finds itself in a nighttime of ignorance, in disarray, and needful of the further assistance of a new Revelation.

It is because of this predictable scheme that the transition to the next Revelation couples the prophecies of the previous one with several subsequent events and divinely inspired prophecies. The following simple illustration demonstrates this idea of the pattern of transitions as human history moves forward:

From "Day" to "Day"

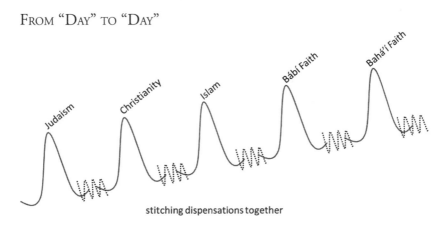

stitching dispensations together

Figure 18. How Dispensation Are Stitched Together

From a Bahá'í perspective of human history, as we can observe, these "Days" or cycles are on an ascent. They do not simply repeat the same information but are progressive. And yet the pattern of each Dispensation follows this same sequence of movement like the sinus wave of a heartbeat. Likewise, we see reflected in each wave the profile of a literal day—the dawning, the rising, the peak effulgence, the setting, the eventide, and the nighttime:*

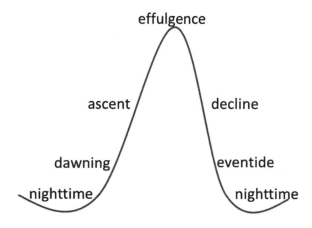

Figure 19. The Course of Past Dispensations

Of course, as we noted very early in our discussion, we will in time collectively come to understand and appreciate this process and recognize our part in the inherently spiritual enterprise that is the construction of a global polity.

As we go about carrying out our individual tasks to bring about the midday splendor of this present Day, the "Day of Days"

---

* "By 'night' is meant the period between two divine Revelations when the Sun of Truth is not manifest among men. In the Persian Bayán, II, 7, the Báb says, 'O people of the Bayan! Act not as the people of the Qur'án have acted, for if you do so the fruits of your night will come to naught'" (cited in the Báb, *Selections from the Writings of the Báb*, footnote, pp. 165–66).

that is the Dispensation of Bahá'u'lláh, it is interesting to note Bahá'u'lláh's assurance that "This is the Day that shall not be followed by night."[4]

This assurance should not be understood to imply that there will be no need for a further Revelation or that this symbolic "nighttime" will not occur.

Shoghi Effendi explains that this statement by Bahá'u'lláh alludes to the inviolable Covenant, the means of which the succession of authority will be ensured and remain intact. Referring to the immediate aftermath of Bahá'u'lláh's ascension, he writes, "The significance of the solemn affirmation that this is 'the Day which shall not be followed by night' was now clearly apprehended. An orphan community had recognized in 'Abdu'l-Bahá, in its hour of desperate need, its Solace, its Guide, its Mainstay and Champion."[5]

In short, unlike every previous religion, the succession of authority by means of authentic written documents had created a secure, durable, authoritative, and inviolable chain between Bahá'u'lláh and the institutions He had ordained to guide the Bahá'í religion. The assertion about there being no "night" did not mean the transition from the Bahá'í era or Dispensation to that of the next Manifestation would not test the people to recognize and follow Him. Bahá'u'lláh makes this abundantly clear: "I am not apprehensive for My own self," and still more explicitly declares, "My fears are for Him Who will be sent down unto you after Me—Him Who will be invested with great sovereignty and mighty dominion." And again He writes in the Súratu'l-Haykal: "'By those words which I have revealed, Myself is not intended, but rather He Who will come after Me. To it is witness God, the All-Knowing.' 'Deal not with Him,' He adds, 'as ye have dealt with Me.'" We must conclude, therefore, that there will be a "nighttime" in due course as the need for a new Revelation approaches. For even though Bahá'u'lláh cautions that a new Manifestation will not appear before "the expiration of a full thousand years," we should note this is the minimal amount of time prior to such an advent.

Four Parts of Transition

While I have represented the transition symbolically with the pattern of thread sewing together the two Dispensations, the fact is that there are distinct parts of that transition, some of which involve the revealed Word while others are expressed through various signs and symbols.

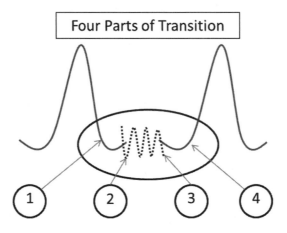

Figure 20. The Transition from One Dispensation to the Next

PART ONE

The first part of the stitching in this transition is, of course, the authoritative prophecies of the previous Manifestation, together with the pronouncements of those whom He has endowed with the power to make authoritative statements. These would be figures such as the minor prophets of the Mosaic Dispensation (Isaiah and Daniel, for example), the twelve Imams of the Islamic Dispensation, and 'Abdu'l-Bahá and Shoghi Effendi for the Bahá'í Dispensation.

As we mentioned at the beginning of the chapter, the first part of Bahá'u'lláh's Kitáb-i-Íqán (pages 1–93) is an amazingly informative analysis of three verses from the words of Christ (Matthew 24:29–31) that prophesy the advent of the next Messenger of God. Elsewhere, Christ designates this next Manifestation with the epithet of Comforter or Counselor:*

> Nevertheless I tell you the truth: it is to your advantage that I go away, for if I do not go away, the Counselor will not come to you; but if I go, I will send him to you. And when he comes, he will convince the world concerning sin and righteousness and judgment: concerning sin, because they do not believe in me; concerning righteousness, because I go to the Father, and you will see me no more; concerning judgment, because the ruler of this world is judged.
>
> I have yet many things to say to you, but you cannot bear them now. When the Spirit of truth comes, he will guide you into all the truth, for he will not speak on his own authority, but whatever he hears he will speak, and he will declare to you the things that are to come.[7]

In another discussion about the "return," Christ explains that this Manifestation will come when least expected, like a thief in in the nighttime—perhaps indicating the night or decline of the Christian Dispensation: "Therefore you also must be ready; for the Son of man is coming at an hour you do not expect."[8]

In the course of His careful exposition in the Kitáb-i-Íqán, Bahá'u'lláh explains that Christ's carefully-devised prophecy regard-

---

* Translated from the Greek *paráklētos*, meaning one who comforts, consoles, advises, like an advocate for someone in a court proceeding.

ing the advent of the Comforter should have been sufficient guidance for the Christians to recognize Muhammad, but only if the Muslims themselves had understood the underlying meaning of these verses sufficiently well to interpret them correctly to the Christians. In this context, we do well to recall the number of occasions on which Christ recites the prophetic verses about the advent of the Messiah to His Jewish audience for this same purpose.

Bahá'u'lláh also demonstrates how the following three verses are actually stating in symbolic and metaphorical terms a sequence that persistently occurs in every transition to the advent of a new Dispensation. A brief explanation helps demonstrate the point. First, let us review the verses Bahá'u'lláh explicates: "Immediately after the tribulation of those days the sun will be darkened, and the moon will not give its light, and the stars will fall from heaven, and the powers of the heavens will be shaken; then will appear the sign of the Son of man in heaven, and then all the tribes of the earth will mourn, and they will see the Son of man coming on the clouds of heaven with power and great glory; and he will send out his angels with a loud trumpet call. . . ."[9] While there is no better interpretation and elucidation of these verses than the text of the Kitáb-i-Íqán itself, the general pattern portrayed here is the darkening or decline of the established religion. During this period, the spiritual luminaries or leaders no longer bestow light to the followers, and their leadership is shaken.

PARTS TWO AND THREE

In Christ's words, the second part of the sequence is heralded by "the sign of the Son of man in heaven." This verse, Bahá'u'lláh explains, has two implications regarding this pattern. The first implication is the fact that prior to the advent of a new Manifestation, a literal celestial phenomenon appears—a comet, in the case of Christ. The second meaning is symbolic and alludes to the advent of a forerunner who announces the imminence of a new Revelation from God:

> By "heaven" is meant the visible heaven, inasmuch as when the hour draweth nigh on which the Daystar of the heaven of justice shall be made manifest, and the Ark of divine guidance shall sail upon the sea of glory, a star will appear in the heaven, heralding unto its people the advent of that most great light. In like manner, in the invisible heaven a star shall be made manifest who, unto the peoples of the earth, shall act as a harbinger of the break of that true and exalted Morn. These twofold signs, in the visible and the invisible heaven, have announced the Revelation of each of the Prophets of God, as is commonly believed.[10]

Bahá'u'lláh examines this pattern as it relates to Abraham, Moses, Jesus, Muhammad, the Báb, and, by implication, Himself. For example, He mentions the soothsayers who informed Nimrod about the rise of a star in the heaven that heralded the coming of Abraham. He then alludes to the soothsayers who warned Pharaoh of a star that "foreshadoweth the conception of Child Who holdeth your fate and the fate of your people in His hand," a sign presaging the advent of Moses.[11]

Bahá'u'lláh then discusses the figurative "stars," the individuals who appear to foretell the advent of a new Manifestation. First, He mentions "a sage," who "in the darkness of the night, brought tidings of joy unto the people of Israel, imparting consolation to their souls, and assurance to their hearts."[12] Here Bahá'u'lláh is not referring to Moses Himself, but to a herald who appeared earlier to forewarn the people about His coming.

The discussion then moves on to a description of the well-known events that presaged the advent of Christ: the star of Bethlehem in the "visible heaven" (fulfilling the prophecies of the Zoroastrian Magi) coupled with a spiritual luminary in the "heaven of divine knowledge," John the Baptist. Indeed, Jesus was one of His followers, and it was Jesus' baptism by John that signaled His assumption of the title of the "Christ," the "anointed one."

Prior to the coming of Muhammad, there were also phenomenal celestial signs as well as four individuals who "successively announced unto the people the joyful tidings" of the advent of the Prophet. According to Bahá'u'lláh, among these was Rúz-bih, later named Salmán: "As the end of one of these approached, he would send Rúz-bih unto the other, until the fourth who, feeling his death to be nigh, addressed Rúz-bih saying: 'O Rúz-bih! when thou hast taken up my body and buried it, go to Hijáz for there the Daystar of Muhammad will arise. Happy art thou, for thou shalt behold His face!'"[13]

Because a major purpose of the Kitáb-i-Íqán is to function as an apologia for, or proof of, the Báb and the Bábí Dispensation,* Bahá'u'lláh expounds extensively on how the pattern of transition alluded to in the verses of Matthew is fulfilled with the advent of the Báb.** Inasmuch as the Revelations of the Báb and Bahá'u'lláh are twin parts of the Day of Days, the long-awaited Resurrection of humankind, this transition is particularly weighty, especially since we have the writings and teachings of the two luminaries who functioned as heralds to both the Báb as Qá'im and Bahá'u'lláh as Qayyúm.†

---

* The work was written a year before Bahá'u'lláh announced to His close followers that He was the One foretold by the Báb and about two or three years before He began sending out epistles to the world's political and religious leaders declaring His station.

** Bahá'u'lláh's explanation of the verses are found in the Kitáb-i-Íqán from ¶71 to the end of Part 1.

† The Báb, Who was the "Qá'im," He who shall arise (from the family of Muhammad), the "Twelfth Imám" and the "Mihdí." Bahá'u'lláh fulfills the

Bahá'u'lláh notes that astronomers acknowledged the celestial phenomenon of twin stars appearing in the heavens (foreshadowing the twin Revelations of the Báb and Bahá'u'lláh), but because the Kitáb-i-Íqán was revealed prior to His formal declaration of His station, Bahá'u'lláh does not elaborate here on the meaning of this phenomenal sign.* He does allude, though, to the two spiritual luminaries, "those twin resplendent lights," who foretold the advent of the Qá'im and the Qayyúm.[14]

The first of these was Shaykh Ahmad-i-Ahsá'í (1743–1828) who lived in Arabia and founded the Shaykhí movement. Most important among his teachings was his explanation that concepts such as the Resurrection, Muhammad's Night Journey to Heaven, and the signs of the advent of the Qá'im should be studied as having allegorical or symbolic importance instead of literal meaning.

One of his students, as well as his appointed successor, was Siyyid Kázim-i-Rashtí (1793–1843), who taught in Karbilá. The main theme of his teaching was that the advent of the Qá'im was imminent. He, in fact, knew the identity of the Qá'im and indicated as much when Siyyid 'Alí-Muhammad (the Báb) was in attendance at one of his classes.** It was also Siyyid Kázim who

---

prophecies of Siyyid Kázim regarding the "*Qayyúm*" Who would arise after the star of the Qá'im had set.

* In his book *Thief in the Night*, Bill Sears offers the following as suggested possibilities fulfilling the phenomenal sign: "1. The star-fall of 1833 and the periodic appearance of this shower of meteors always in November, the month of the birth of Bahá'u'lláh. 2. The beginning of the study of 'double-stars.' 3. The parhelic circles surrounding the sun in 1843. 4. The great comet of 1843. 5. The parhelic circles of 1844. 6. The comet of 1845, which split in two in 1846, and the mingling of the twin-comets into one single shower of light. 7. The belief that the brightest star Sirius had had a twin companion; a belief announced in 1844. It was proved to be true in 1862, on the eve of Bahá'u'lláh's declaration" (William Sears, *Thief in the Night*, p. 3).

** See Nabíl, *The Dawn-Breakers*, p. 27.

announced to his students the appearance of two Manifestations in rapid succession: "Verily I say, after the Qá'im the Qayyúm will be made manifest. For when the star of the Former has set, the sun of the beauty of Husayn [Mirzá Husayn-'Alí, that is, Bahá'u'lláh] will rise and illuminate the whole world."[15]

Through His elucidation of these twin categories of proof—the phenomenal celestial proof and the immaculate heralds who arise to proclaim the imminence of a new Manifestation—Bahá'u'lláh provides evidence of His own station as well as that of the Báb. In fact, toward the end of the work, Bahá'u'lláh forewarns the Bábís that they will be tested to recognize Him Whom God will make Manifest,* even as Muslims were challenged to recognize the Báb as Qá'im: "By His references to their opposition He intended to invalidate the objections which the people of the Bayán might raise in the day of the manifestation of Mustaghátḥ** the day of the Latter Resurrection,† claiming that, whereas in the Dispensation of the Bayán a number of divines have embraced the Faith, in this latter Revelation none of these hath recognized His claim."[16]

PART FOUR

The final part of the transition is the most important because it represents the fulfillment of all that has been veiled by way of prophecy and symbolic language—the appearance of the Manifestation and the proofs He Himself offers. Concluding His discourse about the Divine Plan by which successive Manifestations appear,

---

* The Báb's epithet for the Manifestation Who would succeed Him—that is, Bahá'u'lláh.

** "He Who is Invoked," that is, Bahá'u'lláh.

† A term first used by the Báb to designate the resurrection that would follow His own. According to Islamic belief, the Resurrection would consist of two Trumpet calls, the first of which would dumbfound the peoples and leave them dazed, and the second of which would awaken and revive them.

Bahá'u'lláh provides four proofs of the authenticity of the Manifestation, each consisting of or deriving from the Word.

The first proof He discusses is the revealed Word and the unique power of the Manifestation to produce verses spontaneously without having been educated or tutored by anyone. In the course of His exposition of this proof, Bahá'u'lláh cites Muhammad's own admonition: "And if ye be in doubt as to that which We have sent down to Our Servant, then produce a Surah like it, and summon your witnesses, beside God, if ye are men of truth."[17]* He then continues in a most powerful and eloquent passage to affirm the weighty and incontrovertible proof that the revealed Word establishes, and, by implication, the proof of the Manifestation Who reveals them:

> He, the divine King, hath proclaimed the undisputed supremacy of the verses of His Book over all things that testify to His truth. For compared with all other proofs and tokens, the divinely revealed verses shine as the sun, whilst all others are as stars. To the peoples of the world they are the abiding testimony, the incontrovertible proof, the shining light of the ideal King. Their excellence is unrivaled, their virtue nothing can surpass. They are the treasury of the divine pearls and the depository of the divine mysteries. They constitute the indissoluble Bond, the firm Cord, the 'Urvatu'l-Vuthqa, the inextinguishable Light. Through them floweth the river of divine knowledge, and gloweth the fire of His ancient and consummate wisdom. This is the fire which, in one and the same moment, kindleth the flame of love in the breasts of the

---

* Bahá'u'lláh would later use this same passage to challenge His perfidious half-brother, Mírzá Yahyá.

faithful, and induceth the chill of heedlessness in the heart of the enemy.[18]

Bahá'u'lláh then cites another passage from the Qur'án that attests to the Word as the most mighty proof of God and His Messengers: "Such are the verses of God: with truth do We recite them to thee. But in what revelation will they believe, if they reject God and His verses?"[19]

Effectively, the most lucid and convincing proof to which the Word testifies regarding the validity of the claims and station of the Prophets is contained in this entire section of the Kitáb-i-Íqán. Bahá'u'lláh cites various passages from the Qur'án and explains their meaning, but He also adds His own wonderfully stirring crescendo of observations regarding the power of the Word as proof, and He excoriates those who disdain the clarity of the evidence the verses provide:

> Gracious God! how strange the way of this people! They clamor for guidance, although the standards of Him Who guideth all things are already hoisted. They cleave to the obscure intricacies of knowledge, when He, Who is the Object of all knowledge, shineth as the sun. They see the sun with their own eyes, and yet question that brilliant Orb as to the proof of its light. They behold the vernal showers descending upon them, and yet seek an evidence of that bounty. The proof of the sun is the light thereof, which shineth and envelopeth all things. The evidence of the shower is the bounty thereof, which reneweth and investeth the world with the mantle of life.[20]

Each one of these verses is unto all the peoples of the world an unfailing testimony and a glorious proof of His truth. Each of them verily sufficeth all mankind, wert thou to meditate upon the verses of God. In the above-mentioned verse itself pearls of mysteries lie hidden. Whatever be the ailment, the remedy it offereth can never fail.[21]

Before concluding our brief citation from this extraordinary paean to the proof established by the newly revealed verses, let us repeat a passage we cited earlier—namely, Bahá'u'lláh's statement that the understanding of the Word is open to all, not merely to some body of learned scholars. He begins by noting the erroneous contention by some that "the Book and verses thereof can never be a testimony unto the common people, inasmuch as they neither grasp their meaning nor appreciate their value."[22] If this contention were true, Bahá'u'lláh concludes, then how could the people be expected to shoulder the responsibility of knowing God?

This arrogant contention by those who think themselves learned, He goes on to say, is motivated by the pride of the religious leaders who seek to hold sway over those who, though humble, are, in fact, receptive to recognizing and comprehending the true meaning of the revealed word: "The understanding of His words and the comprehension of the utterances of the Birds of Heaven are in no wise dependent upon human learning. They depend solely upon purity of heart, chastity of soul, and freedom of spirit."[23]

Bahá'u'lláh then presents other proofs, focusing His discussion on how they become evident in the Revelation of the Báb. The second proof He presents is the quality of those souls who arise in the early days of a Dispensation to follow the new Manifestation: "Amongst the proofs demonstrating the truth of this Revelation is this, that in every age and Dispensation, whenever the invisible Essence was revealed in the person of His Manifestation, certain souls, obscure and detached from all worldly entanglements, would seek illumination from the Sun of Prophethood and Moon of divine guidance, and would attain unto the divine Presence. For this reason, the divines of the age and those possessed of wealth would scorn and scoff at these people."[24]

The third proof Bahá'u'lláh notes is the constancy of the Prophet in the face of all obstacles, without regard to personal gain or safety, and in spite of the overwhelming forces arrayed against Him. In the Kitáb-i-Íqán (¶257–262) Bahá'u'lláh describes at great length the sorts of persecution the Báb endured from the very first of the proclamation of His station and mission in 1844 until His execution by firing squad in 1850. Nevertheless, the Báb was relentless and unperturbed in proclaiming His Cause, regardless of the consequence:

> Another proof and evidence of the truth of this Revelation, which amongst all other proofs shineth as the sun, is the constancy of the eternal Beauty in proclaiming the Faith of God. Though young and tender of age, and though the Cause He revealed was contrary to the desire of all the peoples of earth, both high and low, rich and poor, exalted and abased, king and subject, yet He arose and steadfastly proclaimed it. All have known and heard this. He was afraid of no one; He was regardless of consequences. Could such a thing be made manifest except through the power of a divine Revelation, and the potency of God's invincible Will?[25]

Bahá'u'lláh concludes His explication of this proof by extolling the steadfastness of the Báb even though the "whole world rose to hinder Him": "The more severe the persecution they inflicted on that Sadrih of Blessedness, the more His fervour increased, and the brighter burned the flame of His love. All this is evident, and none disputeth its truth. Finally, He surrendered His soul, and winged His flight unto the realms above."[26]

The fourth and final substantive proof Bahá'u'lláh elucidates is the material evidences of the transformative power loosed upon the world when the Manifestation unveils Himself and unleashes His Revelation. While beautifully portrayed over the course of several pages, let it suffice for our present purposes to cite but the opening first paragraph of this weighty testimony:

And among the evidences of the truth of His manifestation were the ascendancy, the transcendent power, and supremacy which He, the Revealer of being and Manifestation of the Adored, hath, unaided and alone, revealed throughout the world. No sooner had that eternal Beauty revealed Himself in Shiraz, in the year sixty, and rent asunder the veil of concealment, than the signs of the ascendancy, the might, the sovereignty, and power, emanating from that Essence of Essences and Sea of Seas, were manifest in every land. So much so, that from every city there appeared the signs, the evidences, the tokens, the testimonies of that divine Luminary. How many were those pure and kindly hearts which faithfully reflected the light of that eternal Sun, and how manifold the emanations of knowledge from that Ocean of divine wisdom which encompassed all beings! In every city, all the divines and dignitaries rose to hinder and repress them, and girded up the loins of malice, of envy, and tyranny for their suppression. How great the number of those holy souls, those essences of justice, who, accused of tyranny, were put to death! And how many embodiments of purity, who showed forth naught but true knowledge and stainless deeds, suffered an agonizing death! Notwithstanding all this, each of these holy beings, up to his last moment, breathed the Name of God, and soared in the realm of submission and resignation. Such was the potency and transmuting influence which He exercised over them, that they ceased to cherish any desire but His will, and wedded their soul to His remembrance.[27]

-10-

THE WORD AS WARP AND WOOF OF HUMAN HISTORY

The formulation of the laws and ordinances of a new-born Dispensation and the enunciation and reaffirmation of its fundamental principles—the warp and woof of a future Administrative Order—had, however, enabled a slowly maturing Revelation, in spite of this tide of tribulations, to advance a stage further and yield its fairest fruit.

Shoghi Effendi, *God Passes By*, p. 643

We have now examined some of the patterns of transition from Revelation to Revelation elucidated by Bahá'u'lláh in the Kitáb-i-Íqán, especially as symbolized in the three verses from the Gospel of Matthew. To study intensely all that Bahá'u'lláh has made so logical and lucid in His treatise is to become aware of how the revealed Word works to bind together all the successive stages in the evolution of human civilization. We could discuss the Kitáb-i-Íqán much more extensively than we have so far without in any way exhausting His explanation of how the revealed Word functions to form the warp and woof of the tapestry of our collective history on this planet. Indeed, it is said that when the great Bahá'í scholar Mírzá Abu'l-Fadl passed away, it was discovered that he had written in his copy of this work, "Am now reading for 29ᵗʰ time—there is still so much to learn."*

I do not think this is hyperbole because, in my own experience, I have discovered within the pages of this work—second in importance only to Bahá'u'lláh's Most Holy Book, the Kitáb-i-Aqdas—that with every reading, an entirely new work seems to appear. Furthermore, this statement follows logically from our previously noted hermeneutical principle no. 5 from Lample's list, that the "meaning of the Book cannot be exhausted." In addition, as the Kitáb-i-Íqán is Bahá'u'lláh's principal doctrinal work, each new reading does indeed provide an entirely new experience, not because the words have changed, but because the reader has.

Now that we have laid a proper foundation about the Word and how this most subtle of creations links the two expressions of reality together,** we can reap the rewards of this preparation by glimpsing how the Word weaves together the fabric of our collective history and portends the joyful future that awaits us.

The Loom as Framework of Reality

My persistence in resorting to the metaphors of stitching, knitting, and weaving to portray the effects of the revealed Word in the process of creation will, with these last three chapters, come to what I hope will be a fulfilling and useful conclusion. What I think we will be better able to behold is a view of history—past, present,

---

* There is no source for this story; it had been recounted to me during my pilgrimage in 1972.

** The two with which we are presently familiar. This is not to say that there may not be others that we will come to understand, as well as countless others that will ever remain beyond our reckoning.

and future—as a magnificent panorama purposefully wrought by the Creator as He employs the Manifestations as His Craftsmen to manifest in social form the vision of His celestial kingdom.

By the time we are done, we should be able to glimpse the perfect ingenuity in a design that could derive solely from these perfect Artisans Who, rather than improvising as They go, operate as a fully coordinated and collaborative team following precisely the framework of reality as expressed in the Eternal Covenant, the loom upon which the tapestry of human history is woven.* In this context, three further lessons about how the divine plan is integral to the progress of human history will perhaps help us understand and appreciate how our present history is gradually, mysteriously, but irresistibly moving toward its predestined consummation.

The first of these lessons, which we will attempt to outline in this present chapter, concerns the warp of the tapestry, the sturdy vertical strands upon which the multicolored threads of the woof are woven. In this extended analogy, the vertical strands of the warp will represent the Dispensations, together with the laws and guidance each Manifestation reveals.

The second lesson (the subject of chapter 11) concerns the proof referred to by Bahá'u'lláh as the constancy of the Manifestations in the face of adversity. This is possibly the most obvious and accessible historical authentication that the Prophets have no ulterior motive. Of course, our knowledge of Their history is also part of the Word, the accounts of what They endure as recorded in the sacred texts. For however humble and forbearing They may be, the Manifestations forthrightly proclaim Their station and hardily defend this proclamation against even the most vehement detractors.

---

* This would be a good point in the discourse for the reader to refer to the Glossary and read the definitions of "Major Plan of God," "Everlasting or Eternal Covenant," "Greater Covenant," "Lesser Covenant," and "Divine Plan."

Finally, in chapter 12, we will examine what I describe metaphorically as the woof or horizontal threads that constitute the ongoing themes which unite the successive Revelations.

The Dispensations as the Warp of the Eternal Covenant

Each Manifestation establishes His own Covenant with His followers. Foremost in this agreement is the twofold obligation cited by Bahá'u'lláh in the first paragraph of His book of laws, the Kitáb-i-Aqdas. The first of these duties is recognition of the Manifestation: "The first duty prescribed by God for His servants is the recognition of Him Who is the Dayspring of His Revelation and the Fountain of His laws." The second is to be obedient to those laws: "It behooveth every one who reacheth this most sublime station, this summit of transcendent glory, to observe every ordinance of Him Who is the Desire of the world."[1]

These laws usually contain a code of social conduct stressing justice for all, the integration of various forms of worship and religious ceremony or commemorations, and some form of guidance regarding the next Manifestation in relation to the abiding plan of God in history. This latter aspect is known, in Bahá'í terminology, as the Greater Covenant "which every Manifestation of God makes with His followers, promising that in the fullness of time a new Manifestation will be sent, and taking from them the undertaking to accept Him when this occurs." In addition, there is a "Lesser Covenant that a Manifestation of God makes with His followers that they will accept His appointed successor after Him."[2]

For practical purposes, I have confined this overview of history to the five Abrahamic Dispensations (Judaism, Christianity, Islam, the Bábí Faith, and the Bahá'í Faith) because we have been discussing them more extensively. In the following graph you will find two symbols from chapter 9: the sinus wave (Figure 19) indicating the stages of ascent and decline of each Revelation, and the "stitching"

(Figure 20) that binds these Revelations together. Each of the five religions thus represents the warp on the loom of the Eternal Covenant God made with humanity.

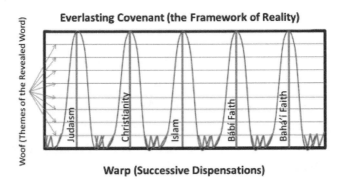

Figure 21. Successive Dispensations on the Loom of
the Everlasting or Eternal Covenant

What I have tried to emphasize in this symbolic portrayal is what we will demonstrate about the warp and the woof of this collective endeavor—that language, and more particularly the Word or the Book revealed by God to man through the Intermediaries of the Manifestations, constitutes the entire arrangement of loom as framework, Covenants (Greater and Lesser) as mainstays of each Dispensation, and the unified themes woven throughout the fabric in ever more rich and varied color and design.

Without stretching the analogy beyond its usefulness, then, we can think of words as the threads that emanate from the Prophets whereby They establish the Covenant and provide the material for weaving these themes* throughout human history to produce an ever more beauteous and coherent tapestry. In more realistic terms, however, we ourselves are the laborers at the loom of history, fol-

---

* These themes, the fundamental verities revealed by the Manifestations, are the subject of chapter 12.

lowing the guidance of the Master Weaver, working one thread at a time from age to age. And while we are not completely aware of what the tapestry will look like after our part is done, the Manifestations assure us that it will be an artful and majestic rendering of the celestial realm expressed as perfectly as ineffable forms and relationships can be portrayed with a material medium.

Of course, we also come to appreciate that the purpose of this project is to educate and unify us as we contribute our part to the artful labors of all those in the past who helped entwine the threads of unity, even as we prepare the way for those workers who will follow in our footsteps. And as we pursue our personal assignment in this undertaking, we need to keep in mind that this project is not simply a tribute to the Creator or His Manifestations—though when accomplished in the right spirit, it is work done for love of the Beauty of the Beloved. This collaborative effort of fashioning the "New Jerusalem," this heavenly kingdom manifest in material form, is the most sublime and efficacious means by which we attain both the "ineffable destiny" of humanity and our own personal advancement.[3]

Reiteration of Spiritual Verities

Spiritual verities, such as kindness, justice, love, and truthfulness, do not change over time—a good person from one era is fundamentally the same as a good person from another. But how these virtues can be implemented in personal and collective practices does change as society evolves, as our individual and collective understanding of these attributes increases, and as the advances in social awareness enable us to express these qualities in a more inclusive and complex manner. Consequently, each Manifestation brings essentially the same truth and spiritual guidance, but over time this guidance must be restated in language befitting a changed civilization, with its new opportunities and challenging exigencies.

Our insight into what constitutes the "good" human being also needs to be explained ever more expansively and completely to meet the more advanced capacity of human society.

Here again, it is important to note the power, flexibility, and infinite variability of language as the conduit by which spiritual concepts and abstract ideas can be transmitted from the divine realm to the minds of human beings. We benefit from remembering that the revealed Word is the crucial source of, and foundation for, this process through which the Manifestation is able to frame His guidance to adequately accommodate the period of time (the "Day" or era) in which His religion will be the principal means for enlightening and uplifting human civilization.

For example, in addition to presenting the concept of spirituality in terms of comprehensible attributes, the revealed Word also sets forth laws that establish for each age those practices best suited to accomplish several important tasks. These may range from a daily regimen of personal conduct to broad and comprehensive objectives about how to establish justice, harmony, and peaceful relationships both within and without the religious community.

In the Hidden Words, His first major work, Bahá'u'lláh articulates the spiritual virtues incumbent upon His followers for this age. But in His own preface to this work, He states that these jewel-like utterances constitute a synthesis of *all* the spiritual teachings that have been conveyed by every previous Revelation. While Bahá'u'lláh went on to reveal hundreds of other works, there is a logical shape to His ministry as indicated by the subjects treated in each. From this perspective, we might well consider the Hidden Words as a sort of review of all that has been previously taught combined with a poetic rendering of the foundational virtues and qualities that must needs be manifest by those who will carry out the plan for global unity He will subsequently outline in His other works.

The Evolving Laws for Human Reformation and Advancement

As we have noted, the laws and the administrative organization revealed by the Manifestations are an inseparable and integral part of His Revelation. Indeed, because the laws about personal behavior and collective social organization update how best to manifest spiritual principles in physical form, they are the means by which the power and meaning of the spiritual principles the Manifestation has set forth are canalized into private and public—individual and collective—patterns of action.

It is precisely in this context that Bahá'u'lláh, at the very beginning of the Kitáb-i-Aqdas, states that our obligations to recognize the Manifestation and "to observe every ordinance" He has mandated for our spiritual conduct are reciprocal and inseparable: "These twin duties are inseparable. Neither is acceptable without the other."[4] We might find it useful, in our examination of the language of laws designed to advance human spirituality, to keep this axiomatic principle in mind.

JUDAISM

While the rationale for many of the changes a new Manifestation introduces may be obvious and quite logical, the wisdom of other mandates may not be. Moses ordained dietary laws that, at first, may have seemed arbitrary. If His followers adhered to these laws, they probably did so out of a basic "fear of God" and their conviction that because Moses had conversed with God, He spoke with authority as God's Emissary.

Of course, the laws of Judaism are plentiful, some of which are indeed believed to have been revealed by Moses as recounted in the Pentateuch. But after Moses, manmade strictures began to be added and collected. In fact, as is commonly known, by the advent of Christ, Judaism was notoriously legalistic, something

Christ Himself decried and demonstrated when, according to the viewpoint of the Pharisees, He violated the law of the Sabbath by healing a suppliant.

Christ and His followers gradually relaxed the stranglehold of those laws and eliminated the ones that the Apostles, especially Paul, considered no longer appropriate—the constraints of circumcision and some of the dietary laws, for example.

Thus, while Moses had introduced those laws and ordinances geared to the exigencies of His "Day," the spiritual principles underlying those laws were eventually forgotten or neglected. Likewise, the ultimate goal of creating a just community focused on the worship of the One True God became subordinated to a plethora of hollow forms and rituals.

CHRISTIANITY

Christ revealed relatively few laws, possibly because His religion evolved within the context of a relatively civilized and codified environment—the rule of the Roman Empire.

He did abolish or change and refine some Judaic laws—the law of divorce and the notion of retributory response to injustice, for example—but He did not give His reasons for doing so. From the perspective of the Judaic clerics, He broke the law of the Sabbath, and yet, in fact, Christ exalted the concept of law and the need to be obedient to it. He especially cautioned His followers that law as an essential part of the spiritual life would never change, a concept that future antinomian misreading of Pauline letters would obfuscate:* "Think not that I have come to abolish the law and the

---

* "Anti-law" passages in Paul have been interpreted by many as meaning that one's actions bear no relationship to one's spiritual condition, especially as regards the concept of salvation. In some passages Paul seems to indicate that one is "saved" or "justified" by faith alone, and not by one's earthly performance.

prophets; I have come not to abolish them but to fulfil them. For truly, I say to you, till heaven and earth pass away, not an iota, not a dot, will pass from the law until all is accomplished. Whoever then relaxes one of the least of these commandments and teaches men so, shall be called least in the kingdom of heaven; but he who does them and teaches them shall be called great in the kingdom of heaven."[5] Christianity thus contains a fairly brief collection of laws. They appear most notably in chapters 5 through 7 in Matthew, though most Protestant sects or denominations contend that Christ left few explicit laws because, they came to believe, one of Christ's purposes was to shatter the legalistic approach to spirituality that had come to dominate the outworn and needless rigor of Judaism.

Nevertheless, Christ concludes His revelation of laws with the strict admonition that those who have heard His articulation of these strictures and neglect to obey them are not truly His followers. This verity is precisely the same one that Bahá'u'lláh seems to convey: "O Son of Spirit! Know thou of a truth: He that biddeth men be just and himself committeth iniquity is not of Me, even though he bear My name."[6]

ISLAM

The Qur'án, though not organized according to topic or category, contains an abundance of laws, admonitions, and personal guidance scattered throughout. The Sharia law is a collection of these laws, plus guidance implicit in the Sunnah, or pattern of life Muhammad led, together with other laws added later by what Muslims consider authoritative clerics. However, the compilation of laws that is the Sharia, together with their interpretation and application, should not be considered in its entirety as the infallible Word of God delivered to humankind by Muhammad or by any sources authoritatively designated by the Prophet. Furthermore, Sharia law has, over the centuries, been applied differently according to sect, culture, and secular governance.

THE BÁBÍ FAITH

The Báb revealed a complex array of laws. We need not discuss them at length because so much of His design for His Faith, especially the plenitude of stringent laws He revealed in the Persian Bayán, never had an opportunity to become enacted, and clearly He foreknew such would be the case. Indeed, the Báb requested that His successor (Him Whom God shall manifest, Bahá'u'lláh) delay revealing Himself as an expression of love for the all the followers of the Báb who had not yet been able to benefit from His teachings: "Shouldst Thou dismiss the entire company of the followers of the Bayán in the Day of the Latter Resurrection by a mere sign of Thy finger even while still a suckling babe, Thou wouldst indeed be praised in Thy indication. And though no doubt is there about it, do Thou grant a respite of nineteen years as a token of Thy favor so that those who have embraced this Cause may be graciously rewarded by Thee."[7]

The Báb had foretold that His Dispensation would last only nine years, as in fact it did (1844–1853). And so it was that Bahá'u'lláh, though having begun to receive His Revelation during the fall of 1852 during His incarceration in the Siyáh-Chál, did not openly proclaim His station as "Him Whom God shall manifest" until the year nineteen of the Bábí Dispensation (1863). He thereby complied with the Báb's request, having in the meantime assisted in transcribing the writings of the Báb and having led the Bábí community as best He could from His place of exile in Baghdad.

It should be further noted that, according to Shoghi Effendi, the elaborate and stringent laws and guidance set forth in the Persian Bayán were never supposed to actually become realized and institutionalized. Nevertheless, the Báb had accomplished His intended break with the Islamic past and prepared the way for the advent of the "Latter Resurrection":

> The laws which were designed, on the one hand, to abolish at a stroke the privileges and ceremonials, the ordinances and institutions of a superannuated Dispensation, and to bridge, on the other, the gap between an obsolete system and the institutions of a world-encompassing Order destined to supersede it, had been clearly formulated and proclaimed. The Covenant which, despite the determined assaults launched against it, succeeded, unlike all previous Dispensations, in preserving the integrity of the Faith of its Author, and in paving the way for the advent of the One Who was to be its Center and Object, had been firmly and irrevocably established.[8]

The Bahá'í Faith

The foundational laws of the Bahá'í Faith are contained in Bahá'u'lláh's Most Holy Book, the Kitáb-i-Aqdas—a relatively brief work, but one replete with guidance that spans every aspect of religious concern, from matters of individual hygiene and comportment to the blueprint for establishing a world commonwealth of nations. Because the structure of the work is more poetic than linear, the laws themselves are scattered like jewels among His various commentaries about society and the human condition.

Fortunately for the student of Bahá'í law, Shoghi Effendi made it a prerequisite for the translation of this work into English from Arabic that a codification of these laws be devised and that the translation be "copiously annotated."[9] Furthermore, the English translation contains a translation of Questions and Answers, a collection of Bahá'u'lláh's responses to question put to Him about specific laws. In its introduction to this translation, the Universal

House of Justice makes the following observation about the most general categories of guidance in this momentous and seminal work:*

> As to the laws themselves, a careful scrutiny discloses that they govern three areas: the individual's relationship to God, physical and spiritual matters which benefit the individual directly, and relations among individuals and between the individual and society. They can be grouped under the following headings: prayer and fasting; laws of personal status governing marriage, divorce and inheritance; a range of other laws, ordinances and prohibitions, as well as exhortations; and the abrogation of specific laws and ordinances of previous Dispensations. A salient characteristic is their brevity. They constitute the kernel of a vast range of law that will arise in centuries to come. This elaboration of the law will be enacted by the Universal House of Justice under the authority conferred upon it by Bahá'u'lláh Himself.[10]

As with the teachings of Moses, Muhammad, and the Báb, the laws of the Bahá'í Faith contain no rigid distinction between the spiritual and the social, or between private and public virtue. The sacred and the secular are thoroughly harmonized, reconciled, and integrated in the Bahá'í teachings. Doubtless this lack of a significant distinction between our obligation to be obedient to civil ordinances and spiritual guidance foreshadows the Bahá'í vision of a world commonwealth in which universally accepted spiritual

---

* These laws are momentous because, unlike the laws penned by the Báb, these laws will actually be enacted, and they are "seminal" because Bahá'u'lláh designs an institution which will use this foundation as "the kernel of a vast range of law that will arise in centuries to come."

principles establish the foundational means by which our diverse global community can become a single collaborative and cohesive neighborhood.

Social Organization and Religious Administration

A third aspect of the guidance provided by the Word of each Manifestation concerns the social order best suited for developing a community life that is safe, just, harmonious, and unified—in other words, the ideal environment for human progress of every sort (mental, spiritual, and physical). As Shoghi Effendi notes, we can discern in retrospect how successive Manifestations guided us through ever more expansive and complex social forms, and as society progressed and human knowledge developed, the enlightenment of the Revelations became increasingly more wide-ranging and complete:

> . . . the discord and separation of the children of men will have given way to the worldwide reconciliation, and the complete unification of the divers elements that constitute human society.
>
> This will indeed be the fitting climax of that process of integration which, starting with the family, the smallest unit in the scale of human organization, must, after having called successively into being the tribe, the city-state, and the nation, continue to operate until it culminates in the unification of the whole world, the final object and the crowning glory of human evolution on this planet.
>
> Just as the organic evolution of mankind has been slow and gradual, and involved successively the unification of the family, the tribe, the city-state, and the nation, so has the light vouchsafed by the Revelation of God, at various stages in the evolution of religion, and reflected in the successive Dispen-

sations of the past, been slow and progressive. Indeed the measure of Divine Revelation, in every age, has been adapted to, and commensurate with, the degree of social progress achieved in that age by a constantly evolving humanity.[11]

Even though the Bahá'í teachings affirm that we are attaining in this present age the stage of maturity of human society and will accordingly develop and implement a global commonwealth and infrastructure capable of ministering to this long-awaited stage, we know that there remains an incalculable amount to learn—knowledge and practices that future Manifestations will reveal and include as part of Their own Revelations: "It hath been decreed by Us," explains Bahá'u'lláh, "that the Word of God, and all the potentialities thereof, shall be manifested unto men in strict conformity with such conditions as have been foreordained by Him Who is the All-Knowing, the All-Wise. . . . Should the Word be allowed to release suddenly all the energies latent within it, no man could sustain the weight of so mighty a Revelation."[12]

One of the main intents of every Manifestation—and the central component of each Dispensation—is that the religion become a source of unity and social order for the community at large, and not solely for the body of believers. Consequently, it would be helpful to recite examples from these same five religions of how carefully concepts of social structure are integrated with spiritual concepts and practices.

JUDAISM

Certainly we observe how Moses viewed His mission to educate a people of former slaves as a method for creating a just tribal society. Indeed, it has been argued—correctly, I am inclined to believe—that the forty years spent wandering in the desert were, in fact, a period of training these unlearned people, who had never known

271

any form of self-governance, in how to establish the foundational ingredients of a social order wherever they might find themselves.

It is in this sense, I feel, that Moses did not get to observe His people establish their stable government in the land of Canaan not because He was being punished but because—according to the plan of God and the wisdom of Moses—His people, having been arduously and meticulously trained and tested about the inextricable relationship between their spiritual beliefs and the establishment of a just social system, would now be tested to see if they could fulfill the objective which God had entrusted to them through their tireless, infallible, and exemplary Teacher.

CHRISTIANITY

Christianity presents us with a problem in regard to this aspect of its teachings. Christ admonishes His disciples to go and spread His teachings to the entire world. However, He does not prescribe any particular methodology for doing this, other than the example of His own teaching. Neither does He leave to His disciples, as far as we know, any explicit plan about how to organize the religion itself or what practices should be required for those who claim allegiance to the Christian cause: "Not one of the sacraments of the Church; not one of the rites and ceremonies which the Christian Fathers have elaborately devised and ostentatiously observed; not one of the elements of the severe discipline they rigorously imposed upon the primitive Christians; none of these reposed on the direct authority of Christ, or emanated from His specific utterances. Not one of these did Christ conceive, none did He specifically invest with sufficient authority to either interpret His Word, or to add to what He had not specifically enjoined." The result was that the early days of Christianity saw heated debates among the disciples about which of the Judaic laws should be retained and which should be abolished. Likewise, while some believed Christ indicated that

Peter would be the head of His Church (Matthew 16:17–18), it is Paul who seemed to take the lead in spreading Christianity. Shoghi Effendi notes that, "[t]heir contention centered around the fact that the vague and inconclusive words, addressed by Christ to Peter, 'Thou art Peter, and upon this rock I will build my Church,' could never justify the extreme measures, the elaborate ceremonials, the fettering creeds and dogmas, with which His successors have gradually burdened and obscured His Faith."[13]

Ultimately, after Christianity became the state religion under Constantine, there emerged a sort of temporary alliance of church and state, but this merging occurred in the fourth century, near the end of the Roman Empire. Beginning in the fifth century, the empire was shattered by tribal migrations and invasions—a period previously designated as the "Dark Ages"*—that effectively ended the Roman Empire. But the confluence of Roman rule with Christianity was hardly the cause of the religion's decline. The administrative order that emerged in the Christian Church prior to the onset of the Dark Ages endured strife among its principal leaders as early as the fourth century. These disputes concerned crucial theological issues, such as the station of Christ and the relationship of Christianity to previous religions, and they eventually resulted in schisms such as the split with the Eastern Church.

In short, there never was one unified administrative order for the Christian religion that endured without controversy or animated dissension regarding doctrine. It is probably for this reason that Christ's promised Comforter (Muhammad) arrived as early as the seventh century.

---

* A darkness now largely regarded as the modern ignorance about the rich culture that many of these tribal societies brought with them and from which emerged such noble governmental enterprises as the reign of Alfred the Great (ninth century in England) and Charlemagne (eighth century in France).

ISLAM

As ample and complete as the Qur'án is in its guidance, and as creatively and ingeniously Muhammad taught His followers how to unify diverse, disunited, and warring tribal peoples, the administrative order of Islam was effectively divided at the death of the Prophet. Of course, the immense and propitious influence of Islam, like that of Christianity, brought into being incredible advances in secular learning, as well as concepts of the Oneness of God, and, even more weighty, the notion of Revelation as a continuous force underlying the whole of human history. In fact, the Bahá'í writings state that it was this influence, especially in places such as Córdoba, Spain, where milestones in learning took place, that brought about the Renaissance in Europe. As a replica of the type of community Muhammad had modeled, during the tenth century of al-Andalus civilization, a vast library was assembled—the library of Al-Ḥakam II, which contained almost half a million volumes.

The seeds of Islam's administrative destruction were planted at the Prophet's death. And while there still remains dispute about how the schism between Sh*í*'ih and Sunní Islam occurred, the Bahá'í texts accord with the Sh*í*'ih version of this unfortunate but doubtless foreordained breaching of Muhammad's Covenant.

According to a tradition accepted by Sunnis and Sh*í*'ih alike, Muhammad stated that He left as guidance for His followers "two weighty things": "Muhammad, Himself, as the end of His mission drew nigh, spoke these words: 'Verily, I leave amongst you My twin weighty testimonies: The Book of God and My Family.'"[14] The first weighty thing (the Book being, of course, the Qur'án) contains a great deal of guidance and laws that could be codified into categories, even as has been done with the Kitáb-i-Aqdas.

By "family," Muhammad was referring to His progeny, designating 'Alí (His son-in-law and first cousin) as the first leader, or

Imam, with the understanding that 'Alí's first male lineal descendants would succeed him. This second weighty thing was lost immediately upon Muhammad's passing and resulted in the grievous schism that undermined the full force of what Islam could have accomplished—even though its bountiful influence spread widely and rapidly. The creation of an elected Caliphate not only split Islam, but also deprived it of the authoritative interpretation of law and text that could have been derived from 'Alí and his successors had they been recognized and their guidance safeguarded and implemented.

From both the Shí'ih and Bahá'í perspective, therefore, a significant part of the Covenant of Muhammad was thus lost or diverted, in part because it was not written down. According to Shí'ih belief, Muhammad on His deathbed called for pen and paper that He might write down these final instructions, but His request was denied by those who wished to seize power for themselves. Thus, while 'Alí was assisting in the preparation of Muhammad's body for burial in another chamber, Umar nominated Abu Bakr as the first Caliph, even though others reminded them that Muhammad had verbally designated 'Alí to be His successor.

In spite of this perversion of what seems to have been the Prophet's intended course for the administrative institution of the religion, Islam exerted an extremely important influence on the advancement of civilization, achieving what is widely acknowledged as its "Golden Age" from the eighth to the thirteenth centuries. But because of the initial schism at the death of Muhammad, the full efflorescence that the religion might have attained was cut short and its unity supplanted by the ceaseless sectarian warfare between the Shí'ih and the Sunní branches. Likewise, what synthesis has occurred between the religion and governance has largely degenerated into tyrannical theocracies upheld by Sharia law, which is composed of substantially improvised or manmade

275

additions to the letter and intent of Qur'ánic law, and literalist misinterpretations and inappropriate applications of the Word itself.

THE BÁBÍ FAITH

Though the Báb is an independent Manifestation in His own right, He considered the principal purpose of His brief Dispensation to prepare the peoples of the world for what He termed the "Latter Resurrection" that would be ushered in by a second Manifestation ("Him Whom God shall make manifest") in the year nineteen of His Dispensation.[15] Therefore, even though He revealed a complex and strict compendium of explicit laws, He considered Himself primarily as the Herald of Bahá'u'lláh, Whose purpose it would be to bring about the long-awaited "Day of Days" when the earth would become one country and would establish a universal and lasting peace. Consequently, He did little by way of designing a religious institution. In this context, it is entirely appropriate to consider the Báb and Bahá'u'lláh as "twin Manifestations," and Their Revelations as one integrated plan. It is for this reason that the Bahá'í Faith dates its beginning with the Báb's declaration of His mission to Mullá Husayn on May 23, 1844.

To vindicate this approach to the religious organization that is the present-day Bahá'í Faith, we need to review briefly the sequence of events and, more importantly, the authoritative documents (the Word) that link together the Cord that is the Covenant of Bahá'u'lláh: "Cling thou to the hem of the Robe of God, and take thou firm hold on His Cord, a Cord which none can sever. Beware that the clamor of them that have repudiated this Most Great Announcement shall not deter thee from achieving thy purpose. Proclaim what hath been prescribed unto thee in this Tablet, though all the peoples arise and oppose thee. Thy Lord is, verily, the All-Compelling, the Unfailing Protector."[16]

At each transition in the succession of authority throughout the evolution of the Bahá'í administrative order, the mettle and logic of the language in the critical documents that bind these links together has been contested, and every time several followers faltered in their allegiance, but the administrative order was able to withstand these assaults and remain secure and inviolable.

It is clear that the Báb was aware that the One Whose advent He foretold was Bahá'u'lláh. Shoghi Effendi mentions that the two Manifestations were in constant communication prior to Bahá'u'lláh's strategic arrangement of the Conference of Badasht:* "Bahá'u'lláh, maintaining through continual correspondence close contact with the Báb, and Himself the directing force behind the manifold activities of His struggling fellow-disciples, unobtrusively yet effectually presided over that conference, and guided and controlled its proceedings."[17]

Another piece of historical evidence of the Báb's designation of Bahá'u'lláh as the Promised Qayyúm for Whom the Báb was both the Qá'im and the "Gate" occurs on the occasion of the execution of the Báb. Though He had designated Bahá'u'lláh's half-brother Mírzá Yahyá as the one whose job it was to secure the Bábí Faith until the appearance of Him Whom God will manifest, the Báb had mandated that crucial documents, His seal rings, and a most telling scroll He had written be conveyed to Bahá'u'lláh:

It was to the date of His impending Revelation that the Lawh-i-Hurúfat, revealed in Chihríq by the Báb, in honor

---

* "The Báb called a gathering of eighty-one of His followers in the early summer of 1848 in the hamlet of Badasht. The primary purpose of the conference was 'to implement the revelation of the Bayán by a sudden, a complete and dramatic break with the past—with its order, its ecclesiasticism, its traditions, and ceremonials'" (Momen, *A Basic Bahá'í Dictionary*, p. 31).

of Dayyán, abstrusely alluded, and in which the mystery of the "Mustaghát̲h̲" was unraveled. It was to the attainment of His presence that the attention of another disciple, Mullá Báqir, one of the Letters of the Living, was expressly directed by none other than the Báb Himself. It was exclusively to His care that the documents of the Báb, His pen-case, His seals, and agate rings, together with a scroll on which He had penned, in the form of a pentacle, no less than three hundred and sixty derivatives of the word Bahá, were delivered, in conformity with instructions He Himself had issued prior to His departure from C̲h̲ihríq.[18]

This may be considered implicit evidence of the Báb's designation of Bahá'u'lláh as the Manifestation for Whom He was the Herald, but through a study of the Báb's Dispensation we can discern other allusions to Bahá'u'lláh as "Him Whom God shall make manifest."

The first of these regards the laws of the Báb. The Persian Bayan* includes an immense collection of explicit, stringent, and astounding requirements for His followers. The Báb well knew that, because His Dispensation was destined to endure no more than nineteen years, it would be impossible for all the teachings in His book to be widely copied and disseminated—let alone discussed, practiced, and enforced.

While some scholars assume that this fact meant that the Dispensation of the Báb must have been intended to endure and His laws to be effected over the coming centuries—that the Qayyúm, therefore, would not appear for some time to come—Shoghi Effendi makes clear that the Persian Bayán and the laws it contain had two main goals.

---

* Composed in 1847, while the Báb was imprisoned at Máh-Kú, this book is the principal repository of His laws.

First, this compendium of radical change symbolized a dramatic, emphatic, and shocking break with the past. As the Bábís at the conference at Bada<u>sh</u>t concluded—with the guidance of Bahá'u'lláh—the Bábí Faith was not a reform movement within Islam, but the first of the two trumpet calls alluded to in the Qur'án. This first call would dumbfound and dismay the peoples of the world, and the second would awaken and bring together (resurrect) humankind and fashion a global commonwealth:

> This Book at once abrogated the laws and ceremonials enjoined by the Qur'án regarding prayer, fasting, marriage, divorce and inheritance, and upheld, in its integrity, the belief in the prophetic mission of Muhammad, even as the Prophet of Islam before Him had annulled the ordinances of the Gospel and yet recognized the Divine origin of the Faith of Jesus Christ. It moreover interpreted in a masterly fashion the meaning of certain terms frequently occurring in the sacred Books of previous Dispensations such as Paradise, Hell, Death, Resurrection, the Return, the Balance, the Hour, the Last Judgment, and the like. Designedly severe in the rules and regulations it imposed, revolutionizing in the principles it instilled, calculated to awaken from their age-long torpor the clergy and the people, and to administer a sudden and fatal blow to obsolete and corrupt institutions, it proclaimed, through its drastic provisions, the advent of the anticipated Day, the Day when "the Summoner shall summon to a stern business," when He will "demolish whatever hath been before Him, even as the Apostle of God demolished the ways of those that preceded Him."[19]

The second goal was much more explicit. In His Persian Bayán, the Báb openly directed the believers' attention to Bahá'u'lláh.

Shoghi Effendi states that this declaration "deserves to rank as one of the most significant statements recorded in any of the Báb's writings": "'Well is it with him,' is His prophetic announcement, 'who fixeth his gaze upon the Order of Bahá'u'lláh, and rendereth thanks unto his Lord. For He will assuredly be made manifest. God hath indeed irrevocably ordained it in the Bayán.'"[20]

THE BAHÁ'Í FAITH

There are several detailed documents that authoritatively forge the links between each successive stage in Bahá'u'lláh's evolving World Order. All we need to do here is note the major points of transition and the revealed documents that navigate those transitions.

First is Bahá'u'lláh's own precise appointment of His son 'Abdu'l-Bahá as His successor. In the brief Book of the Covenant (the Kitáb-i-'Ahd), Bahá'u'lláh confers a specific station and several powers on His "Most Great Branch," among which is conferred infallibility, both in regard to His guidance of the religion and in His interpretation of the revealed Word of Bahá'u'lláh. He also designates 'Abdu'l-Bahá as the "Mystery of God," in part because, unique in the annals of religious history, 'Abdu'l-Bahá was, like his Father, the perfect exemplar of the Bahá'í teachings, even though he was a mortal human being and not a Manifestation of God.[21]

In addition to beginning the construction of the worldwide Bahá'í community during the remainder of His life, 'Abdu'l-Bahá wrote a remarkable Will and Testament in which He created or clarified the establishment of a number of innovative and essential parts of the Bahá'í institutions. First and foremost, he appointed his eldest grandson, Shoghi Effendi, as Guardian, a position antici-pated by Bahá'u'lláh and discussed in detail in this same document by 'Abdu'l-Bahá. Second, 'Abdu'l-Bahá conferred infallibility upon the Guardian with regard both to his guidance of the Bahá'í Faith and to his capacity to render infallible interpretations of the sacred and authoritative texts. In this same crucial document, 'Abdu'l-Bahá empowered the Guardian to appoint Hands of the Cause to assist Him and the Bahá'í community at large. He also established intermediary elected administrative institutions, Secondary Houses of Justice (the present-day National Spiritual Assemblies) and designated them as the electors of the Universal House of Justice. 'Abdu'l-Bahá also delineated the powers of each of these institutions, defined the method of elections for each of the three levels of administrative bodies, clarified the relationship between the Guardianship and the Universal House of Justice, and delineated the powers and authority of this Supreme Institution of the Bahá'í Faith.

Suffice it to say that all the guidance in the authoritative text of this critical document has been effected precisely according to 'Abdu'l-Bahá's design so that now every institution he ordained has been established. The physical structure of the World Centre of the Bahá'í religion now stands resplendent atop Mt. Carmel in Haifa, Israel, and the Faith itself, in little more than a century and a half, has become the second most widespread religion in the world.

A Glimpse of the Future

To conclude our review of how the Word revealed by the Manifestations establishes through Their own Covenants the institutions and principles for social advancement, let us consider briefly the overall vision of the future revealed by Bahá'u'lláh.

As we have mentioned numerous times, Bahá'u'lláh discusses throughout His writings that the "Promised Day" has come in which humanity will collaborate to fashion a global commonwealth. While the details of how this structure will emerge and evolve are discussed fully by Shoghi Effendi in *The World Order of*

Bahá'u'lláh, *The Advent of Divine Justice*, and various other works by him and by the Universal House of Justice, we can effectively summarize this vision by noting how it combines the most salient and efficacious features of all the major systems of governance without being a replica of any one of them.

In the new World Order, there will be no individuals of authority because all governance will be conducted by institutions elected through universal suffrage. The three-tiered hierarchy of this system—the local, the secondary or national, and the international—while provided with a superstructure, will maximize the autonomy of governance at the national or territorial level, as well as at the local level. It will be based upon the spiritual principles articulated by Bahá'u'lláh for this Dispensation, yet it will not take on the unsavory features that have characterized theocracies—primarily because Bahá'u'lláh has abolished the priesthood and the authority of clerics or scholars to make or enforce law.

The most accurate and insightful discussions of this future world polity are found in the statements by the Guardian and the House of Justice. These institutions provide us with a valuable glimpse of how this global system will safeguard world resources, deter wars among nations, yet maximize and secure individual rights and freedoms. It is also crucial to note that the most faithful vision of that future administrative order can best be discerned in the present-day worldwide Bahá'í administration, based entirely as it is on the blueprint designed by Bahá'u'lláh:

> The Bahá'í Commonwealth of the future, of which this vast Administrative Order is the sole framework, is, both in theory and practice, not only unique in the entire history of political institutions, but can find no parallel in the annals of any of the world's recognized religious systems. No form of democratic government; no system of autocracy or of dic-

tatorship, whether monarchical or republican; no intermediary scheme of a purely aristocratic order; nor even any of
the recognized types of theocracy, whether it be the Hebrew
Commonwealth, or the various Christian ecclesiastical organizations, or the Imamate or the Caliphate in Islam—none of
these can be identified or be said to conform with the Administrative Order which the master-hand of its perfect Architect
has fashioned.[22]

The institutions of the present-day Bahá'í Administrative
Order, which constitute the "structural basis" of Bahá'u'lláh's
World Order, will mature and evolve into the Bahá'í World
Commonwealth. In this regard, Shoghi Effendi affirms that
the Administrative Order "will, as its component parts, its
organic institutions, begin to function with efficiency and
vigour, assert its claim and demonstrate its capacity to be
regarded not only as the nucleus but the very pattern of the
New World Order destined to embrace in the fullness of time
the whole of mankind."[23]

- 11 -

THE PROPHET'S CONSTANCY
IN REVEALING THE WORD

Though young and tender of age, and though the Cause He
revealed was contrary to the desire of all the peoples of earth,
both high and low, rich and poor, exalted and abased, king
and subject, yet He arose and steadfastly proclaimed it. All
have known and heard this. He was afraid of no one; He was
regardless of consequences. Could such a thing be made manifest except through the power of a divine Revelation, and the
potency of God's invincible Will?

Bahá'u'lláh, Kitáb-i-Íqán, ¶257

We can conclude our survey of the framework that constitutes
the loom of the Eternal Covenant by alluding to what is both an
invariable proof of the Manifestations, as well as a central bulwark
of the Revelation—the constancy of the Manifestation "in proclaiming the Faith of God" in spite of incalculable tribulations,
persistent rejection, and, in some cases, martyrdom itself.

Their constancy is a major proof of Their claim to be Manifestations because it demonstrates beyond any doubt that They have

no ulterior motive for enduring the scorn and persecution of high and low alike. It is the case with each of Them that to escape from tribulation of physical and spiritual difficulties, They have only to deny Their claims and cease confronting the religious and political leaders who see Them as threats to the status quo. And yet, as Bahá'u'lláh notes about the young Báb, He was fearless, persistent, and fully aware that in the long run, He would be executed for His claim to be the Qá'im:

> To what, We wonder, do they ascribe so great a daring? Do they accuse Him of folly as they accused the Prophets of old? Or do they maintain that His motive was none other than leadership and the acquisition of earthly riches?
>
> Gracious God! In His Book, which He hath entitled "Qayyúmu'l-Asmá'," — the first, the greatest and mightiest of all books — He prophesied His own martyrdom. In it is this passage: "O thou Remnant of God! I have sacrificed myself wholly for Thee; I have accepted curses for Thy sake; and have yearned for naught but martyrdom in the path of Thy love. Sufficient Witness unto me is God, the Exalted, the Protector, the Ancient of Days!"[1]

Their determination to reject anything that would benefit Them and to pursue with unstinting courage the mission God has bestowed upon Them applies equally to every Manifestation. Furthermore, the power unleashed by Their own constancy exerts a "transmuting influence" that raises up spiritual luminaries who are capable of exemplifying a similar detachment. They become "embodiments of purity" Who exhibit "naught but true knowledge and stainless deeds," and whose ultimate reward in this life is usually to suffer "an agonizing death": "Notwithstanding all this, each of these holy beings, up to his last moment, breathed the Name of God, and soared in the realm of submission and resignation. Such was the potency and transmuting influence which He exercised over them, that they ceased to cherish any desire but His will, and wedded their soul to His remembrance." But as the foundation of Their own Covenants, the Manifestations bear witness—long after They have passed from this plane of existence—to the history of Their own constancy. It is then that the fullest expression of the power They have unleashed becomes manifest in social reformation and spiritual practices, even though after Their passing, They continue to guide and nurture humankind from the spiritual realm: ". . . the dissolution of the tabernacle wherein the soul of the Manifestation of God had chosen temporarily to abide signalized its release from the restrictions which an earthly life had, of necessity, imposed upon it. Its influence no longer circumscribed by any physical limitations, its radiance no longer beclouded by its human temple, that soul could henceforth energize the whole world to a degree unapproached at any stage in the course of its existence on this planet."[2]

Let us recall, then, some examples of how the Manifestations' persistence in proclaiming the Word and Their imperviousness to any and all affliction is manifest in Their lives. And as we do, let us consider a particularly important point that we should not allow to escape our attention. Moses was *alone* when the voice of the Holy Spirit emanated from the burning bush. Christ was *alone* during His forty days in the wilderness as Satan tried to tempt Him, even as He was on the evening prior of His arrest when He prayed to the Father, "Not my will but Thine be done." Muhammad was *alone* when the Angel Gabriel appeared to Him as the personification of the Holy Spirit, as was the Báb "when in a dream He approached the bleeding head of the Imam Husáyn, and, quaffing the blood that dripped from his lacerated throat, awoke to find Himself the chosen recipient of the outpouring grace of the Almighty." Finally, when the Maiden appeared to Bahá'u'lláh in a vision witnessed by no one else, He was awaiting execution in the stygian darkness of Tehran's Siyáh-Chál, the infamous Black Pit prison.[3]

My point is this—the only reason we know about the intimate details of these milestones in the lives of the Manifestations is that They share them with us through the Word. Consequently, we must presume that They think it important for us to know the circumstances of the first intimation They receive of Their Revelations, even as They find it important to share with us other details of about Their lives, particularly about the suffering and persecution They subsequently endure.

It would seem, therefore, that They share this information with us so that we might appreciate that Their claim to a Revelation direct from God will bring Them no earthly ascendancy but only persecution and grief. When we contemplate Their foreknowledge of what They will endure, as well as the fact that They have free will, we also come to grasp more completely that the sole motive for Their ceaseless determination to proclaim the Revelation is that They are totally dedicated to advancing the Cause of God and willing to undergo whatever sacrificial course of action is necessary to aid in the enlightenment of humankind. The following portion of a prayer by Bahá'u'lláh is but one of many passages in which the purity of the Manifestation's motives is made plain:

I swear by Thy might! Neither the hosts of the earth nor those of heaven can keep me back from revealing the things I am commanded to manifest. I have no will before Thy will, and can cherish no desire in the face of Thy desire. By Thy grace I am, at all times, ready to serve Thee and am rid of all attachment to any one except Thee.

What I desire, however, O my God, is that Thou shouldst bid me unveil the things which lie hid in Thy knowledge, so that they who are wholly devoted to Thee may, in their long-ing for Thee, soar up into the atmosphere of Thy oneness, and the infidels may be seized with trembling and may return to the nethermost fire, the abode ordained for them by Thee through the power of Thy sovereign might.[4]

While this theme could be endlessly studied and applied to the lives of the Manifestations, let it suffice for our purposes simply to review some highlights from the lives of the Founders of the five religions we have used as principal examples of how the Word of God is conveyed to us by these immaculate altruistic Emissaries.

Moses

The account of Moses' life—especially of the miracles asso-ciated with His ministry—seems to portray Him as an ordinary man placed in extraordinary circumstances, a notion contrary to 'Abdu'l-Bahá's explicit statement that the Manifestations are well aware of Their station and that no change or transformation occurs in Them. They are not ordinary humans suddenly changed into Prophets or Manifestations: "Briefly, the Manifestations of God have ever been and ever will be luminous Realities, and no change or alteration ever takes place in Their essence. At most, before Their revelation They are still and silent, like one who is asleep, and after Their revelation They are eloquent and effulgent, like one who is awake."[5]

It is unnecessary to recall here all the various miraculous episodes associated with Moses, whether we follow the account presented in the books of Exodus, Leviticus, Numbers, and Deuteronomy from the Jewish texts, or the fundamentally same story as narrated throughout the Qur'án and alluded to in Bahá'u'lláh's writings. I am inclined to refer to the Qur'án, partly because I presume it more accurate than the Old Testament, since it represents the story as told by a Manifestation of God, rather than as passed down by the tribal oral tradition until finally being transcribed, as we suppose was the case with the Pentateuch. Also, most of the allusions to Moses in the Bábí and Bahá'í religions are taken from those parts of the life of Moses that are emphasized in the Qur'án.

The life of Moses has inspired writers and artists of every sort through the ages. Indeed, it is the number and consistency of miraculous events performed by Moses that prompted some contemporary theologians to assert that the God of the Old Testament, a Being who personally intervenes in history to set things right, no longer seems to exist, or at least seems content now to leave us to our own devices.

The episodes that compose the life of Moses are no less miraculous than the most compelling adventures of modern popular culture, a reality on which Cecil B. DeMille capitalized in his 1956 movie *The Ten Commandments*. From the ingenuity of Moses' mother in arranging for Him to be raised by Pharaoh's daughter, to His first revelatory experience on Mount Sinai, to His confounding Pharaoh by turning His rod into a snake, followed by His bringing about the ten plagues, parting the Red Sea, receiving the Ten Commandments atop Mr. Sinai, then leading the Israelites in their forty years of wandering in the desert—His life sounds more like the stuff of legends and mythical heroes rather than holy scripture. Consequently, as with the story of Noah, or Jonah, or Job, we are challenged to determine how much of this story should be accepted at face value and how much should be seen as a symbolic or spiritual representation of events.

'Abdu'l-Bahá offers important insight into the miracles associated with the lives of the Manifestations, the essence of which is worth reviewing. First, He notes that because the Manifestations are not ordinary human beings but divinely empowered representatives of God, They clearly possess the power to do whatever They wish: "The Manifestations of God are sources of miraculous deeds and marvellous signs. Any difficult or impossible matter is to Them possible and permitted. For They show forth extraordinary feats through an extraordinary power, and They influence the world of nature through a power that transcends nature. From each one of Them, marvellous things have appeared."[6] However, 'Abdu'l-Bahá notes that the miraculous events associated with the lives of the Manifestations are not an important proof of Their station, nor, by implication, should we consider these events as constituting some integral part of Their Revelations, since

> in the sight of the Manifestations of God these marvels and miracles are of no importance, so much so that They do not even wish them to be mentioned. For even if these miracles were considered the greatest of proofs, they would constitute a clear evidence only for those who were present when they took place, not for those who were absent. . . .
>
> However, in the day of God's Manifestation, they that are endued with insight will find all things pertaining to Him to be miraculous. For these things are distinguished above all else, and this distinction is in itself an absolute miracle.[7]

In other words, what Moses accomplished was to lead a people out of bondage and reveal to them fundamental laws that established the foundation of what it means to be a good person, whether as a member of a family or as a citizen in a community. Then, over the course of forty years, He educated these same former slaves and trained them in the art of governance, justice, and piety. By the time He had accomplished this miraculous transformation, they were ready to cross over the Jordan River and establish a mighty nation without His physical presence, though we can assume He continued His guidance from the spiritual realm.

Finally, it must be said that all portraits of Moses, whether biblical or cinematic, miss the mark in trying accurately to render this Figure in logical terms. Indeed, such would be the failure of any depiction that ignores the special features characterizing the lives of every Manifestation. For if They are portrayed as inspired but ordinary fallible human beings, then such depictions are completely erroneous and deceiving. On the other hand, if They were to be portrayed as impervious to pain and suffering, this portraiture would be no less fallacious. Only with an understanding of the dual stations occupied by these divine Emissaries from the celestial realm can we begin to consider the nature of Their experience, and even then we have only Their own words to give us any clue as to what that experience might be. No doubt it is for this reason that Muhammad, the Báb, and Bahá'u'lláh forbade depictions of the Manifestations, whether in art or on stage.

I feel it necessary to mention this fact because even the best and most artful attempts to portray the Manifestation and what He feels or experiences are so distorted that they utterly belie a reality that is ultimately beyond our comprehension. For example, several movies about the life of Moses take one particular biblical account at face value and depict Him as becoming impatient when tapping the stone to bring forth water. He is shown temporarily disdaining piety and reverence, and because of this "mistake" on His part, Moses is prevented from going with His followers to their new homeland.[8]

And yet, as we noted early on in our discussion, God's Emissaries are always precisely aware of what They are doing, conscious of the example They are setting, and never sin or go astray in Their guidance. More to the point of this chapter, They maintain perfect constancy in revealing the word and in setting forth for Their followers an example of the perfectly lived life.

'Abdu'l-Bahá explains why some of the scriptural accounts seem to portray Them as fallible and why they seem to be attributing to the Manifestations some wrongdoing. He states that these passages are actually an indirect way of condemning the actions of the followers: "How often have the Prophets of God and His universal Manifestations confessed in Their prayers to Their sins and shortcomings! This is only to instruct other souls, to inspire and encourage them to be humble and submissive before God, and to acknowledge their own sins and shortcomings. . . . In brief, our meaning is that the rebukes recorded in the Sacred Scriptures, though outwardly addressed to the Prophets—the Manifestations of God—are in reality intended for the people. Were you to peruse the Bible, this matter would become clear and evident."[9]

Christ

The abiding theme of Christ's ministry is the importance and nature of different levels of love and the nurture and forgiveness available to the people through God the Father. In the context of this theme, Christ has been portrayed in art and even in discussions of Christology as the emblem of loving kindness, forgiveness, and compassion. He is the healer, the One Who offers Himself as a ransom for the sins of humankind. He is the gentle shepherd, the kind teacher who tells His disciples, "Let the children come to me, and do not hinder them; for to such belongs the kingdom of heaven."[10]

And yet He is also the lawgiver, a "warner" like Muhammad,* an astute debater who has little patience with hypocrisy or the dis-

---

* "We have truly sent thee as a witness, as a bringer of Glad Tidings, and as a Warner: In order that ye (o men) may believe in Allah and His Messenger, that ye may assist and honor Him, and celebrate his praises morning and evening" (Qur'án 48:8–9).

ingenuous queries of the Pharisees, Sadducees, and scribes who taunt Him with enigmatic theological questions. He is the forthright condemner of moneychangers whom He physically removes from the sacred steps of the temple. He is not hesitant to rebuke those who are more impressed with His miracles but seem oblivious to the spiritual message underlying these actions:

> "Truly, truly, I say to you, you seek me, not because you saw signs, but because you ate your fill of the loaves. Do not labor for the food which perishes, but for the food which endures to eternal life, which the Son of man will give to you, for on him has God the Father set his seal."
>
> Then they said to him, "What must we do, to be doing the works of God?"
>
> Jesus answered them, "This is the work of God, that you believe in Him whom He has sent."[11]

Of course, except for the so-called "passion of Christ"—the events surrounding His arrest, trial, and execution—the life of Christ is relatively uneventful, particularly inasmuch as His ministry is so brief. Indeed, except for miracles such as the healings, walking on the water, and raising Lazarus from the dead, there is little adventure compared to the life of Moses. What is most memorable and remarkable about His life are His words, whether in the form of challenging parables or in His ingenious responses to the taunting of those who thought their clerical learning could undo the acumen of this untutored son of a carpenter.

But what impresses the crowds as much as the sometimes enigmatic parables He tells is His conduct, as is the case with every Manifestation. Wherever They appear, the magnetism of the power and love that emanates from Them immediately begins to attract followers. At the same time, Each employs a language and manner to befit the circumstances and characteristics of the culture and the people where They appear.

In this sense, the Manifestations seem to maintain a fine balance between appearing human and thoroughly accessible, and yet unequivocally proclaiming the truth about Their station. Each Manifestation boldly asserts that to follow Him and His guidance is to follow God, and to disdain Him or ignore His admonitions is to reject God. Each also articulates the fact that all the teachings of previous Manifestations are consummated in His appearance, even as He prepares humankind for the Manifestation Who will succeed Him: "They are all the manifestation of the 'Beginning' and the 'End,' the 'First' and the 'Last,' the 'Seen' and 'Hidden'—all of which pertain to Him Who is the innermost Spirit of Spirits and eternal Essence of Essences."[12]

That the fullness of this expression is comprehended by so few of Their close followers is evidenced by the fact that most Christians focus entirely on the events surrounding Christ's martyrdom, and too few appreciate the complex moral and theological doctrine He unleashed, whether through His parables or through His explication and elucidation of Jewish scripture in His persistent allusion to verses that, without His explanations, might make little sense at all.

As we have previously noted, one of the best examples of this manner in which Christ demonstrates how His Revelation is an inextricable part of the Eternal Covenant is in His discussion about how the Jews were spared from starvation by the manna from heaven that Moses provided them in the wilderness. He explains that what saved them, and will save them still, is the spiritual nourishment God provides, not the material sustenance. And we could rehearse numerous instances where Christ responds to queries, whether from believers or those who would mock Him, to demonstrate the erudite and sometimes veiled answers in His discourse.

The point is that the collection of His utterances constitutes sophisticated theological doctrine combined with explicit guidance regarding what practices His followers should carry out to make these themes manifest in their individual and collective lives. But for the purpose of alluding to His constancy as a major ingredient in upholding His covenant, it would be a fitting conclusion for us to mention the temptation of Christ in the wilderness immediately after His anointing by John the Baptist.

Even though John Milton tried to make a minor epic of this encounter between Christ and Satan in *Paradise Regained,* there is not much tension in this largely unsuccessful work—we are never really concerned that Satan can offer Christ anything at all that would seriously tempt or deter the Son of God. But the first point for us in the context of the constancy of Christ is that we know about this temptation, and the second is that we know it is symbolic.

As we noted in our initial survey of the major axioms of Bahá'í belief, it is the Bahá'í view that the figure of Satan is a symbolic representation of our selfish and sensual desires, the temptation of the things of this world, whether they be physical possessions or fame and power. With such a view of theology, we are immediately aware that this encounter is a symbolic representation of a point in the life of Christ where He establishes once and for all that He does not have, nor will He ever have, any desire for those things that are most highly prized by ordinary human beings.

And yet, the logical possibility of temptation exists—the Manifestation has free will and, during the course of His mortal experience, He feels the same desires for food, water, and comfort that we experience. This fact is made completely clear when in the Garden of Gethsemane immediately prior to His arrest and fully aware of the trial, torture, and execution He is about to undergo, Christ "withdrew from them about a stone's throw, and knelt down and prayed, 'Father, if thou art willing, remove this cup from me; nevertheless, not my will, but thine, be done.'"[13]

Here again, the main point is not that Christ accedes to God's will in spite of the temptation to escape this fate. This lesson is entirely for our benefit. Christ makes it clear that there is a distinction between what He might desire for Himself were He not content to relinquish His own will to comply with the will of God—something, we must infer, that He is by example demonstrating that all believers must do to the extent that they are able. Similarly, while the temptation in the wilderness is internal and spiritual—as opposed to the very real physical torment He is about to endure at the hands of the Romans—the Gospel shares both struggles with us that we might learn from Christ how to respond to our own internal and external temptations and tests.

And how do we know this and why are such personal and private episodes essential to the Covenant? As mentioned previously, perhaps the most satisfying answer is that no one was with Christ on either occasion—either during His temptation in the wilderness or during His agony in the Garden of Gethsemane—so the reason we know that He confronted and defeated any desires for self-aggrandizement or self-preservation is because He must have conveyed this information to His disciples. In other words, He, like all the Manifestations, is well aware that one of His essential purposes is to exemplify the conduct that characterizes the religious code He is trying to teach.

The articulation, in the writings and utterances of the Manifestations, of the suffering and rejection They are made to endure, is a persistent theme for all the Manifestations, not because They are self-pitying or desire sympathy but as a proof that everything They do is solely for our benefit. Nothing They do gains Them any earthly power. They have no ulterior motive. They are not *forced* to accept their mission or endure the torment we inflict upon them.

They all freely and happily accept Their part in this process of spiritualizing human civilization. For Them, this selfless act of sacrifice and hardship is an expression of Their perfect love of God and us.

Finally, it is valuable for us to emphasize again that the Manifestations are not loathe to profess Their own exemplary model as a paradigm of what their followers should emulate. Christ's most well-known and studied discussion regarding this fact is in one of His final discourses with His disciples as He prepares them for His imminent execution:

> Thomas said to Him, "Lord, we do not know where you are going; how can we know the way?"
>
> Jesus said to him, "I am the way, and the truth, and the life; no one comes to the Father, but by me. If you had known me, you would have known my Father also; henceforth you know him and have seen him."
>
> Philip said to him, "Lord, show us the Father, and we shall be satisfied."
>
> Jesus said to him, "Have I been with you so long, and yet you do not know me, Philip? He who has seen me has seen the Father; how can you say, 'Show us the Father'? Do you not believe that I am in the Father and the Father in me? The words that I say to you I do not speak on my own authority; but the Father who dwells in me does his works. Believe me that I am in the Father and the Father in me; or else believe me for the sake of the works themselves. Truly, truly, I say to you, he who believes in me will also do the works that I do; and greater works than these will he do, because I go to the Father."[14]

Muhammad

We pick up this same theme of suffering with Muhammad by recalling a passage of Bahá'u'lláh demonstrating that the ultimate ascendancy of the religion brought by the Manifestations occurs only after They have undergone all the persecution, rejection, and torment that people in power can inflict upon Them:

> Such sore accusations they brought against Him [Muham-mad] that in recounting them God forbiddeth the ink to flow, Our pen to move, or the page to bear them. These malicious imputations provoked the people to arise and torment Him. And how fierce that torment if the divines of the age be its chief instigators, if they denounce Him to their followers, cast Him out from their midst, and declare Him a miscreant! Hath not the same befallen this Servant, and been witnessed by all?
>
> For this reason did Muhammad cry out: "No Prophet of God hath suffered such harm as I have suffered." And in the Qur'án are recorded all the calumnies and reproaches uttered against Him, as well as all the afflictions which He suffered. Refer ye thereunto, that haply ye may be informed of that which hath befallen His Revelation.[15]

Of course, these events occur in the midst of a life that, like that of Moses, is filled with dramatic episodes as a result of a similarly staggering mission—to reveal a religion capable of unifying possibly the most contentious and diverse array of tribal communities during the period that is categorized as the "Dark Ages" in Europe.

In effect, while all that had once been the stable Roman Empire was being torn apart by the marauding migration of tribes throughout what is now Europe—from the Huns in the east to the Anglo-Saxons and Vikings in the west—Muhammad managed, by contrast, to transform the stark landscape of the Arabian Peninsula into a unified state with a constitution, a shared monotheistic religious belief, and accompanying practices of prayer, piety, and a code of conduct unlike anything the world had heretofore experienced.

Muhammad's life and the Qur'án—in which He comments about the progression of His campaign to bring about stability, peace, and justice—constitute a truly remarkable transformative force that has rarely been appropriately understood or appreciated, whether by those who succeeded Him or, most notably, by most Western scholars of history or religion. In a brief but insightful book *Six Lesson on Islam*, Bahá'í scholar and translator Marzieh Gail begins with the following important observation about contemporary knowledge of and attitudes about Muhammad and Islam: "To study Islam we need new books. We need a re-evaluation by future Bahá'í scholars, of all the available data, in the light of Bahá'u'lláh's Teachings. The Guardian told a pilgrim that the Bahá'ís must vindicate Islam in the West; we must convert people, not to its institutions, now abrogated by the Báb and Bahá'u'lláh, but to its truth as a further step in Divine Revelation, following Christianity."[16]

In 1976, noted Bahá'í scholar Hasan M. Balyuzi published one such book, *Muhammad and the Course of Islam*, a work which not only redeems our understanding of the character and actions of the Prophet but also explains in lucid detail how the intended succession and administration of the religion were diverted from their intended course.

But while some scholars have worked toward a reevaluation of the beneficial influence of the Revelation of Muhammad in the progress of civilization—most notably the forces underlying the Renaissance in Western Europe—much more remains to be done before we can have anything approaching an accurate understanding or appreciation of Who Muhammad was and why the strategies He employed were not only spiritually sanctioned but absolutely necessary to bring about God's mandate for this Revelation. First we need to observe that His primary and enduring objective was not to conquer tribes and thereby gain political power. It is true that one result of His life's work was, in fact, the unification of the Arabian peoples and the establishment of the belief in one God and in progressive Revelation throughout what became the Islamic empire. However, the spread of Islam across North Africa and into the Iberian Peninsula in the West, and throughout the Holy Land, the Byzantine Empire, and the Sassanid Empire in the North and East is to be attributed to the attraction these teachings had for peoples seeking justice and stability. But at no point was the mandate or plan of the Prophet to create a military force capable of subduing nations and coercing people into accepting His teachings.

That Muhammad found it necessary to become involved in a sequence of battles has been one of the most confounding facts of His life for those who perceive Manifestations or Prophets as passive sages rather than active shapers of social order. While we cannot dwell here on the details of the remarkable history that emanates from Muhammad's Dispensation, we should mention the reason the Manifestation chose such a difficult and depraved place to reveal Himself. It was precisely to demonstrate the power of God's religion to transform even the most chaotic and decadent societies into a source of spiritual enlightenment and a model of what others should strive to achieve. However, we cannot abandon even so brief an assessment without noting that that any Manifestation encountering identical circumstances would have resorted to precisely the same tactics to bring about a similar result:

It was among such tribes that Muhammad was sent forth. For thirteen years He suffered at their hands every conceivable tribulation, till at last He fled the city and emigrated to Medina. And yet, far from desisting, these people joined forces, raised an army, and attacked with the aim of extermi-

301

nating every man, woman, and child among His followers. It was under such circumstances and against such people that Muhammad was forced to take up arms. This is the plain truth—we are not prompted by fanatical attachment, nor do we blindly seek to defend, but we examine and relate matters with fairness. You should likewise consider in fairness the following: If Christ Himself had been placed in similar circumstances and among such lawless and barbarous tribes; if for thirteen years He and His disciples had patiently endured every manner of cruelty at their hands; if they were forced through this oppression to forsake their homeland and take to the wilderness; and if these lawless tribes still persisted in pursuing them with the aim of slaughtering the men, pillaging their property, and seizing their women and children—how would Christ have dealt with them? If this oppression had been directed towards Him alone, He would have forgiven them, and such an act of forgiveness would have been most acceptable and praiseworthy; but had He seen that cruel and bloodthirsty murderers were intent upon killing, pillaging, and tormenting a number of defenseless souls and taking captive the women and children, it is certain that He would have defended the oppressed and stayed the hand of the oppressors.[17]

Stated succinctly, Muhammad resorted to physical combat to accomplish what was essentially a spiritual enterprise. But only by studying in depth the historical context of His ministry can one fully appreciate why an immaculate Messenger of God would find it necessary to become involved in any sort of violence.

For the idol-worshiping tribes in Arabia for whom Mecca was a place of pilgrimage, Muhammad's teachings were both an ideological and material threat to the prosperity and control of the city. While initially He and His small following were tolerated, His growing influence eventually forced Him to escape from Mecca to avoid being murdered. His migration (*hegira*) from Mecca to Medina in 622 CE thus marks the beginning of the Islamic Dispensation.

In Medina, over the course of successive defensive battles, He and His followers managed to convert and stabilize the community. Regarded as a trusted leader, He established the Constitution of Medina that set forth a type of federation among the diverse tribes and peoples. The community model (*ummah*) Muhammad devised defined the rights and obligations of the citizenry, regardless of their past religious identity or tribal allegiance. And at the core of this polity was a practical structure with a religious orientation that was not oppressive and that effectively became a model for the first Islamic state. In fact, this may well be regarded as the beginning of the concept of a constitutionally based nation-state.

Along with the explicit laws in the Qur'án, Muhammad's followers also accept the *sunnah* (pattern of life) exemplified by Him as the perfect model for appropriate behavior. But as 'Abdu'l-Bahá points out in the above-cited passage, that behavior, like that of all the Prophets, must be understood in the context and exigencies of historical circumstances.

The Báb

Both the Báb and Bahá'u'lláh are also fully aware that Their behavior is both an essential proof of Their station and an integral part of Their Covenant. But, unlike the previous Manifestations, They are careful to recount Their own lives in detail rather than leave them to the speculation of historians. Likewise, as we have noted, They also share with us, through Their recorded utterances, the trials They endure, the exercise of Their free will in acquiescing to this oppression, and Their repeated efforts to make known precisely Who They are, the lofty purposes with which God has endowed Them, and the surest methods by which society can become transformed.

Put more simply, the Manifestations are fully aware that They exemplify perfectly the spiritual attributes of God, and They are not hesitant to say so. This part of Their Revelation, after all, is essential to everything else They exhort us to do. 'Abdu'l-Bahá—though not a Manifestation, but well aware that part of his function was to model the perfect Bahá'í behavior—delivered this well-known farewell address to some early Bahá'í pilgrims:

> Another commandment I give unto you, that ye love one another even as I love you . . . look at one another with the eye of perfection; look at Me, follow Me, be as I am; take no thought for yourselves or your lives, whether ye eat or whether ye sleep, whether ye are comfortable, whether ye are well or ill, whether ye are with friends or foes, whether ye receive praise or blame . . . Look at Me and be as I am; ye must die to yourselves and to the world, so shall ye be born again and enter the Kingdom of Heaven. Behold a candle how it gives its light. It weeps its life away drop by drop in order to give forth its flame of light.[18]

When declaring Himself and His station to Mullá Husayn on the evening of May 23, 1844, the Báb asked the young student of Siyyid Kázim what he sought. Mullá Husayn explained that, at his teacher's behest, he had set out in search of the Promised One, the Qá'im. The Báb then inquired from His guest what signs would betoken this individual, whereupon Mullá Husayn replied, "'He is of a pure lineage, is of illustrious descent, and of the seed of Fátimih. As to His age, He is more than twenty and less than thirty. He is endowed with innate knowledge. He is of medium height, abstains from smoking, and is free from bodily deficiency.'" The Báb shocked His guest when He responded, "'Behold, all these signs are manifest in Me!' He then considered each of the above-mentioned signs separately, and conclusively demonstrated that each and all were applicable to His person." During the course of that momentous evening, the Báb spontaneously revealed the entire first chapter of the Qayyúmu'l-Asmá', His commentary on the Surah of Joseph, and proclaimed to His young visitor that though He was the Qá'im and "'the mouthpiece of God Himself,'" He was but "the Herald of One immeasurably greater than Himself.'"[19]

As we mentioned earlier, once the Manifestations receive the intimation that it is time for Them to unfold Their station and ministry, They boldly and forthrightly proclaim this truth, even though They accomplish this task wisely, by degrees, and in a manner most effective for the distinctive conditions in which Their ministry must unfold. Thus, while the challenge Muhammad faced was to subdue and train desert peoples living in a state of constant tribal warfare, the Báb over a thousand years later found Himself having to break through the stringent orthodoxy that Islam had assumed, especially in the Shí'ih stronghold of Persia.

As a result, He was arrested less than two years after His public declaration of His mission and spent the remainder of His brief life imprisoned until He was executed, six years later, at age thirty-one. Because He spent the last three years of His six-year ministry in confinement—imprisoned first at Máh-Kú and then at Chihríq, the evidence of His constancy in revealing the Word of God despite His circumstances is as obvious as it is dramatic.

The Báb was well aware that His central role was not to play an active part in constructing a social order but rather to challenge the status quo by instigating a religious movement whose followers would, like a wildfire, sweep across Persia and demonstrate in pitched defensive battles at the Shrine of Shaykh Tabarsí and in the cities of Zanján and Nayríz the power of the Faith to which they had sworn allegiance. Unlike Muhammad, the Báb, imprisoned in strict confinement, was unable to assist His followers directly.

Like Muhammad and Bahá'u'lláh, the Báb was forthright in articulating all that He had been made to endure—again, not as a plaint to God, but as a gift to those who would follow Him, so that there would be no question about His motives or the extent of His suffering. As if the obvious fact that the myriad of works penned by the Báb were written while He was incarcerated was not sufficient proof of His constancy in the face of untold adversity, in a work written shortly before His execution, the Báb rehearses for history an outline of the course of His brief life:

> Thou art aware, O My God, that since the day Thou didst call Me into being out of the water of Thy love till I reached fifteen years of age I lived in the land which witnessed My birth [Shíráz]. Then Thou didst enable Me to go to the seaport [Búshihr] where for five years I was engaged in trading with the goodly gifts of Thy realm and was occupied in that with which Thou hast favored Me through the wondrous essence of Thy loving-kindness. I proceeded therefrom to the Holy Land [Karbilá] where I sojourned for one year. Then I returned to the place of My birth. There I experienced the revelation of Thy sublime bestowals and the evidences of Thy boundless grace. I yield Thee praise for all Thy goodly gifts and I render Thee thanksgiving for all Thy bounties. Then at the age of twenty-five I proceeded to thy sacred House [Mecca], and by the time I returned to the place where I was born, a year had elapsed. There I tarried patiently in the path of Thy love and beheld the evidences of Thy manifold bounties and of Thy loving-kindness until Thou didst ordain for Me to set out in Thy direction and to migrate to Thy

presence. Thus I departed therefrom by Thy leave, spending six months in the land of Sád [Isfáhán] and seven months in the First Mountain [Máh-Kú], where Thou didst rain down upon Me that which beseemeth the glory of Thy heavenly blessings and befitteth the sublimity of Thy gracious gifts and favours. Now, in My thirtieth year, Thou beholdest Me, O My God, in this Grievous Mountain [Chihríq] where I have dwelt for one whole year.[20]

Later that same year, on July 9, 1850, He was taken before a firing squad in Tabriz and executed, but not before He had, like Christ before the Sanhedrin, responded with the following amazing speech to a panel of clerics and government inquisitors assembled to determine His fate. When asked who He claimed to be, "'I am,' He exclaimed, 'I am, I am the Promised One! I am the One Whose name you have for a thousand years invoked, at Whose mention you have risen, Whose advent you have longed to witness, and the hour of Whose Revelation you have prayed God to hasten. Verily, I say, it is incumbent upon the peoples of both the East and the West to obey My word, and to pledge allegiance to My person.'"[21]

Bahá'u'lláh

Just as the previous Manifestations, Bahá'u'lláh revealed His station by degrees. First He helped guide the bereft Bábí community after the imprisonment and subsequent execution of the Báb, and He did so even more directly after He Himself had been imprisoned and then exiled to Baghdad. In 1863, immediately prior to His further exile to Constantinople, He spent twelve days in Najíbíyyih Garden (designated later by His followers as "the Garden of Ridván"), where "His friends and companions, arriving in successive waves, attained His presence and bade Him, with feelings of profound sorrow, their last farewell."[22] During those same momentous days, He disclosed what many had already surmised, that He was Him Whom God would make manifest, the One for Whom the Báb had been the Herald.

After a few months in Constantinople, Bahá'u'lláh was exiled to Adrianople where, during a four-year period, He began the formal announcement of His station, together with His mission to create a world commonwealth, to the most prominent political and religious leaders of the day. Following a still further and final exile to the prison-city of Akká (in present-day Israel) Bahá'u'lláh wrote the Kitáb-i-Aqdas, His Most Holy Book, a compilation of Bahá'í laws and the blueprint for the global commonwealth, a world polity that will signalize the unity and lasting peace of all the peoples of the world.

Because Bahá'u'lláh was a prisoner from 1852 until His death in 1892, He charged His son and successor, 'Abdu'l-Bahá, with the task of being the public face of the community and of tending to the relationship of the Bahá'í community with the government and clerical officials. Aside from taking the lead in reviving and animating the Bábí community in Baghdad, Bahá'u'lláh devoted the majority of the remainder of His life to revealing the hundreds of works that constitute the revealed Word of the Bahá'í Faith. Within them is contained the guidance for humankind in establishing the foundation for those social systems that will be the essential components of a new World Order capable of building planetary governance and social organization as an imprint of the spiritual realm—the "kingdom of God on earth."

The most obvious proof of Bahá'u'lláh's constancy in this process is the worldwide growth of the present-day Bahá'í community, which is the second most widespread religious community after Christianity. Without any outside assistance, financial or otherwise, this religion has grown through individual participation in strategically devised teaching plans, and in the course of a little more than a century it has gone from being represented primarily in Persia (and parts of what was then the Ottoman Empire) to becoming established in all the countries and territories of the planet, with communities based on the administrative order designed by Bahá'u'lláh.

But to return to the theme of how Bahá'u'lláh, like Manifestations before Him, accomplished all this "unaided and alone," without ulterior motive and without the desire for personal gain of any sort, we need only to allude to *Epistle to the Son of the Wolf,* the last major work He penned, which serves both as a sort of autobiography and as a chronological review of His most prominent works.[23] In it, Bahá'u'lláh explicitly challenges the reader* to discover in all He has done and revealed any desire for personal gain or any trace of dissimulation. Interestingly, the theme of this work is how His followers maintained their fidelity and faith despite ceaseless persecution, and how He had no motive in any of His endeavors other than the betterment of the human condition.

Allied to this assertion is His recurring challenge to the recipient of this epistle to examine Bahá'u'lláh's life to discover if He has ever attempted to acquire power or if any outside source or influence for His ideas and writings can be discerned:

The learning current amongst men I studied not; their schools I entered not. Ask of the city wherein I dwelt, that thou mayest be well assured that I am not of them who speak

---

* The work is addressed to Shaykh Muhammad-Taqí who, along with his father, Shaykh Muhammad-Báqir, was not only an adversary of the Bahá'í Faith, but also a collaborator with his father in a policy of murdering Bahá'ís. He was responsible for the grievous purges of Bahá'ís in Isfáhán and Yazd.

falsely. This is but a leaf which the winds of the will of thy Lord, the Almighty, the All-Praised, have stirred. Can it be still when the tempestuous winds are blowing? Nay, by Him Who is the Lord of all Names and Attributes! They move it as they list. The evanescent is as nothing before Him Who is the Ever-Abiding. His all-compelling summons hath reached Me, and caused Me to speak His praise amidst all people. I was indeed as one dead when His behest was uttered. The hand of the will of thy Lord, the Compassionate, the Merciful, transformed Me.[24]

It would take volumes to recount all that Bahá'u'lláh was made to endure as He persisted in carrying out His mission, that He might bring about this turning point in the religious history of humankind. He was fearless in confronting the clerics in Baghdad, and in one of His tablets declared that "'were they to put Him to death God will assuredly raise up One in His stead, and asserts that the Almighty will "perfect His light" though they, in their secret hearts, abhor it.'"[25]

It is in this context that Bahá'u'lláh often alludes to Himself as "this Wronged One," not in a tone of self-pity or lamenting what He has been made to endure, but to emphasize to all the irony that once again humankind has rejected the very Source of assistance that God has sent to save them: "In these days enemies have compassed Us about, and the fire of hatred is kindled. O peoples of the earth! By My life and by your own! This Wronged One hath never had, nor hath He now any desire for leadership. Mine aim hath ever been, and still is, to suppress whatever is the cause of contention amidst the peoples of the earth, and of separation amongst the nations, so that all men may be sanctified from every earthly attachment, and be set free to occupy themselves with their own interests."[26] In the same work He writes:

In these days there are some who, far from being just and fair-minded, have assaulted Me with the sword of hatred and the spear of enmity, forgetting that it behooveth every fair-minded person to succor Him Whom the world hath cast away and the nations abandoned, and to lay hold on piety and righteousness. Most men have until now failed to discover the purpose of this Wronged One, nor have they known the reason for which He hath been willing to endure countless afflictions. Meanwhile, the voice of Mine heart crieth out these words: "O that My people knew!" This Wronged One, rid of attachment unto all things, uttereth these exalted words: "Waves have encompassed the Ark of God, the Help in Peril, the Self-Subsisting. Fear not the tempestuous gales, O Mariner!* He Who causeth the dawn to appear is, verily, with Thee in this darkness that hath struck terror into the hearts of all men, except such as God, the Almighty, the Unconstrained, hath been pleased to spare."[27]

In sum, our brief allusion to the selflessness and courage with which the Manifestations willingly undertake the mission assigned to Them by God should be regarded as but a glimpse into the full extent of the sacrifice They make for us, whether it be the willingness to sacrifice Their own lives—as with Christ and the Báb—or whether it be to endure a lifetime of ceaseless struggle against those who would vehemently reject and attack what they perceive to be a threat to their own stranglehold on the peoples under their sway.

But perhaps we have made the point sufficiently clear that integral to the Covenant They establish as the inviolable cord to con-

---

* This is a reference to the *Tablet of the Holy Mariner*, an allegorical work depicting Bahá'u'lláh as the mariner of the ark of the Covenant Who must guide this Craft over tumultuous seas of enmity, turmoil, and suffering.

nect the peoples of the world to the Creator is Their willingness to endure any and all trials that become Their lot, regardless of how grievous or relentless these afflictions may be.

-12-

UNITY OF MAJOR THEMES IN THE FABRIC OF THE ETERNAL COVENANT

Behold, how lofty is the station, and how consummate the virtue, of these verses which He hath declared to be His surest testimony, His infallible proof, the evidence of His all-subduing power, and a revelation of the potency of His will. He, the divine King, hath proclaimed the undisputed supremacy of the verses of His Book over all things that testify to His truth. For compared with all other proofs and tokens, the divinely-revealed verses shine as the sun, whilst all others are as stars.

Bahá'u'lláh, Kitáb-i-Íqán, ¶226

The final part of our examination of how the revealed Word serves to knit together the counterpart dimensions of reality (the metaphysical and the physical) concerns those threads that traverse every Revelation from age to age, weaving ever more completely the central themes of God's message of understanding and comfort to His creation. These same themes have been extensively elucidated and implemented during the past twenty years by the Universal House of Justice in its guidance for those practices that the present-day Bahá'í community employs throughout the world to establish collaborative neighborhoods which model at the local level those spiritual principles that Bahá'u'lláh portrays as adorning the continuous evolution of His design for a World Commonwealth.

To envision how these themes work, we once again turn to our analogy of the Eternal Covenant as the loom of human history upon which the successive Manifestations of God have guided us as weavers to participate in fashioning the evolving tapestry of an emerging global community:

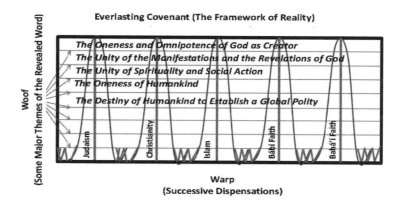

Figure 22. Some Major Themes that Traverse the Progressive Revelations

In this diagram, I have suggested in a prioritized sequence the major themes that constitute the woof of God's plan, those major cords that underlie, support, and reinforce all other spiritual concepts reiterated in the increasingly expansive and encompassing Word revealed by each successive Manifestation of God. Although these themes are readily apparent in all religious scripture—most especially as they are explicated by Bahá'u'lláh in the Kitáb-i-Íqán—it is perhaps useful to conclude our discussion with a brief review of the continuity of these themes.

The Oneness of God

It is not uncommon, when we discuss our belief in God, to have someone ask us, "Which God?" For Bahá'ís and others who believe in the essential unity of the world religions, this query may come as a surprise. In the past I presumed the question to be rhetorical, the sarcastic quip of someone grown tired of the tension among all the various religions' beliefs. Now I realize the question is often a sincere desire to discover one's view regarding the existence and nature of God. Because so many of the extant religions of the world have become so distant in time and clarity from the original verities the Founder established, there has emerged the idea that various religious believe in a distinct or different "God" to accord with their own misperception or misinterpretation of what constitutes "God."

Of course, we are not here referring to what any Manifestation or Founder of a religion articulated; we can safely assume that every Manifestation described the same spiritual realm, the same Deity, and the same changeless spiritual verities that govern reality—albeit in terms that best communicated these metaphysical realities for a given time and a given part of the world. Rather, what we are alluding to are the conflicting beliefs among present-day followers of some still extant religions that endured long past the time and conditions they were created to serve. In all these religions, the teachings have lost their efficacy, and the followers have lost sight of what the Founders once made clear.

For example, some Hindus do not have a concept of a single Creator or personal God, though they may believe in the advent of certain specialized souls, or Avatars, who are great teachers that incarnate the virtues we should try to emulate. Other Hindus, instead, do believe in the Vedic figure of Vishnu as the Supreme Being and the Avatars, such as Krishna, as His Messengers incarnating His divine attributes.

Similarly, most Western followers of Buddhism view their system of belief as a philosophy and not a religion per se. Therefore, some might be Christians or Jews yet also consider themselves as following the Buddhist philosophy. The majority of these advocates of Buddhism will assert that Buddha did not believe in God, that the spiritual path He discussed was a humanistic concept of balance and reflective practices based on natural laws and forces, but not in any way a system of religious belief involving the concept of a Creator or Supreme Being. And yet there is no evidence in any purported statement by the Buddha to uphold such a conclusion. Indeed, it seems clear in even a cursory examination of His influence that His teachings were, among other things, a response to some of the literalism that had become infused into what was intended as symbolic mythology in Hindu philosophy and theology.

The traditional Western view of Zoroastrianism is that this religion, born in Persia, advocates a belief in two warring deities, and that this same religion is the source of the concept of the conflict between God and the Devil. But the fact is that Zoroaster taught belief in a supreme, eternal, and omnipotent God, Ahura Mazda, who created the evil spirit, Angra Mainyu. This evil spirit is thus not the coequal antithesis of God but a mythical concept like unto the Christian concept of Lucifer who, though warring against God, is totally under His control and will ultimately succumb to His power. In short, we can assume this theology employs the same sort of symbolic mythology to portray a complex and logical theology in which a Satanic figure represents the negative aspects of self—pride, licentiousness, greed, and so forth.

In this context, it is well worth noting that the core objective for the followers of all religions is the acknowledgement of the oneness of God. In all religions we must ultimately discern, beyond the myths and symbols, the reality of a single Creator from Whom emanate all the Messengers and divine teachings, as well as reality itself: "We should, therefore, detach ourselves from the external forms and practices of religion. We must realize that these forms and practices, however beautiful, are but garments clothing the warm heart and the living limbs of Divine truth. We must abandon the prejudices of tradition if we would succeed in finding the truth at the core of all religions. If a Zoroastrian believes that the Sun is God, how can he be united to other religions? While idolaters believe in their various idols, how can they understand the oneness of God?"[1]

The Unity of the Manifestations

Because it is more distant in time and has had less influence in the western hemisphere, and because it has not been studied through the lens of the theory of progressive Revelation—as implied in the Bible and as discussed explicitly in the Qur'án and in the revealed works of the Báb and Bahá'u'lláh—the continuity of the Dharmic line of Manifestations is less well understood. Within the sequence of Abrahamic religions, we have a consistent, evolving, and extant discourse regarding God as Creator, as the eternal and omnipotent Lord, singular and alone. This personal God is continually concerned with the fruit of His creation and therefore empowers certain specialized Souls—the Prophets or Manifestations—to advance the progress of human enlightenment and spirituality.

While the extant Abrahamic religions are Judaism, Christianity, Islam, and the Bahá'í Faith, various other Manifestations are mentioned in the authoritative writings of these religions, although They are not always identified as Manifestations.* Nevertheless,

---

* For example, the Bible mentions Adam, Noah, and Abraham. In the Qur'án and in Bahá'í scripture are Húd and Sálih, Prophets who appeared after Noah but before Abraham. Their followers are considered part of the "People of the Book."

we can infer from the brief allusions to them that They also taught the concept of God as Creator at work in history via His Emissaries to unfold "progressive Revelation," the ever more expansive truth about reality, through Their utterances, actions, and religions.[2]

The so-called Abrahamic line of Manifestations, alluded to as the Adamic or Prophetic Cycle of Prophets, began with Adam and concluded with the Báb. Bahá'u'lláh inaugurated a new universal cycle, the Bahá'í Cycle, destined to endure for no less than five hundred thousand years, though the entirety of God's plan for planet Earth encompasses all cycles, including those lost to our collective memory, in a continuous, organic, and coherent process.

That is why, in Genesis, Moses speaks first about the story of the Prophet Noah before starting a lengthy narration of the life and teachings of Abraham. And while we associate Abraham with the establishment of the Covenant between God and humankind, clearly Noah is teaching the same concept. According to the Qur'án, the Covenant between God and man was instigated on the Day of *Yawm-i-Alast*, the Day when God addressed Adam's posterity-to-be and asked them, "Am I not your Lord?" (*a-lastu bi Rabbikum*) and they replied: "Yea! We do verily bear witness!" This response represents the binding Covenant between God and humankind.[3]

Each of the Manifestations alludes to this Covenant being played out in human / religious history. As we noted earlier, the Old Testament intimations about the advent of Christ are plentiful, and Christ Himself is explicit in tying His Revelation to that of Moses and Abraham. In the following exchange with taunting Pharisees, Christ alludes to both the continuity of Revelation and the preexistence of the Manifestations in the realm of the spirit, which, as He later points out, has neither time nor physical dimension:*

---

* See Christ's response to the Sadducees in Mark 12:15–27.

The Jews said to him, "Now we know that you have a
demon. Abraham died, as did the prophets; and you say, 'If
any one keeps my word, he will never taste death.' Are you
greater than our father Abraham, who died? And the prophets
died! Who do you claim to be?"

Jesus answered, "If I glorify myself, my glory is nothing;
it is my Father who glorifies me, of whom you say that he is
your God. But you have not known him; I know him. If I
said, I do not know him, I should be a liar like you; but I do
know him and I keep his word. Your father Abraham rejoiced
that he was to see my day; he saw it and was glad."

The Jews then said to him, "You are not yet fifty years old,
and have you seen Abraham?"

Jesus said to them, "Truly, truly, I say to you, before Abraham was, I am."[4]

We may find it helpful to take note in this passage of the double
entendre in Christ's allusion to His "Day," a term we have already
discussed as representing the cycle or Dispensation of a Prophet.

Interestingly, in the Surah of Húd (Surah 11) Muhammad mentions the sequence of Manifestations beginning with Noah but
includes others not mentioned in Genesis. After Noah, He cites
Húd and Sálih before discussing Abraham, no doubt because They
appeared in the Arabian Peninsula. What is more important, the
theme of this recitation of the sequence of Prophets is not solely
that They, one and all, proclaimed the Oneness of God and His
Prophets, but also that each met a similar sort of rejection.

Muhammad says that when Noah appeared, He preached that
unless the people reformed, God would impose "the Penalty of a
Grievous Day." But inasmuch as the people perceived Noah as but
an ordinary man and not a Manifestation, they rejected His warning: "But the Chiefs of the Unbelievers among his people said: 'We

see (in) thee nothing but a man like ourselves: nor do we see that any follow thee but the meanest among us, in judgment immature: nor do we see in you (all) any merit above us: in fact we think ye are liars!'"[5]

Muhammad reiterates this same theme of rejection with His account of God sending Húd to the people of 'Ad, Sálih to the people of Thamud, Abraham to the land of Hebron, Shoaib to the land of Midian, Moses to Egypt, and Christ to the people of Jerusalem.* He emphasizes that in each case the Manifestations appeared with clear signs and proofs of Their station and that each came with a Book, some form of revealed utterances wherein They guided the people to believe in one God and to employ practices of piety and reverence for God.

Bahá'u'lláh begins the Kitáb-i-Íqán with this same theme. He alludes to the stories of Noah, Húd, Sálih, Abraham, Moses, Christ, Muhammad, and later in this same work, to the Báb and lastly to Himself as Mustagháth ("He Who is invoked"). Similar to the Súrih of Húd, the theme of this catalogue is the rejection of the Prophets by those most responsible for recognizing them and accepting them—the divines or religious leaders of the previous Revelation:

> Leaders of religion, in every age, have hindered their peo-ple from attaining the shores of eternal salvation, inasmuch as they held the reins of authority in their mighty grasp. Some for the lust of leadership, others through want of knowledge and understanding, have been the cause of the deprivation of the people. By their sanction and authority, every Prophet of God hath drunk from the chalice of sacrifice, and winged His

---

* Christ is not mentioned in this Surah, but is discussed in the same vein in numerous other Surah.

flight unto the heights of glory. What unspeakable cruelties they that have occupied the seats of authority and learning have inflicted upon the true Monarchs of the world, those Gems of divine virtue! Content with a transitory dominion, they have deprived themselves of an everlasting sovereignty. Thus, their eyes beheld not the light of the countenance of the Well-Beloved, nor did their ears hearken unto the sweet melodies of the Bird of Desire. For this reason, in all sacred books mention hath been made of the divines of every age.[6]

Even more specifically, the reason for this failure, Bahá'u'lláh goes on to explain, is the inability of religious leaders to grasp the symbolic or poetic nature of the revealed Word. This theme is another thread in the fabric of this abiding continuity of the teachings of every Manifestation:

The denials and protestations of these leaders of religion have, in the main, been due to their lack of knowledge and understanding. Those words uttered by the Revealers of the beauty of the one true God, setting forth the signs that should herald the advent of the Manifestation to come, they never understood nor fathomed. Hence they raised the standard of revolt, and stirred up mischief and sedition. It is obvious and manifest that the true meaning of the utterances of the Birds of Eternity is revealed to none except those that manifest the Eternal Being, and the melodies of the Nightingale of Holiness can reach no ear save that of the denizens of the everlasting realm.[7]

The Unity of Spirituality and Social Action

Another recurring theme in the revealed utterances of every Manifestation is the inseparability of spirituality from social action.

Every Manifestation exhorts His followers to undertake some sort of spiritual regimen whereby their beliefs are practiced personally and collectively. Furthermore, each Manifestation explains, directly or indirectly, that unless belief brings about spiritual refinement among the followers, they really have not understood the essential meaning or purpose of the Revelation.

We have alluded to this tension between the Manifestation and those to whom He appears in the previous theme when the Manifestations function as "Warners" about the consequence of ignoring Their exhortations and guidance They reveal. In some stories from the Judaic texts, disobedience is often portrayed as resulting in some miraculous physical consequence. A familiar example is the story of Lot's wife being turned into a pillar of salt.

And as we have previously noted, as Moses trains His people to rise from their lowly state as slaves to become a refined community of believers, He makes no categorical distinctions between those laws and practices that are secular and those that are spiritual. The believers correctly infer that everything they do ultimately has some spiritual meaning and that failure to comply with this guidance has both immediate and long-term consequences, whether these practices regard personal and private action or relationships with others.

But over the course of centuries, such practice degrades into the recitation and interpretation of a "spiritual life" as a finely regulated and dogmatically codified conduct. The religion loses the sense of its underlying purpose, of its foundational concept of spirituality as an inner reformation rather than a mindless legalistic approach to their relationship with God. Consequently, while Christ alludes to this inability of the people of Jerusalem to understand the spiritual meaning of His teaching, we find the antinomian attitude of authoritative Christian texts played out most dramatically in the letters of Paul to the various congregations.

Christ Himself very explicitly upholds law and obedience to spiritual practices as an eternal component of spirituality. Surely this is the meaning of His statement: "Whoever then relaxes one of the least of these commandments and teaches men so, shall be called least in the kingdom of heaven; but he who does them and teaches them shall be called great in the kingdom of heaven." Of course, in the sequence of laws and practices that Christ then sets forth, He abrogates some of the laws of Moses, introduces new ones, and alters others. But the most resounding affirmation that Christ makes regarding the inseparability of spirituality and adherence to the laws He has revealed is found at the very end of this same sermon: "Everyone then who hears these words of mine and does them will be like a wise man who built his house upon the rock; and the rain fell, and the floods came, and the winds blew and beat upon that house, but it did not fall, because it had been founded on the rock. And every one who hears these words of mine and does not do them will be like a foolish man who built his house upon the sand; and the rain fell, and the floods came, and the winds blew and beat against that house, and it fell; and great was the fall of it."[8]

When Paul contends with the apostles that some of the Judaic laws which Christ did not abrogate should be abandoned, his point is accepted and these constraints are relaxed: "We ourselves, who are Jews by birth and not Gentile sinners, yet who know that a man is not justified by works of the law but through faith in Jesus Christ, even we have believed in Christ Jesus, in order to be justified by faith in Christ, and not by works of the law, because by works of the law shall no one be justified."[9]

However, when Paul seems to reject the overarching concept of obedience to law as having any importance with regard to one's "justification" or "salvation," Peter observes that believers misconstrue what Paul means and run into the danger of being licentious by thinking their behavior has no bearing on their spirituality nor any consequence for their salvation: "Therefore, beloved, since you wait for these [the coming of the Day of God], be zealous to be found by him without spot or blemish, and at peace. And count the forbearance of our Lord as salvation. So also our beloved brother Paul wrote to you according to the wisdom given him, speaking of this as he does in all his letters. There are some things in them hard to understand, which the ignorant and unstable twist to their own destruction, as they do the other scriptures. You therefore, beloved, knowing this beforehand, beware lest you be carried away with the error of lawless men and lose your own stability."[10] James is even more direct and emphatic in his argument that faith is entirely theoretical until it is demonstrated in one's personal conduct, whether in one's private deeds or social relationship with others:

> What does it profit, my brethren, if a man says he has faith but has not works? Can his faith save him? If a brother or sister is ill-clad and in lack of daily food, and one of you says to them, "Go in peace, be warmed and filled," without giving them the things needed for the body, what does it profit? So faith by itself, if it has no works, is dead. But someone will say, "You have faith and I have works." Show me your faith apart from your works, and I by my works will show you my faith. . . . You see that a man is justified by works and not by faith alone. . . . For as the body apart from the spirit is dead, so faith apart from works is dead.[11]

It is worth noting, then—before we examine Muhammad's teachings regarding the relationship between belief and action— that while the generality of Christians may regard the words and teachings in the letters of Paul, Peter, and James as authoritative inasmuch as these apostles were early pillars of the Church and their writings are inseparable parts of the New Testament, there is no logical basis for accepting their words as an inextricable part of Christ's Revelation or even as being infallibly authoritative.

There is no ambiguity about the relationship between belief and social practices in the Qur'án or in the Covenant of Muhammad establishing the line of authority from which additional authoritative utterances about the interpretation of the laws will flow. The Qur'án, being the revealed and infallible Word of God, contains all manner of guidance regarding personal comportment, a complete spiritual regimen, teachings regarding marriage, family, divorce, responsibility to the community, and the community's responsibility to the individual. The Constitution of Medina mentioned earlier might legitimately be considered a paradigm for how the Prophet intended community life to be established—a constitutional covenant between governance and the governed.

And while Muhammad verbally appointed 'Alí and his lineal descendants as leaders of the Faith, one might argue whether or not Muhammad intended that there should be an explicit relationship between these religious leaders and the administration of civil affairs. However, since there was no other universally recognized form of a just social structure during His Dispensation, we can reliably infer from the foundational social structure exemplified in the *ummah* as devised in the Constitution of Medina that, while not establishing a rigid theocracy, Muhammad does envision just governance as arising from the universal acceptance of and allegiance to a single unified religious belief.

In this sense, it would be impossible and needless to attempt to summarize in the brief span of this book how Muhammad synthesizes faith and action, whether in explicit religious practices or in familial and social responsibility. The entirety of the Qur'án is saturated with this theme. For us, the following substantial verses from Surah 2 will suffice as an example of a broad-based overview

of one of the Prophet's statements about the nature of righteousness, the motives that should govern our life as a whole, and how
these motives are to be expressed in concrete action:

> It is not righteousness that ye turn your faces toward East
> or West; but it is righteousness to believe in God and the Last
> Day, and the Angels, and the Book, and the Messengers; to
> spend of your substance, out of love for Him, for your kin,
> for orphans, for the needy, for the wayfarer, for those who
> ask, and for the ransom of slaves; to be steadfast in prayer,
> and practice regular charity; to fulfill the contracts which ye
> have made; and to be firm and patient, in pain (or suffering)
> and adversity, and throughout all periods of panic. Such are
> the people of truth, the God-fearing.[12]

> Those who spend their substance in the Cause of Allah,
> and follow not up their gifts with reminders of their gener-
> osity or with injury, for them their reward is with their Lord;
> on them shall be no fear, nor shall they grieve. Kind words
> and the covering of faults are better than charity followed by
> injury. Allah is free of all wants, and He is Most Forbearing. O
> ye who believe! cancel not your charity by reminders of your
> generosity or by injury, like those who spend their substance
> to be seen of men, but believe neither in Allah nor in the last
> day. They are in Parable like a hard, barren rock, on which is
> a little soil; on it falls heavy rain, which leaves it (just) a bare
> stone. They will be able to do nothing with aught they have
> earned. And Allah guideth not those who reject faith. And
> the likeness of those who spend their substance, seeking to
> please Allah and to strengthen their souls, is as a garden, high
> and fertile: heavy rain falls on it but makes it yield a double

increase of harvest, and if it receives not heavy rain, light moisture sufficeth it. Allah seeth well whatever ye do.[13]

The Word as revealed in the works of Bahá'u'lláh parallels this theme established by Muhammad. To cite but a single example from one of Bahá'u'lláh's first revealed works, we can reflect on the passages that conclude the Persian Hidden Words and how they exalt a profession and work itself as a foundational expression of individual righteousness:

> O My Servants! Ye are the trees of My garden; ye must give forth goodly and wondrous fruits, that ye yourselves and others may profit therefrom. Thus it is incumbent on every one to engage in crafts and professions, for therein lies the secret of wealth, O men of understanding! For results depend upon means, and the grace of God shall be all-sufficient unto you. Trees that yield no fruit have been and will ever be for the fire.[14]

> O My Servant! The basest of men are they that yield no fruit on earth. Such men are verily counted as among the dead, nay better are the dead in the sight of God than those idle and worthless souls.[15]

> O My Servant! The best of men are they that earn a livelihood by their calling and spend upon themselves and upon their kindred for the love of God, the Lord of all worlds.[16]

Perhaps one of the most weighty axiomatic passages by Bahá'u'lláh regarding the relationship between belief and action is the following frank and succinct observation: "The essence of faith is fewness of words and abundance of deeds; he whose words exceed his deeds, know verily his death is better than his life."[17] It sounds almost like a caveat to those to whom Peter addresses his concerns about taking Paul's words too literally.

Of course, Bahá'u'lláh, like Christ and Muhammad, always interlaces His discourses about spiritual attributes with guidance about how these virtues should be manifested in one's private and public life. Even in His book of laws, the Kitáb-i-Aqdas, He often introduces laws, exhortations, and other forms of guidance with salient examples. We can observe in the following passage Bahá'u'lláh's caution about presenting an outward display of piety while inwardly coveting power, or the practice of ingratiating ourselves to others for selfish purposes: "Amongst the people is he who seateth himself amid the sandals by the door whilst coveting in his heart the seat of honour. Say: What manner of man art thou, O vain and heedless one, who wouldst appear as other than thou art? . . . Make not your deeds as snares wherewith to entrap the object of your aspiration, and deprive not yourselves of this Ultimate Objective for which have ever yearned all such as have drawn nigh unto God."[18]

The Oneness of Humankind

People are clearly not equal in inherent abilities or capacity. As Bahá'u'lláh observes, "The portion of some might lie in the palm of a man's hand, the portion of others might fill a cup, and of others even a gallon-measure."[19] True, all are equal in the sight of God, but what exactly does this axiom mean as it plays out in daily life?

As Socrates observes in constructing his fictional republic, all sorts of people with differing capacities, skill sets, and inclinations are needed to have a well-organized and smoothly functioning society. Therefore, in his aristocratic republic, he implies quite literally that the rulers are the "best" (*aristos*, the most "excellent") only in the sense that they have a specialized capacity for the position of

determining laws and social organization. But in his vision of an
utopian republic, they are also "best" in terms of virtues, among
which the most important is the altruism with which they assume
this difficult task.

However, their specialized function does not imply they are
more valuable than those citizens who fill the other equally necessary tasks that serve society. Without the farmers, there would
be no food. Without the teachers, the culture would degenerate.
Without the workforce to maintain all the public utilities, the
infrastructure would soon become defunct. A phrase employed by
the Universal House of Justice regarding the functions within the
family and how the various tasks are divided between the husband
and wife applies equally well to society as a whole:

> The equality of men and women, as 'Abdu'l-Bahá has
> often explained, is a fundamental principle of Bahá'u'lláh;
> therefore the Laws of the Aqdas should be studied in the
> light of this. Equality between men and women does not,
> indeed physiologically it cannot, mean identity of function.
> In some things women excel men, in others men are better
> than women, while in very many things the difference in
> sex is of no effect at all. The differences are most apparent
> in family life. The capacity for motherhood has many far-
> reaching effects. For example, because of this, daughters
> receive preference in education over sons. Again, for physio-
> logical reasons, women are granted exemptions from fasting
> that are not applied to men.[20]

As the Universal House of Justice goes on to discuss, this concept
in no way relegates women to having a discrete arena of function or
service; each family must decide for itself how best to arrange the
different tasks required for its unique situation. But what is clear is

that people can have equal value even though they may be doing completely different sorts of jobs: equality of status does not imply identity of function.

Also implicit in this principle is that we cannot assign some fixed or detailed hierarchical valuation of what tasks in the family or in society are more important than others. In contemporary society, there is a vastly inappropriate allocation of financial resources and prestige to certain professions or functions, whereas in the society envisioned in the Bahá'í writings, special attention is given to those at the heart of a thriving society, vocations such as farming or teaching, for example. Also included in this vision is the abolition of the extremes of wealth and poverty.

The Bahá'í vision of a future economy will doubtlessly be an organically evolving process, not merely some fixed allocation of wages or a single plan. Like every other aspect of this evolving concept of global collaboration and polity, the economic systems will evolve to befit constantly evolving conditions. To give but one example of this principle of flexibility regarding systems and institutions, the governing body of the Local House of Justice (presently titled the "Local Spiritual Assembly") is elected by plurality vote* according to criteria that have little to do with a person's position in society. Among the Guardian's articulations of the necessary qualifications is the following: "it is incumbent upon the chosen delegates [the electorate] to consider without the least trace of passion and prejudice, and irrespective of any material consideration, the names of only those who can best combine the nec-

---

* The ballots are secret, and the election prohibits electioneering or nominations. One simply writes down the nine people he or she thinks are most qualified, and the nine persons receiving the most votes become the members of the Local Spiritual Assembly.

essary qualities of unquestioned loyalty, of selfless devotion, of a well-trained mind, of recognized ability and mature experience."[21] At the level of local governance, the electorate are all adult Bahá'ís within the jurisdictional boundaries of the local community.

The Bahá'í concept of function having no bearing on equality of status is a totally new and innovative concept regarding social order and community standing. Consequently, one's achievements in the secular world are unlikely to have any impact on one's chances of being elected to any administrative body in the Bahá'í community.

Likewise, in the social interaction among community members, whether at regular community gatherings or in other sorts of activities, accepted standards of secular standing (such as vocation or wealth) do not affect the status of the individual within the Bahá'í community. Rather, emphasis is placed on selfless devotion to others, spiritual comportment, and dedication to the public good as borne out in action: "Holy words and pure and goodly deeds ascend unto the heaven of celestial glory. Strive that your deeds may be cleansed from the dust of self and hypocrisy and find favor at the court of glory; for ere long the assayers of mankind shall, in the holy presence of the Adored One, accept naught but absolute virtue and deeds of stainless purity."[22]

Moreover, there are no individual positions of authority in the Bahá'í community. Authority derives solely from elected institutions, and outside the functioning of these institutions, all Bahá'ís have equal status. Neither is there any distinction in standing between someone who has been a Bahá'í for fifty years versus someone who became a Bahá'í yesterday, even though the Guardian states that one qualification for being elected to an institution is "recognized ability and mature experience."

Conceivably, one might have these qualities prior to becoming a Bahá'í, but inasmuch as the election is by secret ballot, without nomination or electioneering, the weight of such a distinction would be entirely up to the private and prayerful reflection of each voting individual. Bahá'í governance is thus a system-driven polity rather than a personality-weighted structure, and the Bahá'í writings affirm that this system—Bahá'í administration as it is presently being modeled in the worldwide Bahá'í community—foreshadows the paradigm for governance of the future.

It is important to note that the Bahá'í Commonwealth as designed by Bahá'u'lláh is not the same as any other political system presently in place, even among the most democratically oriented nations. While in most nations the concept of equality of rights under the law is operant in theory, these societies are still stratified according to more mundane and totally material circumstances and criteria. The wealthy CEO living in a gated community and driving an expensive car will not be considered as having the same social status as a manual laborer who lives in an apartment and uses public transportation. And because election to public office in most countries is driven by financial interests, there is certainly no equal opportunity to be chosen to serve in a position of authority for one who is noble but penniless.

Nevertheless, implicit in all the past religions is the notion of equality of status in terms of spiritual valuation and, in many societies, in terms of civil rights. For example, in the tribal stage of social evolution (i.e. in the Judaic civilization established under Mosaic law) the idea of retributive justice was operant—an eye for an eye and a tooth for a tooth—but this concept of justice was predicated on a person's worth according to social status. At the same time, there was a sense of equity in the retribution, a fixed value placed on that which had been lost so that the extrication of retribution could be settled by remuneration rather than bloodshed. We have surviving documents codifying Anglo-Saxon laws based on that same principle that set the precise monetary value for various parts of the body and the various categories of individuals in the community, such as a slave versus a freeman, for example.

But let us turn to the most often discussed principle underlying the concept of spiritual equality, the so-called "Golden Rule" whereby all humankind is considered equally deserving of what each of us would desire for ourselves. The implicit universality of this standard of justice is demonstrated by the fact that this principle exists in virtually every religious and philosophical tradition.

In the Pentateuch of Moses we find the following admonition: "You shall not take vengeance or bear any grudge against the sons of your own people, but you shall love your neighbor as yourself: I am the Lord."[23] Logically, since Genesis seems to assert that all the people in the world are descendants of Adam, then it follows that all the people of the world should be considered to be one's "own people."

A few verses later, just in case the concept of the brotherhood of the human family is not sufficiently understood or accepted, we find a further specification: "When a stranger sojourns with you in your land, you shall not do him wrong. The stranger who sojourns with you shall be to you as the native among you, and you shall love him as yourself; for you were strangers in the land of Egypt. I am the Lord your God."[24]

Of interest in relation to our previous discussion about authoritative text that is explicitly revealed—text that may be considered divinely inspired but not necessarily a "revelation direct from God"—is how each verse of guidance concludes with the affirmation about the source of these instructions being God Himself. Thus, whether we consider the words as coming directly from Moses or as being passed down by oral tradition from the words of Moses, clearly this phrase is intended to remind the believers that they are to consider these words and the guidance they contain as deriving or emanating from God through the mouth of Moses.

As a principle or standard or touchstone for human justice, this simple advice is as valid and valuable today as it was in the Day of Moses, or as it has been cited in religions before and since. It is for this same reason that parallel statements of this evaluative process are found in all religious and philosophical literature, and explicitly in the revealed utterance of Christ, Muhammad, the Báb, and Bahá'u'lláh.

Christians are most familiar with the principle as stated by Christ in His recitation of the laws for His Dispensation in chapters 5 to 7 of the Gospel of Matthew: "Or what man of you, if his son asks him for bread, will give him a stone? Or if he asks for a fish, will give him a serpent? If you then, who are evil, know how to give good gifts to your children, how much more will your Father who is in heaven give good things to those who ask him! So whatever you wish that men would do to you, do so to them; for this is the law and the prophets."[25]

The same principle is implicit in the Qur'án in any number of verses, especially among explicit instructions about the treatment of other people, regardless of gender, race, or place of origin. For example, we find the following exhortation that people act in accordance with the divine standards: "Let not those among you who are endued with grace and amplitude of means resolve by oath against helping their kinsmen, those in want, and those who have left their homes in Allah's Cause. Let them forgive and overlook. Do you not wish that Allah should forgive you? For Allah is Oft-Forgiving, Most Merciful."[26]

Bahá'u'lláh provides an abundance of verses that apply this same standard both in self-evaluation and in deciding a course of social action. Bahá'u'lláh, however, goes a step further and, moving beyond the simple action or the motive thereof, exhorts His followers to understand that the standard of justice is that we should not even *contemplate wishing for others* what we would not wish for ourselves: "He must not wish for anyone that which he doth not wish for himself, nor speak that which he would not bear to hear spoken by another, nor yet desire for any soul that which he would not have desired for himself."[27]

Whether one accepts in any literal sense the Adamic myth of Genesis or the scientific DNA evidence (mentioned in chapter 1) that we did indeed emerge from a single pair of parents in ancient Africa, the abiding theme underlying this principle or standard of justice in our relationship with others is that all members of the human race are members of a single family, a single creation that has at last emerged as a global community. Thus, when Bahá'u'lláh states, "Ye are the fruits of one tree, and the leaves of one branch," He is not merely exhorting humanity to strive toward attaining this goal; He is, rather, making the factual observation that we are inherently equal in our creation and in the sight of God, and that "the earth is but one country, and mankind its citizens." Of course, while this verity has always been true, it is only in this "Day" that we are privileged to witness it becoming manifest in the foundational beginnings of the establishment of a global polity that can uphold and sustain this inherent equality among humankind.[28]

Finally, in stating the standards and expectations befitting the followers of Bahá'u'lláh, the Guardian employs the same metaphor we have chosen to be the framework for this discussion of how the Word weaves reality together: "Of all the kindreds of the earth they alone [those who recognize Bahá'u'lláh as the Manifestation for this Day] can recognize, amidst the welter of a tempestuous age, the Hand of the Divine Redeemer that traces its course and controls its destinies. They alone are aware of the silent growth of that orderly world polity whose fabric *they themselves are weaving.*"[29] (Italics added)

The Destiny of Humankind to Establish a Global Polity

While the eternal themes of God's Manifestations are manifold, sampling some of the major continuing threads of thought that bind the Days of God together allows us to glimpse the foreshadowing of a dramatic turning point in human history. From the perspective of the followers of some religious beliefs, this is a point when the world will end, when humankind will be judged and its members then accordingly relegated to either Heaven or Hell. For other religious adherents, particularly for the followers of the Bahá'í Faith, this turning point marks the maturation of humankind in our collective journey, a time when all the citizens of the earth will come to recognize our essential unity and purpose and begin weaving together a world polity.

Stated in terms of an "end time"—or eschatology—the Bahá'í view is that this Dispensation is indeed a point of change for which all previous Revelations were necessary stages of preparation. Consequently, Bahá'u'lláh's approach to this theme is virtually the antithesis of that found in other beliefs systems:

> Say: O men! This is a matchless Day. Matchless must, likewise, be the tongue that celebrateth the praise of the Desire of all nations, and matchless the deed that aspireth to be acceptable in His sight. The whole human race hath longed for this Day, that perchance it may fulfil that which well beseemeth its station, and is worthy of its destiny.[30]

> Should the greatness of this Day be revealed in its fullness, every man would forsake a myriad lives in his longing to partake, though it be for one moment, of its great glory—how much more this world and its corruptible treasures![31]

Of course, it would be naïve for Bahá'ís to expect people of other faiths suddenly to recognize the efficacy and logic underlying the Bahá'í view of human history when opposing views have become so pervasive and embedded in literalistic orientations to the eschatological portrayals of this turning point as "the end of the world." After all, until the dramatic changes that transpired with the advent of the Revelation of Bahá'u'lláh, who among us could have imagined that these evocative images could have alluded to anything but something calamitous rather than the emergence of forces capable of forging the foundations for a ceaselessly evolving world community, an "ever-advancing civilization."[32]

Indeed, we would be accurate in asserting that most interpretations of texts referring to the "Day of Days" have become a source of confusion, consternation, and grievous conflict. Yet even a brief glimpse at some of the allusions in the Word as revealed in past Dispensations reveals why such misunderstandings were common. But while there are eschatological allusions in literature of virtually all religious traditions, let us continue here to confine ourselves to some passages from the Abrahamic religions.

In Judaism, we find the prophecy of an apocalyptic upheaval in the book of Daniel where references to "the abomination that makes desolate" appear in three verses. Each of these seems to foretell some catastrophic end time in which humankind will experience the wrath of God. In the Gospel of John we find allusions to the "Second Coming" of Christ and in the Book of Revelation we find the portrayal of Armageddon, both of which are generally interpreted as indicating the literal return of Christ to judge "the quick and the dead."[33]

Many Christian religions have focused on the signs Christ discusses as portending His return—the same verses we have cited regarding Bahá'u'lláh's explication of these prophecies in the Kitáb-i-Íqán—but for many Christians the Book of Revelation is the primary source of the most imaginative speculation about the calamitous events that will precede the return of Christ. This work is also the primary source of literalist versions of the judgment that will be imposed on humankind.

In his description of a complex symbolic dream, John* recounts four visions in which, he affirms, he is privileged to behold the plan of God in order to assist humankind in preparing for the coming turning point in human history. But without any authoritative interpretation of St. John's narrative, Christians have most often attempted to discern in the historical signs portrayed in this narrative how the dream-vision might be applicable to contemporary events. And yet this understandable speculation is somewhat undercut by Christ's own observation that He Himself does not know exactly when these events will come to pass: "But of that day and hour no one knows, not even the angels of heaven, nor the Son, but the Father only."[34]

While the Last Judgment or Day of Resurrection is a major theme in the Qur'án, we find among Muslims the same quandary regarding interpretations about the significance or nature of these events. Generally, these disputes focus on whether or not passages are to be understood literally or figuratively. Because most Muslims believe that Muhammad is the final Prophet or Manifestation, most refuse to accept these allusions as referring to the advent of another Messenger from God or as being a propitious turn of events. Therefore, references to an end time or Day of Days are interpreted as implying a "Last Judgment" and the end of the world.

---

* His exact identity is not established and has produced an abundance of scholarly speculation.

Most Muslims similarly interpret this event as signaling a point in time when deserving believers will be admitted to a physical heaven while evildoers will be consigned to a physical hell according to an exacting and precise assessment of their deeds as assayed by God Himself: "When the Earth is shaken to her (utmost) convulsion, and the Earth throws up her burden (from within), and man cries (distressed), 'What is the matter with her?'—on that Day will she declare her tidings, because thy Lord will have given her inspiration. On that Day will men proceed in companies sorted out, to be shown the Deeds that they (have done). Then shall anyone who has done an atom's weight of good, see it! And anyone who has done an atom's weight of evil, shall see it."[35]

Certainly not all Muslims accept these verses as being literally true. There are numerous passages in the Qur'án where Muhammad alludes to God's eternal mercy, grace, and forgiveness. And yet, balanced against this hope is always the theme that no sinful action is left unrecorded in the "Book of Deeds": "Truly those in sin are the ones straying in mind, and mad. The day they will be dragged through the Fire on their faces, (they will hear:) 'Taste ye the touch of Hell!'. . . All that they do is noted in (their) Books (of Deeds). Every matter, small and great, is on record. As to the Righteous, they will be in the midst of Gardens and Rivers in an Assembly of Truth, in the Presence of a Sovereign Omnipotent (One)."[36]

Like Christ, Muhammad affirms that only God knows when this Day of Days will occur, but Muhammad alludes to several signs of the approach of that time. Among the most frequently cited are the twin trumpet blasts, the first of which will dumbfound the peoples and render them unconscious, while the second will resurrect humankind: "The Trumpet will (just) be sounded, when all that are in the heavens and on earth will swoon, except such as it will please Allah (to exempt). Then will a second one be sounded, when behold, they will be standing and looking on! And the Earth will shine with the glory of its Lord. The Record (of Deeds) will be placed (open). The prophets and the witnesses will be brought forward, and a just decision pronounced between them, and they will not be wronged (in the least). And to every soul will be paid in full (the fruit) of its deeds, and (Allah) knoweth best all that they do."[37]

As we have noted, because the Bahá'í teachings assert that a judgment is imposed upon humankind every time a new Manifestation appears, the advent of the Báb and Bahá'u'lláh might be seen as representing the "Last" of these tests, at least insofar as the severity of the transition from one Dispensation to another is concerned. That is, since in this present period of maturation humanity will come to understand the abiding logic of the divine process we have described as "progressive Revelation," humankind will also come to appreciate the unity of religions, of the Manifestations, and the oneness of humankind.

Therefore, this "Day of Days" is ultimately portrayed in the Bahá'í texts as the most propitious event that will ever occur in human history. This conjuncture represents the universal recognition of the Plan of God for planet Earth, something that all the Manifestations of the past have foreshadowed and longed to behold. In this context, the Bahá'í view of the "Day of Resurrection" refers not to the literal resurrection of dead bodies but to a Dispensation during which the whole of humanity will become awakened to the underlying reality and purpose of creation: "In this most mighty Revelation all the Dispensations of the past have attained their highest and final consummation." Shoghi Effendi writes, "The Faith of Bahá'u'lláh should indeed be regarded, if we wish to be faithful to the tremendous implications of its message, as the culmination of a cycle, the final stage in a series of successive, of preliminary and progressive revelations. These, beginning

340

with Adam and ending with the Báb, have paved the way and anticipated with an ever-increasing emphasis the advent of that Day of Days in which He Who is the Promise of All Ages should be made manifest."[38]

The Bahá'í vision of the ultimate destiny of human civilization is thus entirely positive, even if we must endure the turmoil and suffering of present-day instability. The Bahá'í texts state that while tumultuous and dire, the wrenching trauma of this transitional period will serve not only to enable us to understand that the earth has become one community, but will also help cleanse world civilization of the prejudices and misconceptions that are impediments to constructing world peace and a global infrastructure.

Viewed from a long-term perspective, the process of transition we are presently enduring will provide a major impetus to instigate the unity of humankind under the aegis of a series of collaborative systems. For this reason, at the outset of his work *The Promised Day is Come*, Shoghi Effendi cites several dire and foreboding passages by Bahá'u'lláh concerning what the immediate future holds, though even these remarks significantly assert that the end result of this process will be "unimaginably glorious." For the same reason, I wish to close this chapter with those same words:

A tempest, unprecedented in its violence, unpredictable in its course, catastrophic in its immediate effects, *unimaginably glorious in its ultimate consequences*, is at present sweeping the face of the earth. Its driving power is remorselessly gaining in range and momentum. Its cleansing force, however much undetected, is increasing with every passing day. Humanity, gripped in the clutches of its devastating power, is smitten by the evidences of its resistless fury. It can neither perceive its origin, nor probe its significance, nor discern its outcome. Bewildered, agonized and helpless, it watches this great and mighty wind of God invading the remotest and fairest regions of the earth, rocking its foundations, deranging its equilibrium, sundering its nations, disrupting the homes of its peoples, wasting its cities, driving into exile its kings, pulling down its bulwarks, uprooting its institutions, dimming its light, and harrowing up the souls of its inhabitants.[39] (Italics added.)

CONCLUSION

While we cannot know exactly what the remainder of this panoramic tapestry of our collective history on planet Earth will look like, we are assured in the revealed Word of Bahá'u'lláh that this "ever-advancing civilization" will increasingly reflect the divine attributes of the celestial realm. That this promise is not a vain hope but the assurance from One capable of both foreseeing that future and assisting in its actualization is spelled out in wonderful detail in authoritative Bahá'í texts such as Shoghi Effendi's *The World Order of Bahá'u'lláh* and *The Advent of Divine Justice*.

However, the abiding logic in these studies of how such a just and stable world polity will evolve and become inviolable can be understood and appreciated only if all the constituent ingredients of the Bahá'í perspective are examined and assembled into a holistic view of the past, the present, and the future of human history. Only then can the threads of themes that have characterized the Word throughout all the religions in our collective history be perceived not as a tangled web of haphazard struggles for power, but as a beauteous panorama, exquisitely designed by the mind of the Creator and woven together by the selfless efforts and sacred utterances of His successive Emissaries.

Endowed solely with the perspective regarding human possibilities that we had but a century ago, even the wisest and most visionary sages among us could not have imagined what sorts of material transformation lay ahead. Neither could anyone have foreseen the dramatic contraction of the diverse countries and cultures into an interdependent global economy, nor that it would be accompanied by contention regarding working collaboratively to deter global warming, to preserve our natural resources, and to find a collective mechanism for securing the world from nuclear disasters. Of course, we also could never have imagined the gross inhumanity of the two world wars, the subsequent numerous instances of massive genocide, nor the needless slaughter of innocents in terrorist attacks perpetrated in the name of religious piety. How infinitely more strange might it be were we privileged to behold what world civilization will be like a century or two from now. For while we are unaware of the often imperceptible forces at work that are weaving threads of reformation into the fabric of a revised and revisioned world civilization, we can see even now, in every corner of the world, embryonic models of that future. These are neighborhoods in which the worldwide Bahá'í community is building a core of essential spiritual activities to construct the foundation for community life.

Among these practices are devotional meetings in the homes of friends and family, neighborhood children's classes focusing on spiritual virtues, junior youth gatherings in which service activities and discussions about the life of the spirit provide a festive banquet for thirsting young souls, and study circles formed around a sequence of courses aimed at exploring the spiritual fabric of both the human heart and the life of society at large. These activities, far from being merely an end in themselves or a short-term means of providing needed spiritually-based activities for individuals in the neighborhood, have the overarching and far-reaching objectives of instigating community development so that a literal collaboration in every aspect of daily life assumes a spiritual tenor.

And yet these activities are not aimed at creating large, central, congregational gatherings where someone in authority and endowed with oratorical prowess provides periodic injections of enlightenment and guidance. Central to all of these community activities is the spoken word: consultation with friends and neighbors; the almost forgotten art of in-depth conversation and the exchange of ideas; and a reflection and consultation whose objective is community action and incremental renewal of the quality of life at the local level.

Of course, at the heart of this discourse, empowering it and guiding its progress, is the Word, the revealed guidance of the Messenger mandated by God to guide us with a vision of a world commonwealth in which the "God particle," the essential building block of our global community, is the family, dwelling in neighborhoods of diverse people who live and work together to forge a reality that has never before been imagined, let alone attempted:

> The Bahá'í Commonwealth of the future, of which this vast Administrative Order is the sole framework, is, both in theory and practice, not only unique in the entire history of political institutions, but can find no parallel in the annals of any of the world's recognized religious systems. No form of democratic government; no system of autocracy or of dictatorship, whether monarchical or republican; no intermediary scheme of a purely aristocratic order; nor even any of the recognized types of theocracy, whether it be the Hebrew Commonwealth, or the various Christian ecclesiastical organizations, or the Imamate or the Caliphate in Islam—none of these can be identified or be said to conform with the Administrative Order which the master-hand of its perfect Architect has fashioned.[1]

NOTES

1 / Roots, Diaspora, and a Family Reunion

1. 'Abdu'l-Bahá, *Foundations of World Unity*, p. 60.
2. Genesis 11:1–9.
3. Qur'án 28:37–40.
4. Bahá'u'lláh, *Gleanings*, no. 87.3–4.
5. Shoghi Effendi, *The World Order of Bahá'u'lláh*, pp. 203–4.
6. Shoghi Effendi, *The Advent of Divine Justice*, ¶28.
7. The Universal House of Justice, *Messages from the Universal House of Justice*, no. 42.24.

2 / In the Beginning Was the Word

1. 'Abdu'l-Bahá, *Some Answered Questions*, no. 47.1.
2. 'Abdu'l-Bahá, *Promulgation of Universal Peace*, p. 12.
3. Genesis 1:27.
4. Bahá'u'lláh, The Kitáb-i-Aqdas, ¶63.
5. Bahá'u'lláh, *Gleanings*, no. 75.1.
6. Bahá'u'lláh, The Kitáb-i-Aqdas, p. 176.
7. Bahá'u'lláh, The Hidden Words, Arabic no. 5.
8. John 1:1, 1:14.
9. Qur'án 6:101, 7:54.
10. Bahá'u'lláh, *Gleanings*, no. 27.4.

11. Shoghi Effendi, *High Endeavours*, p. 49.

12. 'Abdu'l-Bahá, *Some Answered Questions*, no. 7.7.

13. Bahá'u'lláh, The Kitáb-i-Íqán, ¶171–73.

14. Bahá'u'lláh, *Gleanings*, no. 113.13.

15. Bahá'u'lláh, *Prayers and Meditations*, no. 141.1.

16. Bahá'u'lláh, The Kitáb-i-Aqdas, ¶176.

17. Ibid., ¶177.

18. Shoghi Effendi, *The World Order of Bahá'u'lláh*, p. 163.

3 / The Word that Was the Beginning

1. Bahá'u'lláh, *Prayers and Meditations*, no. 183.10.

2. Ibid., no. 4.1; Qur'án 2:117.

3. Bahá'u'lláh, *Prayers and Meditations*, no. 183.10.

4. Shoghi Effendi, quoted in Bahá'u'lláh, The Kitáb-i-Aqdas, p. 245.

5. Bahá'u'lláh, *Gleanings*, no. 84.4.

6. John 14:6–7.

7. John 14:8–11.

8. Bahá'u'lláh, *The Summons of the Lord of Hosts*, "Súriy-i-Haykal," ¶44.

9. Bahá'u'lláh, *Gleanings*, no. 93.1.

10. Ibid., no. 78.2.

11. Ibid.

12. John 1:1; 'Abdu'l-Bahá, *Some Answered Questions*, no. 42.3.

13. Bahá'u'lláh, The Hidden Words, Arabic no. 67.

14. Bahá'u'lláh, Epistle to the Son of the Wolf, p. 33.

15. 'Abdu'l-Bahá, *Some Answered Questions*, nos. 10.3, 10.4.

16. Bahá'u'lláh, The Kitáb-i-Íqán, ¶78.

17. Ibid., ¶283.

18. Ibid., ¶180, ¶185.

19. Ibid., ¶53, ¶233.

20. Bahá'u'lláh, *Gleanings*, no. 80.2.
21. Ibid.
22. Ibid., no. 81.1.
23. Alexander, *Proof of Heaven*, p. 46.
24. Bahá'u'lláh, The Kitáb-i-Aqdas, ¶176.
25. Bahá'u'lláh, *Gleanings*, no. 81.1.
26. Ibid.

4 / The Mind as Intermediary

1. Bahá'u'lláh, The Kitáb-i-Íqán, ¶233; Bahá'u'lláh, *The Summons of the Lord of Hosts*, "Súriy-i-Haykal," ¶193.
2. Shoghi Effendi, *The Promised Day Is Come*, ¶303.
3. Harmon, *A Handbook to Literature*, p. 473.
4. Shoghi Effendi, quoted in Helen Hornby, *Lights of Guidance*, no. 1543; 'Abdu'l-Bahá, *Selections from the Writings of 'Abdu'l-Bahá*, no. 15.6.
5. Bahá'u'lláh, *Gleanings*, no. 93.15.
6. 'Abdu'l-Bahá, *Foundations of World Unity*, p. 41.
7. Qur'án 2:33.

5 / The Process of Creating Words

1. Chomsky, *Powers and Prospects*, p. 30.
2. 'Abdu'l-Bahá, *The Promulgation of Universal Peace*, p. 49.
3. Chalmers, *The Character of Consciousness*, p. 5.
4. Ibid., pp. 16–17.
5. 'Abdu'l-Bahá, *Some Answered Questions*, no. 42.3.
6. Ibid., no. 49.8–9.
7. Ibid., no. 3:8, 3:10.
8. Ibid., no. 3:15.
9. Bahá'u'lláh, *Gleanings*, no. 86.4.
10. Ibid., no. 83.1.

11. Ibid., no. 83.2.
12. Ibid., no. 83.3–83.4.
13. Ibid., no. 80.2.

6 / The Word and the Divine Methodology

1. Luke 12:48.
2. The Báb, *Selections from the Writings of the Báb*, no. 7:38:2.
3. Bahá'u'lláh, The Kitáb-i-Íqán, ¶283.
4. John 14:11.
5. Bahá'u'lláh, *Gleanings*, no. 84.4.
6. 'Abdu'l-Bahá, *Selections from the Writings of 'Abdu'l-Bahá*, no. 96.1.
7. Matthew 7:15–20.
8. 'Abdu'l-Bahá, *Selections from the Writings of 'Abdu'l-Bahá*, no. 35.5.
9. 'Abdu'l-Bahá, *Some Answered Questions*, no. 14.7.
10. John 14:6.
11. Bahá'u'lláh, The Kitáb-i-Íqán, ¶151.
12. John 14:6.
13. Bahá'u'lláh, *Gleanings*, no. 29.1.
14. Shoghi Effendi, *High Endeavours*, p. 71.
15. Ibid., p. 49.
16. Mark 4:3–8, 4:9.
17. Mark 4:11–12; Isaiah 6:9.
18. Mark 4:13.
19. Mark 4:14–20.
20. Bahá'u'lláh, The Kitáb-i-Íqán, ¶3; Bahá'u'lláh, The Hidden Words, Arabic no. 2.
21. Bahá'u'lláh, The Kitáb-i-Íqán, ¶185.
22. Qur'án 10:47.
23. 'Abdu'l-Bahá, quoted in Ethel Jenner Rosenberg, p. 81.
24. 'Abdu'l-Bahá, *Some Answered Questions*, no. 41:3.

25. Bahá'u'lláh, *Tablets of Bahá'u'lláh*, p. 149.

26. Bahá'u'lláh, *Gleanings*, no. 84.4.

27. Veccia Vaglieri, Laura. "Ghadīr Khumm." *Encyclopedia of Islam*. Brill Online. 2012. http://referenceworks.brillonline.com/entries/encyclopaedia-of-islam-2/ghadir-khumm-SIM_2439?s.num=7

28. Ibid.

29. Gail, *Six Lessons on Islam*, p. 29.

30. Matthew 28:19–20.

31. Shoghi Effendi, *The Promised Day is Come*, ¶294.

32. Shoghi Effendi, *God Passes By*, p. 41.

33. Bahá'u'lláh, *Gleanings*, no. 166.1; Shoghi Effendi, *Bahá'í Administration*, p. 103; 'Abdu'l-Bahá, *Will and Testament*, p. 20.

7 / Indirection in the Language of the Manifestations

1. John 6:32.

2. John 6:35.

3. Matthew 16:26–28.

4. John 1:1, 1:14.

5. Qur'án 4:171–72.

6. Bahá'u'lláh, The Hidden Words, Arabic no. 2.

7. Lample, *Revelation and Social Reality*, pp. 35–46.

8. 'Abdu'l-Bahá, *Some Answered Questions*, no. 30.4.

9. Bahá'u'lláh, The Kitáb-i-Íqán, ¶78.

10. 'Abdu'l-Bahá, *Some Answered Questions*, no. 30.5.

11. Ibid., no. 30.6.

12. Bahá'u'lláh, The Kitáb-i-Íqán, ¶75, ¶232.

13. Ibid., ¶233.

14. John 6:35.

15. John 3:16; Qur'án 4:171.

16. Genesis 11:1–9, Exodus 16:1–36, Numbers 11:1–9.

17. Matthew 27:45–46; Psalms 22:1–2.

18. Qur'án 5:72–73.

19. Matthew 4:19; Maurice Hassett, "Symbolism of the Fish," in *Catholic Encyclopedia*. http://newadvent.com/cathen/06083a.htm.

20. Mark 4:2–9.

21. John Milton, "Paradise Lost," *The Complete Poetical Works of John Milton*, IV: 689–705, p. 291.

22. Abdu'l-Bahá, in *Bahá'í Prayers*, p. 202.

23. Bahá'u'lláh, *Prayers and Meditations*, no. 165.1–2.

24. Bahá'u'lláh, *Gleanings*, no. 125.9.

25. Ibid., no. 81.1.

26. Ibid., nos. 17.3, 43.6; Bahá'u'lláh, *Tablets of Bahá'u'lláh*, p. 177.

27. Bahá'u'lláh, The Kitáb-i-Íqán, ¶118.

28. Deuteronomy 9:10; 'Abdu'l-Bahá, *Some Answered Questions*, no. 16:10.

29. Shoghi Effendi, *God Passes By*, p. 157.

30. Bahá'u'lláh, Epistle to the Son of the Wolf, p. 15.

31. Bahá'u'lláh, The Hidden Words, p. 3, Arabic no. 4.

32. Ibid., Persian no. 13.

33. Bahá'u'lláh, "Súriy-i-Haykal," *The Summons of the Lord of Hosts*, ¶192.

34. Bahá'u'lláh, "Súriy-i-Mulúk," *The Summons of the Lord of Hosts*, ¶58.

35. Bahá'u'lláh, *Prayers and Meditations*, no. 25.2.

36. Ibid., no. 176.43, 176.45.

37. Psalms 23:1–4.

38. Bahá'u'lláh, *Gleanings*, no. 159.4.

8 / Weaving Reality Together

1. Bahá'u'lláh, Gleanings, no. 72.1.

2. Abdu'l-Bahá, *The Promulgation of Universal Peace*, p. 12.

3. Bahá'u'lláh, *Gleanings*, no. 109.2.

4. 'Abdu'l-Bahá, quoted in Shoghi Effendi, *The Advent of Divine Justice*, ¶40.

5. Shoghi Effendi, *The Advent of Divine Justice*, ¶47.

6. Bahá'u'lláh, *Gleanings*, no. 81.1.

7. Ibid., no. 66.4.

8. Bahá'u'lláh, quoted in *Bahá'í Prayers*, p. iii.

9. Bahá'u'lláh, The Kitáb-i-Íqán, ¶185.

10. Shoghi Effendi, *Citadel of Faith*, pp. 130–31.

11. Bahá'u'lláh, The Kitáb-i-Aqdas, ¶149.

12. Bahá'u'lláh, The Hidden Words, Persian no. 82.

13. Bahá'u'lláh, The Kitáb-i-Aqdas, ¶33.

14. Letter written on behalf of Shoghi Effendi, quoted in Bahá'u'lláh, The Kitáb-i-Aqdas, ¶36.

15. Bahá'u'lláh, The Hidden Words, Arabic no. 31.

16. Shoghi Effendi, *The World Order of Bahá'u'lláh*, p. 5.

17. Shoghi Effendi, *Bahá'í Administration*, p. 66.

18. 'Abdu'l-Bahá, *Paris Talks*, no. 54.8–54.13.

19. Bahá'u'lláh, *Gleanings*, no. 136.2.

20. Ibid., no. 153.6; see for example "Miscellaneous Laws, Ordinance and Exhortations," in Bahá'u'lláh, The Kitáb-i-Aqdas, pp. 156–62.

21. Bahá'u'lláh, *Gleanings*, no. 77.1.

22. Bahá'u'lláh, *Tablets of Bahá'u'lláh*, p. 27.

9 / How the Word Stitches Dispensations Together

1. Bahá'u'lláh, The Kitáb-i-Íqán, ¶266.

2. 'Abdu'l-Bahá, *Some Answered Questions*, no. 69.3.

3. Ibid., no. 47.7.

4. Bahá'u'lláh, "Súriy-i-Haykal," *The Summon of the Lord of Hosts*, ¶63.

5. Shoghi Effendi, *God Passes By*, p. 387.

6. Bahá'u'lláh, quoted in Shoghi Effendi, *The World Order of Bahá'u'lláh*, p. 117; Bahá'u'lláh, The Kitáb-i-Aqdas, ¶37.

7. John 16:7–13.
8. Matthew 24:44.
9. Matthew 24:29–31.
10. Bahá'u'lláh, The Kitáb-i-Íqán, ¶66.
11. Ibid., ¶68.
12. Ibid.
13. Ibid., ¶71.
14. Ibid., ¶72.
15. Siyyid Kázim, quoted in Nabil, *The Dawn-breakers*, pp. 41–42.
16. Bahá'u'lláh, The Kitáb-i-Íqán, ¶256.
17. Qur'án 2:23, quoted in Bahá'u'lláh, The Kitáb-i-Íqán, ¶226.
18. Bahá'u'lláh, The Kitáb-i-Íqán, ¶226.
19. Qur'án 45:5, quoted in Bahá'u'lláh, The Kitáb-i-Íqán, ¶228.
20. Bahá'u'lláh, The Kitáb-i-Íqán, ¶230.
21. Ibid., ¶231.
22. Ibid., ¶232.
23. Ibid., ¶233.
24. Ibid., ¶246.
25. Ibid., ¶257.
26. Ibid., ¶262.
27. Ibid., ¶263.

10 / The Word as Warp and Woof of Human History

1. Bahá'u'lláh, The Kitáb-i-Aqdas, ¶1.
2. Letter from the Universal House of Justice, dated March 3, 1975, to an individual believer, in *Guidelines for Local Spiritual Assemblies: Developing Distinctive Bahá'í Communities*, 5:1.
3. Shoghi Effendi, *God Passes By*, p. 148; Shoghi Effendi, *The Promised Day Is Come*, ¶302.
4. Bahá'u'lláh, The Kitáb-i-Aqdas, ¶1.
5. Matthew 5:17–19.
6. Bahá'u'lláh, The Hidden Words, Arabic no. 28.

7. The Báb, *Selections from the Writings of the Báb*, 1:2:4.
8. Shoghi Effendi, *God Passes By*, p. 93.
9. Shoghi Effendi, quoted in Bahá'u'lláh, The Kitáb-i-Aqdas, p. viii.
10. The Universal House of Justice, quoted in Bahá'u'lláh, The Kitáb-i-Aqdas, pp. 4–5.
11. Shoghi Effendi, *The Promised Day is Come*, ¶289–91.
12. Bahá'u'lláh, *Gleanings*, no. 33.1.1.
13. Shoghi Effendi, *The World Order of Bahá'u'lláh*, pp. 20, 21.
14. Muhammad, quoted in Bahá'u'lláh, The Kitáb-i-Íqán, ¶222.
15. The Báb, *Selections from the Writings of the Báb*, 1:2:4.
16. Bahá'u'lláh, *Gleanings*, no. 141.5.
17. Shoghi Effendi, *God Passes By*, p. 50.
18. Ibid., p. 108.
19. Ibid., pp. 39–40.
20. Ibid., p. 41.
21. Bahá'u'lláh, *Tablets of Bahá'u'lláh*, p. 222; Bahá'u'lláh, quoted in Shoghi Effendi, *God Passes By*, p. 381.
22. Shoghi Effendi, *The World Order of Bahá'u'lláh*, p. 152.
23. Bahá'u'lláh, The Kitáb-i-Aqdas, note 189.

11 / The Prophet's Constancy in Revealing the Word

1. Bahá'u'lláh, The Kitáb-i-Íqán, ¶257–58.
2. Ibid., ¶263; Shoghi Effendi, *God Passes By*, pp. 385–86.
3. Luke 22:42; Shoghi Effendi, *God Passes By*, p. 144.
4. Bahá'u'lláh, *Prayers and Meditations*, no. 110.2–3.
5. 'Abdu'l-Bahá, *Some Answered Questions*, no. 16:10.
6. Ibid., no. 22.2.
7. Ibid., nos. 22.3, 22.5.
8. See Numbers 20:1–12.
9. 'Abdu'l-Bahá, *Some Answered Questions*, no. 44:12–13.
10. Matthew 19:14.

11. John 6:26–29.

12. Bahá'u'lláh, The Kitáb-i-Íqán, ¶196.

13. Luke 22:41–42.

14. John 14:5–12.

15. Bahá'u'lláh, The Kitáb-i-Íqán, ¶114–15.

16. Gail, *Six Lesson on Islam*, p. 1.

17. 'Abdu'l-Bahá, *Some Answered Questions*, no. 7:7.

18. 'Abdu'l-Bahá, quoted in Hasan M. Balyuzi, *'Abdu'l-Bahá: The Centre of the Covenant*, p. 73.

19. Mullá Husayn, quoted in Nabíl-i-A'zam, *The Dawn-Breakers*, p. 57; the Báb, quoted in Nabíl-i-A'zam, *The Dawn-Breakers*, p. 57; the Báb, quoted in Shoghi Effendi, *God Passes By*, p. 9.

20. The Báb, *Selections from the Writings of the Báb*, 7:12:1.

21. The Báb, quoted in Shoghi Effendi, *God Passes By*, p. 34.

22. Shoghi Effendi, *God Passes By*, p. 235.

23. Bahá'u'lláh, The Kitáb-i-Íqán, ¶263.

24. Bahá'u'lláh, Epistle to the Son of the Wolf, pp. 11–12.

25. Bahá'u'lláh, quoted in Shoghi Effendi, *God Passes By*, p. 277.

26. Bahá'u'lláh, Epistle to the Son of the Wolf, pp. 32–33.

27. Ibid., p. 36.

12 / Unity of Major Themes in the Fabric of the Eternal Covenant

1. 'Abdu'l-Bahá, *Paris Talks*, no. 41.5.

2. Bahá'u'lláh, *Gleanings*, no. 31.1.

3. Qur'án 7:172.

4. John 8:52–58.

5. Qur'án 11:26–27.

6. Bahá'u'lláh, The Kitáb-i-Íqán, ¶15.

7. Ibid., ¶16.

8. Matthew 5:19, 7:24–27.

9. Galatians 2:15–16.

10. 2 Peter 3:14–17.
11. James 2:14–26.
12. Qur'án 2:177.
13. Ibid., 2:263–65.
14. Bahá'u'lláh, The Hidden Words, Persian no. 80.
15. Ibid., no. 81.
16. Ibid., no. 82.
17. Bahá'u'lláh, *Tablets of Bahá'u'lláh*, p. 156.
18. Bahá'u'lláh, The Kitáb-i-Aqdas, ¶36.
19. Bahá'u'lláh, *Gleanings*, no. 5.4.
20. The Universal House of Justice, *Messages from the Universal House of Justice*, no. 145.5.
21. Shoghi Effendi, *Bahá'í Administration*, p. 88.
22. Bahá'u'lláh, The Hidden Words, Persian no. 69.
23. Leviticus 19:18.
24. Ibid., 19:33–34.
25. Matthew 7:9–12.
26. Qur'án 24:22.
27. Bahá'u'lláh, *Gems of Divine Mysteries*, ¶84.
28. Bahá'u'lláh, *Gleanings*, no. 132.3, no. 117.1.
29. Shoghi Effendi, *The World Order of Bahá'u'lláh*, p. 194.
30. Bahá'u'lláh, *Gleanings*, no. 16.1. Italics added.
31. Ibid., no. 96.3.
32. Ibid., no. 109.2.
33. Daniel 9:27, 11:31, and 12:11; from the "Apostles Creed" as translated in the *Book of Common Prayer* of the Church of England. https://www.churchofengland.org/prayer-worship/worship/book-of-common-prayer.aspx
34. Matthew 24:36.
35. Qur'án 99:1–8.
36. Ibid., 54:47–55.
37. Ibid., 39:68–70.

38. Bahá'u'lláh, *Gleanings*, no. 115.10; Shoghi Effendi, *The World Order of Bahá'u'lláh*, p. 103.

39. Shoghi Effendi, *The Promised Day Is Come*, ¶2.

Conclusion

1. Shoghi Effendi, *The World Order of Bahá'u'lláh*, p. 152.

BIBLIOGRAPHY

Works of Bahá'u'lláh

Epistle to the Son of the Wolf. Translated by Shoghi Effendi. 1ˢᵗ pocket-sized ed. Wilmette, IL: Bahá'í Publishing Trust, 1988.

Gems of Divine Mysteries. Haifa, Israel: Bahá'í World Centre, 2002.

Gleanings from the Writings of Bahá'u'lláh. Translated by Shoghi Effendi. New ed. Wilmette, IL: Bahá'í Publishing, 2005.

Prayers and Meditations. New ed. Wilmette, IL: Bahá'í Publishing Trust, 2014.

Tablets of Bahá'u'lláh Revealed after the Kitáb-i-Aqdas. Compiled by the Research Department of the Universal House of Justice and translated by Habib Taherzadeh with the assistance of a Committee at the Bahá'í World Center. Wilmette, IL: Bahá'í Publishing Trust, 1988.

The Hidden Words of Bahá'u'lláh. Translated by Shoghi Effendi. Wilmette, IL: Bahá'í Publishing, 2002.

The Kitáb-i-Aqdas: The Most Holy Book. 1ˢᵗ pocket-sized ed. Wilmette, IL: Bahá'í Publishing Trust, 1993.

The Kitáb-i-Íqán: The Book of Certitude. Translated by Shoghi Effendi. Wilmette, IL: Bahá'í Publishing, 2003.

The Summons of the Lord of Hosts: Tablets of Bahá'u'lláh. Wilmette, IL: Bahá'í Publishing, 2006.

Works of the Báb

Selections from the Writings of the Báb. Compiled by the Research Department of the Universal House of Justice. Translated by Habib Taherzadeh et al. 1st pocket-sized ed. Wilmette, IL: Bahá'í Publishing Trust, 2006.

Works of 'Abdu'l-Bahá

Foundations of World Unity: Compiled from Addresses and Tablets of 'Abdu'l-Bahá. Wilmette, IL: Bahá'í Publishing Trust, 1972.

Memorials of the Faithful. New ed. Translated by Marzieh Gail. Wilmette, IL: Bahá'í Publishing Trust, 1996.

Paris Talks: Addresses Given by 'Abdu'l-Bahá in Paris in 1911. Wilmette, IL: Bahá'í Publishing, 2006.

Selections from the Writings of 'Abdu'l-Bahá. Wilmette, IL: Bahá'í Publishing, 2010.

Some Answered Questions. Compiled and translated from the Persian by Laura Clifford Barney. Newly Revised by a Committee at the Bahá'í World Center. Reprinted with the permission of the Bahá'í World Center. Wilmette, IL: Bahá'í Publishing, 2014.

Tablets of the Divine Plan: Revealed by 'Abdu'l-Bahá to the North American Bahá'ís. 1st pocket-sized ed. Wilmette, IL: Bahá'í Publishing Trust, 1993.

The Promulgation of Universal Peace: Talks Delivered by 'Abdu'l-Bahá during His Visit to the United States and Canada in 1912. New ed. Wilmette: Bahá'í Publishing Trust, 2007.

The Secret of Divine Civilization. Wilmette, IL: Bahá'í Publishing, 2007.

Will and Testament of 'Abdu'l-Bahá. Wilmette: Bahá'í Publishing Trust, 1991.

Works of Shoghi Effendi

Bahá'í Administration, Selected Messages, 1922–1932. 7th ed. Wilmette, IL: Bahá'í Publishing Trust, 1974.

Citadel of Faith: Messages to America, 1947–1957. Wilmette, IL: Bahá'í Publishing Trust, 1965.

God Passes By. Eighth printing. Wilmette, IL: Bahá'í Publishing Trust, 1974.

High Endeavours: Messages to Alaska. Bahá'í Publishing Trust Alaska, 1976.

Messages to the Bahá'í World, 1950–1957. Wilmette, IL: Bahá'í Publishing Trust, 1971.

Messages to Canada. National Spiritual Assembly of the Bahá'ís of Canada, 1965.

The Advent of Divine Justice. New ed. Wilmette, IL: Bahá'í Publishing Trust, 2006.

The Promised Day is Come. 1st pocket-sized ed. Wilmette, IL: Bahá'í Publishing Trust, 1996.

The World Order of Bahá'u'lláh. First pocket-sized edition. Wilmette, IL: Bahá'í Publishing Trust, 1991.

The Unfolding Destiny of the British Bahá'í Community: The Messages from the Guardian of the Bahá'í Faith to the Bahá'ís of the British Isles. London: Bahá'í Publishing Trust, 1981.

This Decisive Hour: Messages from Shoghi Effendi to the North American Bahá'ís, 1932–1946. Wilmette, IL: Bahá'í Publishing Trust, 2002.

Works of the Universal House of Justice

Century of Light. Commissioned by the Universal House of Justice. Haifa, Israel: Bahá'í World Center, 2001.

Messages from the Universal House of Justice 1963–1986: The Third Epoch of the Formative Age. Compiled by Geoffry Marks. Wilmette, IL: Bahá'í Publishing Trust, 1996.

The Constitution of the Universal House of Justice. Haifa, Israel: Bahá'í World Center, 1972.

The Institution of the Counsellors. Haifa, Israel: Bahá'í World Center, 2001.

The Promise of World Peace. Haifa, Israel: Bahá'í World Center, 1985.

Turning Point: Selected Messages of the Universal House of Justice and Supplementary Material 1996–2006. West Palm Beach, FL: Palabra Publications, 2006.

Compilations of Bahá'í Writings

Bahá'u'lláh, 'Abdu'l-Bahá, Shoghi Effendi, and the Universal House of Justice. *The Compilation of Compilations: Prepared by the Universal House of Justice, 1963–1990.* 2 vols. Australia: Bahá'í Publications Australia, 1991.

Hornby, Helen, comp. *Lights of Guidance: A Bahá'í Reference File.* 6th ed. New Delhi: Bahá'í Publishing Trust, 2001.

National Spiritual Assembly of the Bahá'ís of the United States. *Guidelines for Local Spiritual Assemblies: Developing Distinctive Bahá'í Communities.* Evanston, IL: Office of Assembly Development, 2009.

Other Works

Abdullah Yusuf Ali. *The Holy Qur'án: Text, Translation and Commentary.* Elmhurst, NY: Tahrike Tarsile, Inc., 2001.

Alexander, Eben. *Proof of Heaven: A Neurosurgeon's Journey into the Afterlife.* New York: Simon and Schuster, 2012.

Balyuzi, H. M. *'Abdu'l-Bahá: The Centre of the Covenant of Bahá'u'lláh.* London: George Ronald, 1971.

Chalmers, David J. *The Character of Consciousness.* New York: Oxford University Press, 2010.

Chomsky, Noam. *Power and Prospects: Reflections on Nature and the Social Order.* London: Pluto Press, 1996.

Gail, Marzieh. *Six Lessons on Islam.* Wilmette, IL: Bahá'í Publishing Trust, 1976.

Harmon, William. *A Handbook to Literature.* Upper Saddle River, New Jersey: Pearson, 2006.

Hatcher, William S., and J. Douglas Martin. *The Bahá'í Faith: The Emerging Global Religion.* Wilmette, IL: Bahá'í Publishing, 2002.

Lample, Paul. *Revelation and Social Reality: Learning to Translate What is Written into Reality.* West Palm Beach, FL: Palabra Publications, 2009.

Milton, John. *The Complete Poetical Works of John Milton.* Edited by Douglas Bush. Boston: Houghton Mifflin Company, 1965.

Momen, Wendi. *A Basic Bahá'í Dictionary.* Oxford: George Ronald, 1989.

Nabíl-i-A'zam. *The Dawn-Breakers: Nabíl's Narrative of the Early Days of the Bahá'í Revelation.* Wilmette, IL: Bahá'í Publishing Trust, 1932.

The Holy Bible: Revised Standard Version. New York: Thomas Nelson & Sons, 1953.

INDEX

M